# Economics of Space and Time

*Scientific Papers of Tönu Puu*

Springer
*Berlin*
*Heidelberg*
*New York*
*Barcelona*
*Budapest*
*Hong Kong*
*London*
*Milan*
*Paris*
*Santa Clara*
*Singapore*
*Tokyo*

Åke E. Andersson · Martin J. Beckmann
Karl-Gustaf Löfgren · Anders Stenberg (Eds).

# Economics of Space and Time

*Scientific Papers of Tönu Puu*

Springer

Professor Dr. Åke E. Andersson
Institute for Future Studies
P.O.Box 591
S-101 31 Stockholm, Sweden

Professor Dr. Martin J. Beckmann
Brown University
Department of Economics
P.O.Box B
Providence, RI 02912, USA

Professor Dr. Karl-Gustaf Löfgren
M.A. Anders Stenberg

University of Umeå
Department of Economics
S-901 87 Umeå, Sweden

Springer-Verlag would like to thank the original publishers of Tönu Puu's papers for granting permission to reprint them in this book.

ISBN-13: 978-3-642-64596-9 e-ISBN-13: 978-3-642-60877-3
DOI: 10.1007/978-3-642-60877-3

Cataloging - in - Publication Data applied for
Die Deutsche Bibliothek - CIP-Einheitsaufnahme
**Puu, Tönu:**
Economics of space and time : scientific papers of Tönu Puu / Åke E. Anderson ... (ed.). - Berlin; Heidelberg; New York; Barcelona; Budapest; Hong Kong; London; Milan; Paris; Santa Clara; Singapore; Tokyo : Springer, 1997
ISBN-13: 978-3-642-64596-9


Softcover reprint of the hardcover 1st edition 1997



Hardcover design: Erich Kirchner, Heidelberg
SPIN 10636073 42/2202-543210 - Printed on acid-free paper

*Professor Töno Puu, a passionate music lover, with one of his viole di gamba*

## Table of Contents

## Preface and Acknowledgements

### The Editors

This book is a collection of articles by Professor Tönu Puu presented to him on the occasion of his $60^{th}$ birthday. Not included are some innovative papers whose contents were subsequently included in Tönu Puu's well-known book "The Allocation of Road Capital in two-dimensional Space" (North Holland 1979). Unfortunately those papers are no longer available in print.

The complete bibliography (p 261) lists many more articles that would have been worth reprinting, but we had to observe a certain limit on space.

The editors wish to thank Mikael Bask, a graduate in Engineering, for a unique effort in the final stages of the editing process.

## Tönu Puu - Economic Analyst and Cultural Activist

*by Åke E Andersson*

In Tönu Puu one finds the rare combination of creativity, learning and wide ranging interest in the arts and cultural affairs. Over the years he has contributed distinctively creative ideas, while extending economics both into continuous two-dimensional space and time.

Building upon Beckmann's paper -"A continuous Model of Transportation", published in 1952, Tönu Puu and Martin Beckmann have developed the general two-dimensional theory of spatial economies. This is a remarkably creative contribution. Instead of concentrating on optimality as is conventionally done, Tönu Puu there used properties needed to ensure structural stability as well as a powerful use of bifurcation theory to show under what conditions spatial flow and location patterns might undergo fundamental structural change. In this respect the whole theory was brought into a close and potentially fruitful contact with evolutionary economics.

His wide ranging cultural interests have been demonstrated at a theoretical level in his forthcoming book *Economics and Culture - a Safari*. In this, richly illustrated, extensive essay he covers such seemingly unrelated themes as civilisation as analysed by Frazer, Vivaldis Oevre, cultural scenes of Paris, Vienna, and Florence. And among the figureheads of science, philosophy and the arts, he analyses Poincaré, Bolzmann as well as Bach, Hernoncour and Albrecht Dürer. And all this is brought to a unified treatment in an analysis of the dynamics of the development in society and the arts.

But Tönu Puu is not only a creative economic theoretician and an analyst of culture, arts and society. His interest in the arts has been practical and entrepreneurial as well. His deep interest in music in general, the current revival of early music and especially interpretation of baroque composers has directed his creation and development of the best baroque music festival of Northern Europe. All of his friends and most of his colleagues have been impressed by the capacity to combine major scientific achievements with Tönu and Gertrud Puu's creation, innovation and production of these musical highlights every second year in the north of Sweden. To those of us who know that sometimes musicians in these concerts play on instruments built by Tönu, it gives a natural addition to the picture of this multi faceted personality.

## Tönu Puu and I - in collaboration

*by Martin Beckman*

The last thing a reader would want from me here is a piece purporting to explain or evaluate Tönu Puu's work in location theory and "spatio-economics". It would be difficult reading and biased, to boot. Instead let me give you some notes towards the story of our collaboration.

It starts with Tönu becoming interested in the calculus of variations upon reading Courand and John's book on the calculus. When in 1972 Tönu Puu looked through Tord Palander's papers at the request of his widow, he came across a reprint of mine on the "Continuous Model of Transportation" (Econometrica, 1952), which used variational methods in location theory. Tönu Puu was intrigued by this piece and impressed by the attempt to capture the essence of spatial equilibrium in two differential equations. As a student of Palander's, Tönu was of course familiar with Location Theory, but now he was hooked. Here was some unusual mathematics - vector analysis of the grad, div, curl type usually taught only to engineers and physicists - applied to the "transportation model" that had just emerged with linear programming as a hot new subject for economic theory.

We did not meet in person until 1977 but had some correspondence about a manuscript of his on structural stability in spatial markets which dealt a severe blow to the theory of market areas by August Lösch and which I rejected for the "Lecture Notes in Mathematical Systems and Economics", (Springer-Verlag) of which I was then managing editor.

In the summer of 1980 Tönu and I were together at IIASA in Laxenburg near Vienna for a whole month. At this time IIASA was actively involved in regional science research and hosted a significant part of the "Swedish Regional Science Mafia" (as it was called irreverently later on). In the span of three weeks we managed to write the first draft "Spatial Economics: Density Potential and Flow" that was published five years later as a IIASA monograph by North-Holland.

It must not be thought that we spent the three weeks in hectic activity or in a frenzied atmosphere. It was neither that nor a chummy, easy going sort of thing. As I recall, I had set myself a daily goal of ten handwritten pages and would announce to Tönu not without glee when I had fulfilled my quota. At times we each suffered from writer's block, but the challenge of not falling behind while the other moved ahead kept us going. At this stage it was more competition than cooperation. Critique and cooperation came later.

We often took the afternoons off. Luckily our typist kept up with our pace and we could watch with satisfaction how the manuscript grew steadily.

Rewriting the first draft was much less fun. It has been said that writing a book is like siring a child: conceived with pleasure, carried out in discomfort and born with great labor pains. Over the next five years we meet for one or two weeks at the time in places like SPUR (in Louvain-la-Neuve) in 1982 and CERUM in 1983. If it had been for longer periods and not spaced out as much, the final result might have been a more cohesive, better reasoned, and more readable book, a smoother and more polished product than what we presented to the world, which did not exactly jump for it. I still think that the book's substance is good while its form is unfinished, alas.

Our next book "Spatial Structures" (Springer 1990) in the same general area but less ambitious, had not been planned in advance. It came about almost accidentally when I was visiting the Umeå University as a visiting professor during Tönu's sabbatical in 1989. It turned out that there was no call for me to teach while there. We filled the time by looking at the Hotelling migration model, coming up with ideas for solutions and moving on from there. Once we got going, the pace was fast again. Tönu's wizardry with computers was essential in this enterprise. We had a book manuscript at the end of two months. This book might be a better introduction to the subject of continuous flow models in economics, at least for the mathematically inclined reader, but it is still tough going.

On another occasion, when Tönu was visiting the Center of Economic Studies (CES) in Munich in 1994 the opportunity was there, but we did not come up with a joint product. By then Tönu was captivated by non-linear dynamics which he had, already, discovered in spatial structures.

As a student of the economics of science - at the Institute for Futures Studies in Stockholm - I should perhaps try to draw some lessons from this case of a collaboration in social science, which has added one data point to scientific collaboration between Sweden and foreign countries. I am afraid, there are no clear cut lessons: getting to know each other, inevitable from hindsight, is often enough a chance event for potential collaborators, and good intentions are never enough. In the end success is just as much of a surprise as it is in all research.

Collaboration has been productive and deeply satisfying to us. As regards its outward success, the last word is not in yet. But then, Tönu Puu has many strings to his bow, as this collection of papers amply demonstrates.

## Professor Tönu Puu at the Department of Economics, Umeå University

*by Karl- Gustaf Löfgren*

Tönu Puu was appointed to the chair in Economics at Umeå University in 1971.Prior to that he was an Associate Professorship at the University of Uppsala. However, his influence in Umeå had started much earlier. The department of economics came into existence in the autumn of 1964. Two years later the first chair filled by Professor Hugo Hegeland. He tried to run a regular seminar by inviting guests from other universities. Most of the speakers were quite established economists like Professor Sune Carlsson at Business Administration in Uppsala, Professor Harald Dickson from the Department of Economics in Gothenburg, and Professor Karl G Uhr from the University of Davis, California. Most of them gave well prepared lectures, but in this respect they were all out-performed by the young Associate Professor from Uppsala, Tönu Puu. He gave lectures on the Slutsky equation in the theory of production (see paper 2),on the Philosophy of Science (see paper 12), but above all he showed us the techniques through which the calculations were made. In other words, he made it crystal clear that mathematical and statistical techniques had come to Economics to stay, and that there were no alternatives open to a young economist, but to try to achieve a full understanding of Samuelson's "Foundations of Economic Analysis". Although I never made that level, I have, now and then, been able to fool an editor or two that this is the case, and, no doubt, I owe this to Tönu.

His thesis on "Studies in Optimal Portfolio Selection" published 1964 in Swedish was awarded the highest grade by the Faculty of Philosophy in Uppsala. This hampered Tönu's career for a long time. Only two people before him had accomplished this, and the world renowned "Swedish envy", which has been particular important in academic circles, came into effect. The evaluations were of the following type: "It is quite clear that the book is pretty good, but in no way is it worth an A".

What did it contain? It started with a chapter on investment theory, which discussed investment decisions in imperfect capital markets, where the lending and borrowing rates differ. Tönu showed that an investment is objectively preferable (independent of the preferences of the investor) under these circumstances, if, and only if, all the $2^n$ possible present values are positive. I have elsewhere named this Puu's Theorem , and it was undoubtedly a correct and, at the time, a completely new result. However, as was pointed out by the faculty opponent Harald Dickson, the proof contained one slight slip. Hence, some people used two articles in The Scandinavian Journal of Economics (at the time Ekonomisk Tidskrift) to show how the proof could be shortened. The reason they had to write two articles, was that Tönu in his comments to the first pointed out that the new proof was wrong. Paper 1 in this volume made his result available to an international audience. This paper was delayed somewhat, and it is not inconceivable that Erich Schneider, who was at the time the editor of Weltwirtschaftliches Archiv, did not like it, because it slightly criticized some of his own work on investment decisions.

Tönu's thesis also contained a portfolio theory, which differed from that of Markowitz (1959) in at least one important aspect. By using a conic section, Tönu was able to make the analysis in the "quantity space" instead of the "mean variance space" used by Markowitz. He had developed this theory prior to 1964, and it had been published in Swedish in Ekonomisk Tidskrift. He also had ideas on how to treat increasing risk, although he did not end up in Blackwell's and later Rotschild and Stiglitz's ideas on statistical dominance.

Moreover, he derived difference equations for the relationship between short-term and long-term interest rates, under a condition of non-arbitrage. This must be one of the first comprehensive analyses of this problem, but since it was only published in Swedish he will never get the credit he deserves. Tönu probably thought that because the result, that nothing qualitative can be said about the relative magnitudes of the two, was not an empirically meaningful theorem, it was not worth publishing. The truth is, however, that people in finance tend to forget this, and now and they relate short- and long-run interest rates in a rather mechanical manner.

Most of his best papers are, of course, contained in the present volume, and one of my favorites is an early work on the profitability of exhausting natural resources. The paper not only contains an early post Hotelling analysis, but, to my knowledge, is the first to recognize the fact that the metal content of ore varies, and that it sooner or later becomes low enough to make mining unprofitable. This may seem to be a trivial observation, but in the context of the model it contributes to making mining very different from what Hotelling's rule teaches us.

I also have a special relationship with paper 5 "Towards a Theory of Optimal Roads". When Tönu wrote this he needed simulations of transports within the unit circle. Back in those days, the autumn of 1976, we did not have our own PC:s, but we could sit in a computer room close to the office, and do simulations on a smaller, and much slower, computer then the main frame. The problem was that there was a time limit after which the computer stopped. It could be circumvented, and I told Tönu about the trick. Now he could go shopping, go to the dentist or sleep while the program threw needles within the unit circle and computed a measure of transportation cost. The rate of convergence was slow and the simulation became very expensive. When Tönu was ready to go to Germany for a sabbatical in January 1977, he was told by "Doris" at the computer center, that we owed them 40000 Swedish crowns. Tönu in turn had to tell me, who was supposed to be acting chair during his sabbatical, that we not only had no computer time available for the spring semester, but that we also owed the University our allocation of computer time for the autumn. He was a little embarrassed to say the least.

We managed fairly well by diligently pointing out to Doris that the shadow price of computer time is zero, as long as the capacity utilization is less than full. She, however, neither appreciated the innovative nature of Tönu's paper. nor our sound but less innovative ideas about shadow prices, and she had no confidence at all in Tönu's programming capabilities

Tönu has many strings on his Viola di Gamba, and I will be reckless and suggest that his recent work in cultural economics will turn out to be one of his most influential. He is just finishing a book on the topic, and a little taste of what is in it is given by paper 13 "On Progress and Perfection in the Arts and Sciences".

What the papers in this volume demonstrate to the readers is Tönu's excellence as a scientist. What they cannot tell you is what it means to be a friend of his. I happen to be one of them and, with respect to real friendship, Hotelling's simplyfying assumption about a grade of ore that does not decline over time, is an apt picture. Moreover, the gold content is not only constant, it is also high.

# PART I

# Microeconomics

# Some Reflexions on the Theories of Choice Between Alternative Investment Opportunities

By

**Tõnu Puu**

The following discussion concerns the conditions for existence of criteria by the help of which investment decisions may be made by objective calculations — without reference to subjective time-preferences of the particular investor concerned. While applications of the criteria of "capital value" and "internal rate of interest" are affluent in economic theory, theorists seem to have been interested in the justifications for use of these criteria to a surprisingly small extent. As maximization of the internal rate of interest in general is inconsistent with maximization of capital value, the former procedure is nowadays regarded as inadequate[1]. But maximization of capital value seems to be accepted on pragmatic grounds, as the reasons for using this criterion are seldom explicitly brought forward, but at most treated implicitly in the discussion of which rate of interest one should use for calculations of capital value. Fisher has very clearly stated the reasons why every economic subject, regardless of time-preferences, should maximize capital value when unrestricted amounts of money may be lent or borrowed at one market rate of interest. However, later publications do seldom use so clear formulations. A symptom of this is the existence of discussions on the rate of interest which one should use as "target rate" in calculations of capital value when there are different rates for borrowing and lending. In this connection it has been proposed that some weighted average of the different rates might be used — or that the target rate should be regarded as a subjective rate of interest "required" by the investor.

[1] Erich Schneider, *Investering og rente*, Kjøbenhavn, 1944. — German Ed.: *Idem, Wirtschaftlichkeitsrechnung, Theorie der Investition*, 5. Aufl., unveränd. Nachdr. der 4., durchges. Aufl., Hand- und Lehrbücher aus dem Gebiet der Sozialwissenschaften, Tübingen u. Zürich, 1964. — F. A. Lutz, "The Criterion of Maximum Profits in the Theory of Investment", *The Quarterly Journal of Economics*, Vol. LX, Cambridge, Mass., 1945/46, pp. 56sqq.

Weltwirtschaftliches Archiv, Kiel (1967) Bd. 99, Heft 1:107-125

This may be contrasted to Fisher's position. In his treatment it is clear that the calculations must be carried out by the single market rate of interest — because the existence of a single rate is the very justification for the use of capital value as objective criterion of choice between alternative investment projects. If there are several different rates of interest for borrowers and lenders of various kinds there is no longer any obvious reason for maximization of capital value — simply because in that case no objective ranking of investment projects exists in the sense that the ranking is independent of subjective time-preferences of particular investors. As will be seen objective ranking of a set of investment alternatives may exist, provided that certain conditions are fulfilled. But the ranking is not complete, i.e., it does only apply to certain sets of investment alternatives. The aim of this article is to state explicitly the conditions to be satisfied by the alternative investments in order that objective ranking will exist. Thus the aim of this paper is a little less destructive than Hirshleifer's brilliant criticism. While Hirshleifer[1] takes the position that investment and consumption decisions may not be separated when there are different rates of interest for borrowers and lenders, the purpose of the present treatment is to find a class of cases where the decisions may be in fact separated — even if we accept Hirshleifer's general proposition that investment activity is only a means of redistributing the investor's consumption expenditures over time.

In the following discussion every investment opportunity is represented by a certain sequence of revenues and costs accrueing at different dates during the life-time of the investment considered — from the first costs in connection with construction of the plant necessary for production to the last revenues from selling the plant at its scrapvalue when production is definitely interrupted. In order to simplify the picture of the sequence of payments connected with a certain investment we divide the whole time of activity into time-periods of equal length, and we reason as if all the payments occurred at the ends of these time-periods. Thus, every time-period is represented by a net revenue — positive or negative — made up of the difference of all revenues and costs occurring in the period considered and attributed to the end of the period, and the whole investment is represented by a sequence of net revenues paid with regular intervals. The description has been made for an investment in real productive property. Of course the discussion may also concern financial investments in bonds and shares. In that case the time-periods are naturally intervals between coupon payments, while the periods in the former case are determined by the payment practice of the firms considered.

[1] J. Hirshleifer, "On the Theory of Optimal Investment Decision", *The Journal of Political Economy*, Vol. LXVI, Chicago, Illinois, 1958, pp. 329sqq.

All this is a description of the usual assumptions made in the theory of investment. As I am going to criticize the theory, I have no need to defend the statements made. I have merely put down my conception of the current assumptions made by investment theorists in order to avoid misunderstanding.

However, I have to make some notes about uncertainty. There are no difficulties to regard the history of an investment as a sequence of net revenues afterwards. But when the decision has to be made the sequences of net revenues associated with different investments have to be estimated in advance, and such estimations — or expectations — are always connected with uncertainty. The results of production processes, requiring time to be carried out, are often dependent on factors over which the producer has no control and about which he cannot even have any certain anticipations. The prices of factors to be bought and the prices of products to be sold in future depend on market conditions about which the producer can have not certain knowledge in advance. In case of corporation shares the payments associated with an investment depend on the results of the real production processes and market conditions which concern the firm issuing the shares. Thus the same sources of uncertainty encounter the investor in shares as the investor in real production processes. Moreover, there is another source of uncertainty arising from the instable behaviour of speculators if selling shares on the stock exchange market is contemplated. In case of bonds the uncertainty is only occurring when selling before the date of redemption is considered — provided of course that the ability of the issuing authority to fulfil its promises is beyond doubt.

When uncertainty prevails the treatment of rational behaviour is complicated by the fact that the investor's planning of his future dispositions in connection with the investment activity will not involve fixed plans — but conditional plans for all possible courses of events. The decisions which have to be realized immediately depend in a complicated way on the uncertain expectations and on the strategies of conditional planning for the future.

These problems are ignored in the theory of investment discussed in this paper. Often there are attempts to justify looking upon investments as certain sequences of net revenues, but these are not very convincing. Some authors assume perfect foresight about all future events. This is obviously unrealistic. Others mean that investors themselves assume perfect foresight even if they have none. The problem is then to explain how their belief in perfect foresight can be preserved when they realize the failure of their anticipations. The third and most popular expedient is the assumption that the investors — even if they are aware of the uncertainty prevailing in reality — act "as if" each investment led to a certain sequence of net revenues. Net revenues are then regarded as certainty equivalents to the uncertain revenues of the periods concerned, i.e. as means of probability distributions discounted by some premium on account of risk[1]. This argument is not convincing, because there is hardly any reasonable specific interpretation of the thesis of investors acting as if each investment were represented by a certain sequence of net revenues, besides the obvious interpretation that a certain investor is indifferent in a choice between an investment project with uncertain revenues on one hand and a sequence of certain revenues on the other. Such a sequence of certain net revenues might be determined experimentally by offering a number of choices to the investor. The problem is, however, that it is not possible to determine a *unique* sequence of certain net revenues — because every sequence of net revenues is a member of an infinite indifference class of different sequences. It is not possible to determine a certainty equivalent to the uncertain net revenue of each separate time-period — because the investment opportunity means an option to choose the sequence of uncertain net revenues in entirety and not separate options to choose uncertain net revenues for each time-period in isolation. But these difficulties are no problem of this discussion, because we want the negative result that investment decisions may only be made by way of objective calculations in a restricted number of cases even if the net revenues of each investment project may be anticipated with perfect foresight.

Thus the problem is to choose between different certain sequences of net revenues. The criteria proposed to be used in making an objective decision are of two kinds. One type is based on the idea that on the whole the investments yield more in revenue than is required in expenditure, which introduces the phenomenon of "interest." It would be a matter of measuring this "internal rate of interest" for the alternatives compared, after which one might let its level decide the alternative to be selected[2]. The meaning of this "internal rate of interest" might in plain words be explained by the following analogy. At the end of each period, when the net revenue in the sequence representing a certain investment is negative, an equal amount is imagined as being deposited in a bank account; in the same way, at the end of each period, when the net revenue is positive, an equal amount is imagined as being drawn from this account. The amount on deposit grows by compound interest. The internal rate

[1] Friedrich and Vera Lutz, *The Theory of Investment of the Firm*, Princeton, 1951, pp. 179sqq.

[2] K. E. Boulding, "The Theory of a Single Investment", *The Quarterly Journal of Economics*, Vol. XLIX, 1934/35, pp. 475sqq.

of interest is then equal to the interest which would have had to be paid in order that this bank account might again be reduced to zero by the last withdrawal in the sequence of transactions described, provided that the account began with zero before the first payment. Several problems arise in the precise interpretation of this definition. Since the amount on deposit is to grow by compound interest, we must state the intervals between the moments when interest is added to capital. These need not necessarily coincide with the periods used in the description of the net revenue sequence of the investment. Furthermore we must assume that the same interest will be paid for a debit balance as for a credit balance, if it can be expected that an overdraft on the "bank" will arise in any time period. Finally it is possible that we may get several values for the internal rate of interest from a given sequence of net revenues, provided that the sequence is sufficiently irregular. However, it may be shown that there only exists a unique value of the internal rate of interest, if the sequence of payments is such that there will be no debit balance in any time-period with the imaginary bank. From these complications it ought be clear that the internal rate of interest is an artificial concept defined for investments with *fixed* sequences of net revenues by an obscure analogy between, on the one hand, these investments with fixed sequences of net revenues and, on the other, bank deposits with considerable freedom of choice among an infinity of sequences of deposits and withdrawals being possible at a fixed rate of interest.

For deposits in a bank account, the rate of interest is, of course, fixed by the bank, whilst the depositor himself can determine the time distribution of deposits and withdrawals within a wide framework, which may consist, for example, in the stipulation that the account must not be overdrawn or exceed a certain amount, in stated requirements as regards the period of notice for large withdrawals, etc. The interest paid is then conceived of as a price paid for a homogeneous good. This good is the right of disposal over cash for a certain time-period. When the "price" is given, the depositor may himself determine the amounts over which he will transfer the right of disposal for different periods.

Investments in production processes or in securities, such as bonds and shares, do not give such freedom of choice. In the absence of uncertainty such commitments have been assumed to lead to definite sequences of negative and positive net revenues. We can, it is true, calculate the internal rate of interest in the way mentioned above, but the investor can no longer himself determine the distribution in time of the amounts over which he will transfer the right of disposal at a given rate of interest. The opportunity of engaging in an investment thus involves a fixed option, in the same way as the offer to buy a certain quantity of goods for a certain sum of money. It is not self-evident that we shall choose one of two alternative quantities of goods offered for sale merely because the unit price happens to be lowest; it should be no more self-evident that we shall choose a certain investment alternative merely because the internal rate of interest happens to be the highest. To put it in another way, the investments cannot be reduced to the homogeneous category of "goods" which we have called "right of disposal over cash for a unit period" with a price which has real meaning, since they represent positive and negative payments distributed in time in a definite manner. This would only be possible in either of two cases. If in each period there was a market for the different investments and the future prices on these markets could be predicted with certainty all complicated calculations of internal rates of interest would be pointless, as it would be trivial to decide which investment would be most profitable in each period when every investment only involves two payments — one at the beginning and one at the end of the period. The other case is when every investment project may be worked out on a continuously variable scale — in such a way that the scale factor affects every net revenue in the same proportion — and the different projects — in number at least equal to the number of time-periods considered — may be combined with each other. Then it is possible to compute implied "shadow" rates of interest for each time-period — and those rates of interest have a real meaning because the situation is then the same as when it is possible to borrow from and lend to banks with fixed rates of interest.

One reason which particularly argues against the use of the internal rate of interest as a criterion for the choice made among the alternative investment opportunities is that the procedure of maximizing the internal rate of interest corresponds to a preference ordering of net revenue sequences which is non-transitive. This may be seen in the following way. The value of the internal rate of interest expressed as a decimal fraction added to unity, i.e. the one period accumulation factor, is computed by solving a polynomial equation, the coefficients of which are the net revenues in the sequence corresponding to a certain investment. As we have pointed out such an equation may have several different and economically reasonable solutions. In the economic context considered a polynomial equation, of course, always has as many solutions as there are time-periods in the life-time of the investment considered. But some solutions of the accumulation factor may be complex and some negative. A complex accumulation factor means a complex rate of interest and a negative accumulation factor means a real rate of interest, which is less than —100 percent. Nevertheless it is possible that there is more than one internal rate of interest which is real and does not have the absurd property of converting debits to credits and credits to debits, provided that there is some irregularity in the sequence of net revenues in the meaning that positive net revenues alternate with negative ones. When the internal rate of interest determines the order of preference, some investments may thus correspond to several indifference classes. Thus two investments may be both indifferent — because they yield the same internal rate of interest — and non-indifferent — because they also yield different internal rates of interest. As a particular case it is true that a polynomial equation whose coefficients are all zero is satisfied for any real value of the variable. This means that a sequence of net revenues which are all zero represents an investment which yields any conceivable value of the internal rate of interest. This case is not economically uninteresting, as might be thought at a first glance at the problem, as it corresponds to the alternative of abstaining from any investment activity. Thus abstaining from investment activity will be indifferent to any conceivable investment. Such a preference ordering obviously does not fulfil the most elementary rationality properties required to be fulfilled by preference orderings.

From the preference point of view a sequence of net revenues may be regarded as having the same character as a collection of quantities of physically different kinds of goods. The different "goods" are represented in this case by amounts of money located in different time-periods. This type of analogy leads to the other suggested main criterion for an objective ordering of net revenue sequences. Just as heterogeneous collections of goods can be valued with the aid of the market prices of the different goods, it should conceivably be possible to value sequences of net revenues in the same way. When we value a collection of physically different goods, we do so, as a rule, by calculating its equivalent in money. However, we could just as well have calculated the equivalent as a quantity of one of the different kinds of goods included in the collection. The valuation would then, of course, not have been carried out with the aid of the money prices of the different goods but instead with the aid of their respective exchange rates in relation to the kind of goods in which the value of the collection was expressed, which means this value would have come to depend on which kind of goods was chosen as "numéraire." This is also the way we proceed to calculate the capital value of a net revenue sequence, which, of course, expresses the equivalent of the whole sequence as a sum of money located in some definite period. The capital value must be referred to some particular period, just as the kind of goods in which the heterogeneous collection is valued must be particularly stated. Thus it is not sufficient to state that the valuation shall be made in money, for all the different "goods" are amounts of money and only differ as regards the time-period to which they belong. Often it is usual to calculate the capital value at the time when the investment activity is planned to begin, when it is given the name of "present value." The exchange rates for the net revenues of the later periods in relation to the net revenue of the period immediately preceding the first period of investment activity are then called "discount factors." The investment, amongst several alternatives, which has the highest present value is assumed to be chosen. In this connection it should be observed that the capital values of the alternatives compared should be calculated in terms of the net revenue of one and the same time-period. Otherwise the comparison will be equivalent to a comparison of the equivalents of alternative collections of goods calculated as quantities of different kinds of goods, i.e. a comparison of incommensurables. But so far as this rule is observed it is immaterial which time-period is used for calculation of capital values compared.

The reason for preferring collections with greater market value when the exchange rates of the market between different goods are constant is obvious. It is true that we do not wish, as a rule, to receive as much as possible of the kind of goods in which the valuation is made in order to satisfy our ultimate desires, but, whichever ultimate desires — or preferences — about collections of goods we want to satisfy, we can obtain objectively more desirable collections by market exchange, if we originally have at our disposal a larger quantity of the kind of goods in which the valuation is made. In this connection, an objectively more desirable collection is assumed to be one which contains more of at least one kind of goods without containing less of any one of the other kinds of goods. This applies, however, only if all desired exchanges of goods can really be made at constant exchange rates.

The same can be said about a choice between different net revenue sequences, i.e. that the capital values objectively express the "profitability" of different sequences, provided that borrowing and lending can take place in any period without limitations at a constant rate of interest. In reality, however, these conditions are hardly fulfilled. On the markets for buying and selling promises to pay certain sums of money in the future the prices vary depending on whether one is a buyer or seller and also on the amounts one wants to buy or sell. In simplified theories, in which only one rate of interest is assumed to exist for each period, the prospect that capital value will be maximized seems quite reasonable, but the conclusion cannot simply be assumed to apply under more realistic assumptions of different lending and borrowing rates. The search for a "valid" target rate of interest, by the help of which capital values might be calculated under the more complicated and realistic assumptions is meaningless. The discussion also implies that the capital values in the cases when they may be used as objective criteria must be calculated with the aid of interest rates in real perfect markets, which the investor is assumed to have access to. Thus, it is generally not possible to make the calculations with some subjective rates of interest, which the investor is assumed to "require."

One exception is the case in which the preference ordering of net revenue sequences is such that all indifference loci are parallel hyperplanes. This is a very special case in which the subjective "rate of time preference," i.e. the rate of interest at which the investor is indifferent about infinitesimal substitutions of the net revenue of one period for another, for any pair of time-periods, is constant at movements both along a specific indifference locus and between different indifference loci. There is no reason why the preferences of any investor should have such specific properties. Moreover, if such a system of preferences would be used to determine the optimal time-distribution of consumption outlays of a consumer planning for several time-periods, no optimum can be determined when there is one single rate of interest in every time-period. The problem is the usual one treated in multi-period theory of a consumer's optimum. The reason why no optimum can be determined is the following. Either the rate of time preference coincides with the market rate of interest — and then all alternatives on the consumer's budget constraint are indifferent. Or the rate of time-preference does not coincide with the market rate of interest — and then the stimulus to borrowing or lending remains in unaltered force irrespective of the extent of borrowing and lending which has already occurred. But this is a completely theoretical problem, because the assumption of a coincident rate of interest for borrowing and lending is not very realistic. However, the assumption of maximization of capital value calculated by a subjective rate of interest is unreasonable, because it corresponds to a preference ordering of net revenue sequences so arbitrary that there is no reason why all investors should have preferences with such characteristics.

Hirshleifer has taken the opposite position in relation to those who use the criterion of maximal capital value as a generally applicable method, by arguing that "their common error lay in searching for a rule or formula which would indicate optimal investment decisions *independently of consumption decisions*. No such search can succeed, if Fisher's analysis is sound which regards investment as not an end in itself but rather a process for distributing consumption over time"[1]. Hirshleifer agrees that in a specific case treated by Fisher where there

[1] Hirshleifer, *op. cit.*, p. 329.

is one market rate of interest the investment decision may in fact be separated from the consumption decision. Fisher's own argument for separating the decisions in this case is that since "any time shape may be transformed into any other time shape, nobody need be deterred from selecting an income because of its time shape, but everyone may choose an income exclusively on the basis of maximum present value. It will then happen that his income, as finally transformed, will be larger than it would have been if he had chosen some other ... time shape." With a "larger income" Fisher must obviously mean the same that we mean by "objectively more desirable" or "objectively preferable" in ordering "net revenue sequences." Fisher is quite clear about the limitations of his conclusion, because he states that "all this is true under the assumptions ... that after the most valuable option has been chosen, you can borrow and lend or buy and sell *ad libitum* ... If this assumption is not true, if a person were cut off from a free loan market, the choice among optional income streams might or might not fall upon that one having the maximum present value, depending on the other circumstances involved, particularly his preferences as regards time shape"[1]. In the following discussion we are going to show that even if these assumptions are not fulfilled there may be still an objective ordering in some cases.

We are going to do so by starting from the proposition that each investor has a complete subjective ordering for all conceivable sequences of net revenues. Different investors have, of course, in general different orderings — depending on different preferences for the distribution of consumption outlays in time and depending on different expectations about the distribution in time of expected net revenues from other activities than those considered in the investment decision. But all those different preference orderings will have some features in common. All of them are assumed to fulfil the requirements for rational preference orderings currently made in the theory of a consumer's optimum. Moreover one sequence of net revenues is objectively preferred by all investors in comparison with another, provided that it involves a more favourable — i.e. a greater positive or a smaller negative — net revenue for at least one time-period and does not involve a less favourable — i.e. a greater negative or smaller positive — net revenue for any other time-period. Likewise two sequences of net revenues are indifferent to all investors, provided that they involve exactly equal net revenues for every time-period, and this may thus be called objective indifference. Thus the objective preference ordering is the part of the subjective preference orderings common to all of them. It is not complete, as the absence of

[1] Irving Fisher, *The Theory of Interest, As Determined by Impatience to Spend Income and Opportunity to Invest it*, New York, 1930, pp. 138sq.

objective preference relations in any direction between two sequences of net revenues does not imply objective indifference. This is the case when one sequence of net revenues involves greater net revenues for some time-periods and another sequence involves greater net revenues for other time-periods. Then the decision made will depend on which investor has made the choice. If one investment is objectively preferred to another then it is true that its capital value will be greater whichever sequence of interest rates is assumed to be applicable for the sequence of time-periods concerned. The converse is also true. But it is not true that one sequence of net revenues will be objectively preferable to another sequence when it is only true that its capital value is greatest when calculated by one single sequence of interest rates. In all these discussions the rates of interest used in calculation are assumed to be real and not less than —100 percent.

The treatment sketched above, however, only applies when there are no possibilities of transforming the sequences of net revenues corresponding to different investments by way of loans to or from a bank. The treatment does not even allow hoarding from one time-period to the following. Thus we must modify the criteria of objective preference to cases where the choice of an investment alternative does not mean a choice between two fixed sequences of net revenues — but a choice between two sets of sequences of net revenues, each consisting of the fixed net revenue sequence associated with investment activity as well as the transformations of the fixed sequence by way of hoarding or loans to or from a bank. After one of the investments has been chosen there is still option of choice within the set of transformations. This necessitates a change of the definition of objective preference relation between two investment opportunities in the following way. One of two alternative investment opportunities is said to be objectively preferable if and only if the two corresponding sets of net revenue sequences stand in such a relationship to each other that for every sequence in the set corresponding to the non-preferable investment there is at least one sequence in the set corresponding to the preferable investment which is objectively preferable in the sense defined above for a pair of fixed net revenue sequences. It may be recalled that a fixed sequence of net revenues was assumed to be objectively preferred to another fixed sequence, provided that it involved a better net revenue for at least one time-period without involving a worse net revenue for any other time period.

It will be seen from the mathematical argument below that we may obtain precise interpretations in terms of capital values of the conditions for existence of an objective preference relation for investments with possible transformation, when the transformations may be made by way of loans from and to a bank which has different lending and borrowing rates for all time-periods but no other restrictions. A special case occurs when only hoarding is possible. Then the "bank's" borrowing rate of interest will have zero value and its lending rate of interest will have infinite value, but otherwise it does not differ from the former case described. When there is a borrowing rate and a lending rate for each period, then the calculations by which capital values are obtained may be carried out for every period by two possible methods, i.e. by using either the borrowing rate or the lending rate. As this may be done for every time-period involved, the total number of different sequences of interest rates used in calculation of capital values is an exponential expression with the number two as its base and the number of periods involved as its exponent. This number of different sequences of interest rates is also the number of different methods of calculating a capital value from a certain sequence of net revenues. For a two-period analysis the number of different calculation methods is 4, for a three-period analysis it is 8, for a four-period analysis 16, etc. Generally with n time-periods the number of different ways of calculation is $2^n$. The theorem proved is that an investment with a fixed sequence of net revenues will be objectively preferred to another investment, in the sense defined when we had to consider also sets of transformations, provided that the capital value of the former investment is greatest when calculated in every possible way. This is a necessary as well as sufficient condition for objective preference. Thus, it is necessary to carry out $2^n$ calculations in order to make an objective choice among investment alternatives. Moreover it is perfectly possible that there will be no objective preference relation between a pair of arbitrary investment alternatives. This occurs when one investment yields higher capital value by some ways of calculation while another investment yields higher capital value by other ways of calculation. A special case of interest is the case when only hoarding is possible. Then an investment will be objectively preferable in relation to another, provided that the cumulated simple sums of the fixed net revenues in the sequence of the former are greater for every sub-sequence of time-periods from the first one up to any period from the first one to the last one as compared to the corresponding cumulated simple sums of the fixed net revenues in the sequence of the latter. Another special case is when the borrowing and lending rates coincide. Then there is only one way to calculate a capital value from a sequence of net revenues, and there are only three possibilities when two investments are compared. Either the first investment has a greater capital value, or the second investment has a greater capital value — or if neither is true then the capital values must be equal. In this special case there must always be an objective preference relation between two arbitrary investments, provided that they are not objectively indifferent.

A special kind of choice is the case when a decision has to be made to accept a certain investment opportunity or not. Then the choice may be said to be made between two investment alternatives — one represented by the fixed sequence of net revenues and its transformations corresponding to the investment alternative and the other represented by a fixed sequence of zero net revenues and its transformations corresponding to the non-investment alternative. If we apply the rule of greater capital value in every way of calculation, we find that the capital value of the non-investment alternative will be zero in every way of calculation. The conclusion is thus that an investment should rather be accepted than refused, provided that the capital value of the fixed sequence of net revenues associated with the investment is positive in every way of calculation.

This is however not everything that can be said about the choice of investment when the borrowing and lending rates are different. Provided that a certain transformation — made up by a sequence of deposits into and withdrawals from a bank account — is chosen at the same time as a certain investment is chosen, then we may specify conditions that must not be fulfilled if the choice has to be rational. And these conditions apply even if no objective preference relation applies to the decision made. If the choice has been between two alternative investments, the capital value of the "difference investment" from the investment chosen to the investment not chosen must not be greater in every way of calculation than the capital value of the transformation sequence, where bank withdrawals are taken as positive items and bank deposits as negative items. If these conditions apply then it would have been objectively better to have chosen the alternative which in fact was not chosen. These conditions apply, as has been already pointed out, even if no objective preference relation prevails. But this is all we can say about objective choice between investment alternatives. There is still a large class of choice situations where nothing can be said about which investment should be chosen without knowledge of the circumstances of the investor involved and particularly his time-preferences as regards the distribution of consumption over time. In these cases Hirshleifer's proposition is true that the decision to invest may not be separated from the decision to consume.

We will next make a mathematical treatment of the problem in order that some of the new ideas proposed will be somewhat clearer.

## Mathematical Appendix

Denote first the net revenue which a certain investment yields at the end of the t:th time-period by $x_t$. In this connection payments from the investment project to the investor have positive signs and payments in the opposite direction have negative signs. Assume that the duration of the investment project is n time-periods in all. Thus, if we provide for the possibility of an initial payment at the beginning of the first period, i.e. the end of the period 0, we are concerned about $x_t$ for $t = 0, 1, \ldots, n$. The sequence of all net revenues emanating from the investment project considered may be expressed as a vector $x = [x_0, \ldots, x_n]$. When two investment projects are compared they will be distinguished by a suffix. Thus we denote by $x^{(1)}$ a vector whose elements are $x_t^{(1)}$ and by $x^{(2)}$ a vector whose elements are $x_t^{(2)}$.

A sequence of deposits into and withdrawals from a bank account is similarly denoted by a vector $z = [z_0, \ldots, z_n]$ where payments from the bank to the investor have positive signs and payments in the opposite direction have negative signs. This vector of payments has to satisfy certain conditions which depend on the borrowing and lending rates of interest, but as far as those conditions are satisfied, the investor has a wide latitude of choice within a set of vectors, denoted T. It is our next purpose to state the conditions which determine T, but before we proceed there is another matter of notation which has to be dealt with immediately. As it is possible that different sequences of deposits into and withdrawals from a bank account will be associated with different choices of investment projects the z-vectors too have to be distinguished by the help of a suffix. Thus we denote by $z^{(1)}$ a vector whose elements are $z_t^{(1)}$ and by $z^{(2)}$ a vector whose elements are $z_t^{(2)}$.

Assume now that there is in every time-period one lending and one borrowing rate of interest, denoted $i_{Lt}$ and $i_{Bt}$ respectively and specified for $t = 1, \ldots, n$. It is quite in order that we deal with rates of interest specified for n time-periods, while there are payments specified for $(n + 1)$ time-periods. For every sequence of n time-periods there are namely $(n + 1)$ moments indicating beginnings or ends of the periods considered — and for every such moment a payment may occur. Even if payments are attached to moments and not to periods, we may unambiguously identify a payment by a period specification, provided that we use our convention, introduced above, about payments occurring at the ends of the time-periods for which they are specified. If we do not want to specify which rate of interest is applied for a certain time-period we will write $i_{r_t}$, where for every period either $r_t = L_t$ or $r_t = B_t$. When we want to specify a certain method of computing capital value we have to state for each time-period separately if the lending rate or the borrowing rate of interest is used. Identification of a certain calculation method will thus be made by means of a vector of indices $r = [r_1, \ldots, r_n]$. As every element of the vector may have two interpretations there are in total $2^n$ different r-vectors. They constitute together a set index-vectors, denoted M.

We are now able to calculate capital values from vectors x or z. The capital value functions will be denoted by $K_r(\ )$ and they carry an index r in order to specify the method of calculation. In all there are $2^n$ different capital value functions to be considered. The capital value calculated to the end of the time-period n by the method of calculation specified by r will be:

$$K_r(z) = \sum_{t=0}^{n} z_t \cdot \prod_{s=t+1}^{n} (1 + i_{r_s})$$

where the product

$$\prod_{s=n+1}^{n} (1 + i_{r_s}) = 1$$

by definition. We should further observe that all capital value functions are linear with positive coefficients.

Under the assumption that there are different lending and borrowing rates of interest, but no other market imperfections, the investor may choose any vector z, such that $K_r(z) \leq 0$ for all r in the set M, in addition to and independently of his choice of investment project. All the vectors z, which satisfy the conditions stated, constitute the set of possible transformations T. The verbal interpretation of the proposition is that when there are different rates of interest for borrowers and lenders in every time-period, then, as there are $2^n$ different ways to compute a capital value from a sequence of deposits into and withdrawals from a bank account during n periods, all those sequences are possible whose capital values are non-positive by every way of calculation. This proposition is intuitively plausible. Moreover, it may be formally proved, but because the proof is complicated the reader is directed to my doctoral dissertation or to Dr. Odhnoff's mathematical note about my dissertation[1].

Next we have to specify some vector operations and vector relations. As usually we mean by addition or subtraction of vectors the composite operation of addition or subtraction carried out on all vector elements belonging to the same time-period. Thus $x + z = [x_0 + z_0, \ldots, x_n + z_n]$.

[1] Tönu Puu, *Studier i det optimala tillgångsvalets teori*, Uppsala, 1964, pp. 61sqq. — Jan Odhnoff, "A Mathematical Note to Some Results by Tönu Puu", *The Swedish Journal of Economics*, Vol. LXVII, Uppsala, 1965, pp. 80sqq.

Moreover, we want to extend the relation "is greater than" to vectors. This is accomplished by stating that a vector is greater than another, provided that at least one element is greater and no element is smaller. The connection of this relation to the objective preference relation, introduced in the verbal discussion, is obvious. Formally we write for a pair of vectors $x^{(2)} + z^{(2)}$ and $x^{(1)} + z^{(1)}$ that the relation $x^{(2)} + z^{(2)} > x^{(1)} + z^{(1)}$ is true when $x_t^{(2)} + z_t^{(2)} > x_t^{(1)} + z_t^{(1)}$ is true for at least one t and $x_t^{(1)} + z_t^{(1)} > x_t^{(2)} + z_t^{(2)}$ is not true for any t.

We are now able to state formally the objective preference relation between investments (2) and (1). The former is said to be objectively preferable in relation to the latter when for every $z^{(1)}$ in T it is possible to find at least one $z^{(2)}$ in T, such that the relation $x^{(2)} + z^{(2)} > x^{(1)} + z^{(1)}$ is true.

By the following argument it will be proved that this is equivalent to the conditions that $K_r(x^{(2)}) > K_r(x^{(1)})$ for every r in M. The equivalence will be proved in two stages.

First, assume that for any arbitrary $z^{(1)}$ in T we can find at least one $z^{(2)}$ in T, such that $x^{(2)} + z^{(2)} > x^{(1)} + z^{(1)}$. As this must be true for any vector $z^{(1)}$ in T, it must also hold for the vector of zeros. But then $K_r(z^{(1)}) = 0$ for all r in M. Moreover, as $x^{(2)} + z^{(2)} > x^{(1)} + z^{(1)}$, the vector $x^{(2)} + z^{(2)} - x^{(1)} - z^{(1)}$ will be a "positive" vector in the meaning that it has at least one positive and no negative element. Because all capital value functions are linear with positive coefficients it will then be true that $K_r (x^{(2)} + z^{(2)} - x^{(1)} - z^{(1)}) > 0$ for all r in M. Remembering the linear property of all capital value functions and considering the fact that we have chosen $z^{(1)}$ so that $K_r(z^{(1)}) = 0$ for all r in M, we conclude that $K_r(x^{(2)}) - K_r(x^{(1)}) + K_r(z^{(2)}) > 0$ for all r in M. But as $z^{(2)}$ has to belong to T, we know that $K_r(z^{(2)}) \leq 0$ for all r in M. Thus, finally we see that it must be true that $K_r(x^{(2)}) > K_r(x^{(1)})$ for all r in M. This completes the first part of the proof.

The second part runs as follows. Assume that $K_r(x^{(2)}) > K_r(x^{(1)})$ for all r in M. Next, choose a small positive number d such that $K_r(x^{(2)}) > K_r(x^{(1)}) + d$ for all r in M. Then, starting from any vector $z^{(1)}$ in T, construct a vector $z^{(2)}$ such that $z_t^{(2)} = x_t^{(1)} - x_t^{(2)} + z_t^{(1)}$ for $t = 0, \ldots, n-1$ and $z_n^{(2)} = x_n^{(1)} - x_n^{(2)} + z_n^{(1)} + d$. This vector $z^{(2)}$ will obviously be such that $x^{(2)} + z^{(2)} > x^{(1)} + z^{(1)}$ is true. Thus, it only remains to prove that $z^{(2)}$ constructed above is a member of the set T, i.e. that $K_r(z^{(2)}) \leq 0$ is true for all r in M. Remembering that all capital value functions are linear, and especially that the last coefficients of all those functions are equal to unity, we find that $K_r(z^{(2)}) = K_r(x^{(1)}) - K_r(x^{(2)}) + K_r(z^{(1)}) + d$ for all r in M. Because, according to our assumptions, it is true that $K_r(z^{(1)}) \leq 0$ and $K_r(x^{(1)}) - K_r(x^{(2)}) + d < 0$

for all r in M, the conclusion must be that $K_r(z^{(2)}) \leq 0$ or that $z^{(2)}$ belongs to T. This concludes the proof.

Thus investment (2) has to be objectively preferred in comparison to investment (1), provided that $K_r(x^{(2)}) > K_r(x^{(1)})$ for all r in M. Likewise investment (1) has to be objectively preferred to investment (2), provided that $K_r(x^{(1)}) > K_r(x^{(2)})$ for all r in M. In other cases the choice depends on the time-preferences of the investor.

When the choice is between accepting a certain investment and rejecting it, the conclusion is that it has to be objectively accepted when $K_r(x) > 0$ for all r in M and objectively rejected when $K_r(x) < 0$ for all r in M.

* * *

Zusammenfassung: Einige Bemerkungen über die Theorie der Wahl zwischen alternativen Investitionsmöglichkeiten. — Die vorliegende Abhandlung stellt eine Untersuchung der Rechtfertigung der Verwendung des höchsten Kapitalwerts als Kriterium für die Wahl zwischen alternativen Investitionsmöglichkeiten dar und führt damit zur Annahme alternativer Nettoeinnahmen-Reihen. Der Grund, warum das Kriterium des höchsten Kapitalwerts von allen rational kalkulierenden Investoren verwendet werden sollte, und zwar unabhängig von ihren subjektiven Zeitpräferenzen und den Einnahmen aus anderen Aktivitäten als denen, die bei der Investitionsentscheidung berücksichtigt werden, wurde von I. Fisher für den Fall dargelegt, bei dem unbegrenzte Geldbeträge zu einem einzigen Zinssatz verliehen und geborgt werden können. Spätere Autoren, die sich mit diesem Thema beschäftigten, versuchten, das Prinzip des höchsten Kapitalwerts auf Fälle auszudehnen, bei denen die für Kreditnehmer und Kreditgeber relevanten Zinssätze verschieden sind, indem sie einen einzigen »Soll«-Zinssatz in ihre Berechnungen einbezogen, wobei dieser »Soll«-Zinssatz entweder den gewogenen Durchschnitt der angebotenen und nachgefragten Zinssätze oder einen »subjektiven« Zinssatz darstellt, der von dem Investor erwartet wird. Dieses Vorgehen wurde durch Hirschleifer sehr scharf kritisiert, der mit einiger Berechtigung darauf hinwies, daß die Investitions- und Konsumentscheidungen nicht getrennt werden dürfen.

Der vorliegende Artikel versucht, die Bedingungen für die Fälle ausdrücklich anzugeben, bei denen diese Entscheidungen tatsächlich getrennt werden können, auch wenn Hirschleifers Behauptung im allgemeinen richtig ist. Es wird gezeigt, daß sogar in dem Fall, bei dem die Zinsen für Kreditnehmer und Kreditgeber verschieden sind, die objektive Präferenz durch den Kapitalwert ausgedrückt werden kann, und es wird nachgewiesen, daß eine notwendige und ausreichende Bedingung für die objektive Präferenzbeziehung zwischen zwei Investitionen darin besteht, daß der Kapitalwert der vorgezogenen bei jeder angewendeten Kalkulationsmethode größer sein muß. Wie leicht einzusehen ist, gibt es aber noch eine große Zahl von Fällen, bei denen diese Bedingungen nicht erfüllt sind und für die Hirschleifers allgemeine Kritik zutreffend ist.

*

Résumé: Quelques réflexions au sujet des théories du choix entre possibilités alternatives d'investissement. — L'article examine la justification de l'emploi de la valeur capital maxima comme critère du choix entre possibilités alternatives d'investissement, possibilités qui conduiraient à des suites alternatives et parfaitement prévues de revenu net. C'est Irving Fisher qui a exposé les raisons pour lesquelles le critère de la valeur capital maxima devrait être employé par tout investiteur rationnel, sans égard pour ses préférences subjectives de terme, ni pour les revenus provenant d'activités autres que celles envisagées par la décision d'investir. Il l'a fait pour le cas où des sommes illimitées d'argent peuvent être prêtées et empruntées à un seul et identique taux d'intérêt. Plus tard, d'autres auteurs ont essayé d'étendre le principe de la valeur capital maxima aux cas où les taux d'intérêt des prêts diffèrent de ceux des emprunts. A cet effet ils ont introduit dans leurs calculs un taux d'intérêt «visé» («target»), qui fut une moyenne pondérée des taux d'intérêt des prêts et des emprunts, ou un taux «subjectif» qu'exigerait l'investiteur. Ces procédés ont été sévèrement critiqués par Hirschleifer, qui prétend avec une certaine justification qu'on ne peut pas séparer la décision de consommer de celle d'investir. L'article que voici cherche à préciser les conditions des cas dans lesquels ces deux décisions peuvent en effet être séparées, même si l'affirmation de Hirschleifer reste généralement correcte. Il est démontré que la préférence objective peut être exprimée en termes de la valeur capital même dans le cas où les taux d'intérêt des prêts et des emprunts diffèrent. Il est prouvé que, pour qu'une préférence objective existe entre deux investissements possibles, la condition nécessaire et suffisante est que la valeur capital de l'investissement préféré soit plus grande, quelle que soit la méthode de calcul. On comprend facilement qu'il y a bon nombre de cas où ces conditions ne se trouvent pas être remplies, et que, par conséquent, la critique de Hirschleifer reste, en général, valable.

*

Resumen: Algunas observaciones sobre la teoría de la elección entre posibilidades alternativas de las inversiones. — El presente estudio hace un análisis de la justificación del empleo del supremo valor del capital como criterio para elegir entre posibilidades alternativas de las inversiones, llegando a la aceptación de listas alternativas de ingresos neto. La razón de por qué el criterio del supremo valor del capital debería ser empleado por todos los inversores que calculan racionalmente — y por cierto con independencia de sus preferencias subjetivas respecto de un tiempo y con independencia de ingresos de otras actividades que de aquellas que son tenidas en cuenta al decidir una inversión — fue expuesta por I. Fisher respecto del caso en que cantidades ilimitadas de dinero puedan ser otorgadas y prestadas a un único tipo de interés. Autores que posteriormente se han ocupado de este tema han intentado extender el principio del supremo valor del capital al caso en que sean diversos los tipos de interés relativos a prestatarios y prestamistas, no habiendo incluido en sus cálculos sino un sólo tipo de interés del debe, en cuyo caso, dicho tipo de interés del debe representa, o el término medio de los tipos de interés ofrecidos y demandados, o un tipo de interés subjetivo esperado por el inversor. Este procedimiento ha sido muy criticado por Hirschleifer, quien no sin razón hizo notar que no es posible separar las decisiones de invertir de las decisiones relativas al consumo.

El presente artículo intenta indicar expresamente las condiciones referentes a los casos en que dichas decisiones puedan de hecho ser separadas, si bien la afirmación de Hirschleifer es cierta en general. El autor muestra que incluso en el caso de que sean distintos los intereses para el prestatario y para el prestamista, puede ser expresada por el valor del capital la preferencia objetiva; y así se muestra que una condición necesaria y suficiente para la relación de preferencia objetiva entre dos inversiones consiste en que el valor del capital de la preferida sea mayor en cualquier método de cálculo que se emplee. Como fácilmente se echa de ver, existe todavía un gran número de casos en que tales condiciones no se cumplen, y para los que es acertada la crítica general de Hirschleifer.

*

Riassunto: Alcune osservazioni intorno alla teoria della scelta tra possibilità alternative di investimento. — Il presente saggio presenta un'analisi della giustificazione dell'uso del massimo capitale di valore come criterio per la scelta tra possibilità alternative di investimento e porta all'ammissione di serie di entrate nette alternative. Il motivo per cui il criterio del massimo valore di capitale dovrebbe essere usato da tutti gli investitori che calcolano in modo razionale e cioè indipendentemente dalle loro soggettive preferenze temporali e dalle entrate di altre attività, prese in considerazione per decidere un investimento, è stato dimostrato da I. Fisher per il caso in cui illimitate somme siano date e prese in prestito a un unico tasso d'interesse. Altri che si sono occupati più tardi di questo tema hanno cercato di allargare il principio del massimo valore di capitale a casi in cui i rilevanti interessi sono diversi per il debitore e per il creditore, includendo nei loro calcoli un unico tasso obbligato, dove questo interesse «obbligato» rappresenta o la media degli interessi offerti o richiesti o un interesse oggettivo, atteso dagli investitori. Questo procedimento è stato assai criticato da Hirschleifer che ha con una certa legittimità fatto notare che le decisioni di investimento e di consumo non possono essere divise.

Il presente articolo cerca di presentare le condizioni di quei casi in cui queste decisioni effettivamente non si possono separare, anche se il parere di Hirschleifer è in generale giusto. Viene dimostrato che addirittura nel caso che gli interessi del creditore e del debitore siano diversi, la preferenza obiettiva può essere espressa mediante il valore di capitale. E la condizione necessaria e sufficente all'obiettivo rapporto di preferenza tra due investimenti consiste nel fatto che il valore di capitale di quelli preferiti deve essere più grande in ogni metodo di calcolo usato. Naturalmente c'è ancora un grandissimo numero di casi in cui queste condizioni non si realizzano e per cui rimane valida la critica generale di Hirschleifer.

# Complementarity, Substitutivity and Regressivity in the Theory of Production [1]

## I. The analogy of the theory of consumer behaviour and the theory of the firm.

Since Hicks and Allen (A Reconsideration of the Theory of Value 1934) awakened from oblivion the ideas first expressed by Slutsky (Sulla teoria del bilancio del consumatore 1915), those ideas have gained popularity and ultimately grown a part of every economist's theorical equipment. The essence of those ideas is that in the familiar indifference curve analysis of consumer behaviour the effect on the quantity demanded of any consumer good, caused by a change of the price of the same or of another consumer good, may always be split up in two well-defined parts. Those additive parts are commonly called " substitution effect " and " income effect ". The " substitution effect " is the change, due to the adjustment to changed relative prices, which would emerge if the level of satisfaction was not affected. The level of satisfaction is not affected, provided that the price change is accompanied by an income change of a magnitude adequate to keep the consumer's optimum to the initial indifference curve. In the absence of such a compensatory income change, the substitution effect is modified by such a change as would be caused by an isolated income change (at constant prices) of a magnitude adequate to shift the consumer's optimum to the new indifference curve. This modifying change is called " income effect. "

As the substitution effect is proved to be negative under the assumptions of the theory considered, provided that the demand of a good is concerned whose own price has changed, the splitting of effects yields some of the very few empirically

[1] The author is indebted to Professor Tord Palander for many stimulating discussions on the subject.

controllable assertions of the theory of consumer behaviour. Furthermore, this splitting of effects provides an intelligible explanation of the famous " Giffen's paradox " and furnishes a convenient basis for the definitions of the " complementarity " and " subsitutivity " relations and the " inferiority " property of consumer goods according to a single consumer's preferences.

Surprisingly, the obvious analogy of this for the theory of the firm has not been commonly used. This is the more astonishing, as economists otherwise have been very anxious to emphasize every formal likeness between the theories of consumer's optimum and producer's optimum. An exeption is provided by Makower and Baumol (The Analogy of Producer and Consumer Equilibrium 1950), where a distinction between " substitution effect " and " resources effect " is made for the theory of the firm. The distinction is, however, only applicable in a very special version of the theory of the firm ; framed in such a way that the firm is assumed to obtain maximum of output under a constraint of a fixed initial endowment of production factors, which may be made different from the factor combination actually used only by way of market exchange. As variable costs are fixed, profits will be maximized when output is maximized. The theory seems to apply only to firms that hold all their assets as stocks of factors of production. Thus, every optimizing decision has to be made within the possibilities supplied by fixed initial factor quantities, which may be used directly in production or sold in order to obtain more than the fixed quantities of other factors. Moreover, all borrowing possibilities must be excluded. In support of their theory the authors argue that, as the product may be sold only after the factors are bought and used up in production, the factors of production must be rewarded from some other source than the revenue from the sale of the product. This argument is not very strong as far as short period optimizing decisions are concerned, where the costs of factors bought and the revenues of products sold may be assumed to be payable simultaneously. Thus, in the general short-term theory of the firm, production possibilities are usually not assumed to be limited by liquidity constraints otherwise than by the sole condition that production is only carried on as long as at least the variable costs are covered by the revenues. (However, this condition need not be regarded as a liquidity constraint, as it is also implied by the general assumption of profit maximization when the option of suspending production altogether is taken into consideration.) The assumption that assets are kept as stocks of raw materials or claims on productive services paid in advance, seems very unrealistic. Moreover, even if the theory by Makower and Baumol were realistic, the most interesting problem would be the determination of the factor quantities which are afterwards regarded as fixed.

As the author of this paper has shown (Les effets de substitution et d'expansion dans la théorie de la production 1966), there is an obvious analogy, as to the splitting of effects, between the theory of consumer's optimum and the theory of producer's optimum, both taken in their ordinary text-book forms. The profit-maximizing firm is assumed to produce one product in accordance with a production function by employing an arbitrary number of production factors, and is assumed to be too small to influence the prices of output or inputs. In such a case, the effect on the quantity demanded of any factor, caused by a change of the price of the same or of another factor, may always be split up in an « effet de substitution » and an « effet d'expansion ». The « effet de substitution » is defined as the change of factor demand which would occur as a consequence of the price change considered, provided that the scale of production was not altered. Production is not affected, when the change of factor price is combined with a change of product price of a magnitude, adequate to have this effect of constant output. However, when there is an isolated change of a factor price, i.e. when there is no compensatory change of the price of the product, the scale of production will be affected. The « effet de substitution » will then be modified by such a change, as would be caused by an isolated change of product price (at constant factor prices) of a magnitude adequate to cause the actual change of the scale of production. This latter change is called « effet d'expansion ». In this paper the terms used will be « substitution effect » and « scale effect », the latter without the connotation of one way change of output, inherent in the « effet d'expansion ». These definitions apply to the general theory of the firm, where no other restrictions are placed on the choice of production scale and production technique than those expressed by a production function of given form.

For some reason, this obvious analogy, however, is lacking in the current treatises on economic theory. On the contrary, many authors express some supposition (without further discussion) that a splitting of effects in the theory of production in the same way as this is done in the theory of consumption is not possible or interesting. This point of view, which is not held by the author of this paper, may be recognized in Hicks (Value and Capital 1939) (1), where it is asserted that « the principles which govern the market conduct of a firm ... differ from those governing the conduct of a private individual » because « the income effect is lacking ». This assertion is too trivial if it is conceived literally. Rather, it seems, the assertion ought to be so understood that Hicks for the theory of the firm does not believe in a splitting of effects after the pattern he uses himself for the theory of consumer behaviour. This comprehension of the assertion made by Hicks is also supported by some more explicit statements in text books influenced by his work. Thus, Henderson and Quandt (Microeconomic Theory 1958) (2) assert : « There is no counterpart of the consumer's nonsymmetric income effect in the theory of the firm. The total effect is a symmetric substitution effect. » Moreover the authors have headed the section of their book, considered at present, by the expression « substitution effects » in spite of the fact that complete variability of the scale of production is assumed throughout the section.

A definition by which the total effect of a factor price change is called « substitution effect » seems to be unconvenient, because of the associations between this term and the term « substitution elasticity ». The latter term has got a commonly recognized meaning in Hicks (Theory of Wages 1932), (3) where it is

(1) P. 98.
(2) P. 75.
(3) PP. 92-93.

obviously used to characterize technical substitution of production factors at constant scale of production. However, his own classification of pairs of inputs as technical complements and technical substitutes, according to the effects of factor price changes on factor demands at variable scale of production (Value and Capital 1939) (1), gives some support to this ambiguosity.

Henderson and Quandt are right in asserting that there is no counterpart of the *nonsymmetric* income effect in the theory of the firm, as the effect, above called scale effect, is *symmetric*. Moreover, while it according to the theory of consumer behaviour is possible, provided that an « inferior good » is concerned, that demand of a consumer good may increase as well as decrease when its own price is raised, it is according to the theory of the firm not possible that the demand of a production factor may increase when its own price is raised. The fact that scale effects have the same direction as substitution effects, when effects on factor demands caused by changes of their own prices are considered, and that scale effects are symmetric, may account for the lack of interest in effect splitting in the theory of the firm. But it does not follow from these facts that such a splitting is completely without interest. As the author of this paper hopes to show a splitting of effects may be used to clear up some obscure points of the theory of the firm.

## II. Regressivity.

The fact that, under the assumptions of the theory of the firm, in the total effect on a factor demand, caused by a change of its own price, the substitution and scale effects have the same direction, emerges from the fact that, under the same assumptions, the direction of the scale effect is independent of whether the factor considered reacts like an « inferior » consumer good or not. With « inferiority », or « regressivity » according to Hicks (Value and Capital 1939) (2), is meant the property of some

(1) PP. 92-93.
(2) PP. 93-96.

production factors that they are used in smaller quantities when the scale of production increases at constant factor prices. This property should obviously emerge in cases where some factors are suitable for production in small scale and some factors for production in large scale. That « regressivity » has this meaning is obvious, because Hicks defines it by the case where a fall of a factor price causes the supply of the product to be contracted. As is demonstrated below, this is the case if, and only if, an expansion of product supply at constant factor prices decreases the demand of the factor considered.

For some reason the possibility, that factors of production may be regressive, is usually neglected by writers on the theory of the firm, albeit regressivity of production factors in no way seems to be a stranger property than inferiority of consumer goods. Having asserted that regressivity requires some degree of « substitutivity » between the factors of production and that regressivity is a phenomenon of « increasing returns », Hicks concludes that regressivity « does not yet appear to be a possibility of which we need to take much account ». (1) The argument is also supported by an appendix, where « complementarity » is shown to be the only possible relation between the factors with a linearly homogeneous production function, and this is taken as an indication of a tendency to complementarity also among the production factors in the general case. (2) As Hicks uses alternating distinctions between the cases of complementarity and substitutivity, the meaning of his argumentation is not quite clear. If the distinction is made according to the direction of change of the demand of one production factor, caused by a change of the price of another production factor *at constant scale of production*, there is no reason why the possibilities of regressive factors should be limited by the existence of complementarity (at constant production) among the factors of production. If, on the other hand, the distinction is made according to the direction of change of the demand of one production factor, caused by a change of the price of another production factor *at variable scale of production*, it is true that *existence* of substi-

(1) P. 96.
(2) PP. 322-323.

tutivity (at variable production) among the factors of production is a necessary condition for the possibility of regressive factors. But, it seems to be an impossibility to draw any logically necessary conclusions about the possibility of substitutivity (at variable production) in the general case from conclusions about this in the special case of linearly homogeneous production functions.

The argumentation is the more questionable, because, with linearly homogeneous production functions, no such determinate optimum does exist, the changes of which Hicks investigates in order to demonstrate the necessity of complementarity among factors (at variable production).

Nor does the assertion by Hicks that regressivity is a phenomenon of « increasing returns » seem to be justified. If « increasing returns » means that the marginal productivities of individual factors increase when the uses of the respective factors are increased in isolation, then it is easy to show that second order conditions for profit maximum imply decreasing marginal productivity of each factor. As those maximum conditions do not preclude regressivity of factors, this interpretation of Hicks is obviously not valid. If " increasing returns " means " increasing returns to scale " in the sense that a proportional increase of all inputs causes a more than proportional increase of output, then one may argue that this is an impossibility when the requirement, that variable costs must be covered by revenues, is fulfilled. As the fulfilment of this condition does not seem to preclude inferiority of factors, it is impossible to see on which grounds Hicks maintains that regressivity is a phenomenon of " increasing returns ".

Not even Frisch (Theory of Production 1965) (1) treats the case of regressivity, but is content with a laconic statment that regressivity " generally speaking " and " as a rule " does not occur. As this great work on the theory of the firm, since 1926, has been in circulation among german and scandinavian economists, Frisch has of course inspired several authors on the subject a long time before his own work was printed in any language of widespread use. Works influenced by Frisch, such as

(1) P. 56 and 164.

Schneider (Theorie der Produktion 1934) and Carlson (A Study on the Pure Theory of Production 1939), do not even comment the problem of regressivity. The text-book by Schneider (Einführung in die Wirtschaftstheorie II 1948) (1) is most suitable for a demonstration of how the tradition of neglecting regressivity is continued. Typical formulations are : " Steigt der Preis eines kompensatorischen Faktors bei Konstanz der Preise aller übrigen faktoren, so steigen zunächst die Grenzkosten. Diese ... Verschiebung der Grenzkostenkurve nach oben macht eine verminderung des Einsatzes sämtlicher Produktionsmittel vorteilhaft. ... Ingesamt nimmt mithin die Nachfrage nach dem teurer gewordenen Faktor ab, weil es sich lohnt, a) die Produktion einzuschränken, und b) den relativ teurer gewordenen Faktor durch relativ billiger gewordene faktoren zu substituieren " That Schneider does not consider regressivity as possible may be seen in two ways. First, it is seen directly from the assertion that reduced scale of production causes demand of every factor of production to be contracted. Secondly, it is seen indirectly from the assertion that a raised factor price always raises marginal costs (at a fixed scale of production). According to Samuelson (Foundations of Economic analysis 1947) (2) the direction of change of marginal costs, caused by a raised factor price (at constant production), is the same as the direction of change of the demand of the same factor, caused by an increased production (at constant factor prices). Thus, when a factor price is raised, marginal costs increase if, and only if, the factor whose price is raised is not regressive. Likewise, when a factor price is raised, marginal costs decrease if, and only if, the factor whose price is raised is regressive. This has been noticed by D.T.V. Bear (Inferior inputs and the Theory of the Firm 1965). (3).

The conclusion, that the scale of production is contracted when the price of a factor is raised, therefore, has no general validity, but is correct only when the factor in consideration is not regressive. When the price of a regressive factor is raised, then the scale of production is expanded, because the curve

(1) PP. 201-202.
(2) P. 67.
(3) PP. 287-289.

of marginal costs shifts downwards. However, as the author of this paper has pointed out (Les effets de substitution et d'expansion dans la théorie de la production 1966) (1), it is true that the effect on the demand of any factor, caused of a rise of its own price via the intermediary change of the scale of production, reinforces the substitution effect. The conclusions, that the total of substitution and scale effects on the demand of a factor, caused by a rise of its own price, is in adverse of demand of this factor, is not limited to the case where production scale is reduced in the process, but generally valid. If the factor whose price is raised is not regressive, then the marginal cost curve shifts upwards and production is decreased. The decrease of production causes the demand of the factor whose price has risen to be decreased too, because the factor *is not* regressive. If the factor whose price is raised, on the other hand, is regressive, then the marginal cost curve shifts downwards and production is increased. But, now it is the increase of production which causes the demand of the factor whose price has risen to be decreased, because the factor *is* regressive. Anyhow, the demand of a factor whose price is raised will be reduced according to the scale effect, regardless of whether production is increased or decreased, and thus the substitution effect is reinforced to yield a total effect of definite direction. All this argumentation, of course, presupposes that the marginal cost curve is rising. Otherwise, it is impossible to connect a shift downwards with increased production and a shift upwards with decreased production. But this is a justified line of reasoning, because a rising marginal cost curve is implied by second order conditions for profit maximum. Thus, also the conclusion " une hausse du prix du facteur conduit à une réduction de l'emploi de ce facteur, lorsque l'on considère les répercussions par l'intermédiaire du niveau de la production, et ceci que le niveau de la production se trouve accru ou réduit " is justified. The writers on the theory of the firm have long ago noticed the fact that the total effect has a definite direction, and this is probably a reason why a splitting of effects has not been attempted.

(1) PP. 62-63.

The conclusion about the definite direction of the total of substitution and scale effects, because of the common direction of the separate effects, is only valid when demand of a factor is considered whose own price has been changed. When the changes of demand investigated concern some other factor of production than the one whose price has been changed, then the direction of the total effect depends on whether the factor, the demand of which is considered, and the factor, the price of which is changed, are complementary or substitutive (at constant scale of production) as well as on whether none, one or both of the factors are regressive. In this case a splitting of effects is of the same importance in the theory of the firm as in the theory of consumer behaviour, because the direction of total change is not fixed by the general assumptions of the theory.

## III. Technical complements and substitutes.

It is now necessary to discuss the different senses which have been given the words " technical complementarity " and " technical substitutivity " by different writers on the theory of the firm. There are three different systems of definitions. Frisch (Theory of Production 1965) (1) uses as a criterion the direction of change of the marginal productivity of one production factor caused by an increase of another production factor. If marginal productivity increases, the factors are said to be " complementary ", if marginal productivity decreases, the factors are said to be " alternative " or " competitive ". (The term " substitutive " has been reserved by Frisch to denote the relation between two factors of production where both have positive marginal productivities, so that one factor may be substituted for another while constant production is maintained.) This use of the terms corresponds closely to their use in the older utility theory of consumer behaviour. Thus, the classification of consumer goods into complementary and substitutive pairs in Pareto (Manuel d'économie politique 1909) is made according to whether increased consumption of one good increases or decreases the marginal utility

(1) P. 60.

of another good. But the ordinal utility theory, introduced by Pareto himself, implies that the signs of those second order derivatives of the utility function, that are used as classification criteria, are not independent of the transformations of the utility function, permissible in the ordinal representation of given preferences. Thus, those criteria are not suitable for the theory of consumer behaviour. They have therefore been abandoned. No such problem arises with the definitions used by Frisch in the theory of the firm, as the quantity of products manufactured is a cardinally measurable quantity, and as no transformations of the production function are permissible with given technical conditions. Nevertheless those definitions are less suitable than the following, provided that a maximal degree of formal similarity is desirable between the theory of the firm and the theory of consumer behaviour.

The other two systems of definitions have already been mentioned, as both are used by Hicks (Value and Capital 1939) (1). In both, the criterion used is the direction of change of the demand of one factor of production, caused by a rise of the price of another factor of production. If the demand increases, the factors are said to be " substitutive " or " competitive ", if the demand decreases the factors are said to be " complementary ". The difference between the two systems of definitions is that in one case the scale of production is assumed to be held constant, the constancy being maintained by a compensatory change of the price of the product, while in the other case the scale of production is assumed to be variable, the variability being necessary because the price of the product is constant. Constant scale of production is assumed in some parts by Hicks (Value and Capital 1939) (2) as well as by Allen (Mathematical Analysis for Economists 1938) (3) and (Mathematical Economics 1956) (4). Optimally variable scale of production is assumed in other parts of the work by Hicks mentioned (5). It seems to

(1) PP. 92-93.
(2) P. 92.
(3) P. 509.
(4) P. 611.
(5) P. 93.

be profitable to make a distinction between the two different definition systems used by Hicks. This may be done simply by adding " at variable production " or " at constant production " to the terms " complementary " and " substitutive ". When this addition is omitted, the definitions are assumed to be based on *constant production.*

It might be worth stressing that the three systems of definitions by no means are equivalent. By a complicated mathematical argumentation, it has been demonstrated by Bjøntegård (Etterspørsel etter produksjonsfaktorer 1965) and D.T.V. Bear (Inferior Inputs and the Theory of the Firm 1965) that all factors of production will be complementary (at variable production) in the sense used by Hicks, provided that they are *all* complementary in the sense used by Frisch. Moreover it is proved in the following formal argumentation that, as far as only the senses used by Hicks are considered, complementarity at variable production is implied by complementarity at constant production, provided that no factors are regressive. But besides such special cases there are no clear-cut relations between the different systems of definitions.

The difference between the two definition systems used by Hicks reflects a similar difference between two definition systems in the theory of consumer behaviour. The difference is that in one case the level of satisfaction is assumed to be constant, the constancy being maintained by a compensatory income change, while in the other case the level of satisfaction is assumed to be variable, the variability being necessary because income is constant. Both systems of classifying pairs of consumer goods as complementary or substitutive, according to the direction of the change of the demand of one good, caused by a change of the price of another good, have considerable disadvantages. Because of the asymmetric property of income effects, the demand of one good may be complementary (at variable utility) with respect to changes of the price of another good, while the demand of the latter good is substitutive (at variable utility) with respect to changes of the price of the former good. Thus, it is generally impossible to classify a pair of consumer goods as complementary or substitutive, when variable utility (or, which is the same, constant income) is taken as a basis for the definitions. Nevertheless, it may seem desirable to be able to make such a classification. The reason for this may be that the classification is expected to express a definite and symmetric relation between consumer goods according to their role in the satisfaction of consumer preferences. On the other hand, it also seems desirable to be able to use the classification for a description of the conditions on a market where a great number of individual consumers together are responsible for those conditions. For such a purpose the definitions on basis of constant utility are not suitable, as there is no meaningful definition of " constant utility " for an aggregate of individual consumers.

The difficulties are less serious in the theory of the firm. The counterpart to the income effect, i.e. the scale effect, is symmetric. Thus, there is no logical difficulty in making a definite classification of all pairs of production factors as complements or substitutes on a basis of definitions assuming variable production. Nevertheless, if it is desired to make a classification according to the ways different factors cooperate with eachother or replace eachother in technical processes, it may not be appropriate that the classification depends on whether product supply is elastic or inelastic. But, as will be demonstrated, this is the case if variable production is taken as a basis for the classification. Neither are there any formal difficulties with a classification in complements and substitutes based on constant total production for a whole market, thanks to the possibilities of aggregation over individual firms in an industry. As the author of this paper has shown (Les effets de substitution et d'expansion dans la théorie de la production 1966) (1), however, a specific problem will arise. The problem is that technical complementarity in every firm within the branch is neither a necessary nor a sufficient condition for technical complementarity according to the aggregate production function. In the same way, technical substitutivity in every firm within the branch is neither a necessary nor a sufficient condition for technical substitutivity according to the aggregate production function. This depends on all the changes in the distribution of a fixed total product

(1) P. 83.

quantity between individual firms which may occur without being visible in the aggregate production function, and which will be among the factors determining the classification in complements and substitutes on the basis of constant aggregate production. The classification will for this reason not be solely determined by the purely technical relationships among the factors of production. The obvious conclusion seems to be that it is a vain thing to look for *one* system of definitions which will meet all the requirements, that the use of the words ,, complement " and " substitute " in ordinary language may pose on such a system. It seems to be impossible to find a definition which at once characterizes the relations in technical processes and the conditions on markets. Moreover, it is of course impossible to make the classification according to some notion of " necessary " relations between factors of production attached to the " characters " of the factors themselves. The classification must, in the contrary, depend on the production techniques in actual use or on conditions in actual markets ; and the classification will always have to be made on the basis of marginal changes from a given initial position.

## IV. The returns to scale.

In the preceding discussion there has been some mention of " increasing returns to scale " and of " decreasing returns to scale ". There seems to be general agreement among the writers on the theory of the firm as to how the cases will be defined. The distinction is made with the help of the elasticity of product output with respect to a proportional change of all factor inputs. The " returns to scale " are said to be " increasing ", " constant " or " decreasing ", according to whether this elasticity has a value greater than, equal to or less than unity. As is familiar from elementary text-books, the elasticity must be less than unity if variable costs are covered by revenues. Likewise, under the general tacit assumptions of the theory of the firm about the forms of cost curves, explicitely stated in Frisch (The Theory of Production 1965) under the name " regular ultra passum law ", the elasticity may only be less than unity provided that the marginal cost curve is rising. However there is no general agreement about the name to be used for this important elasticity. Frisch (1) calls it " passus coefficient ". Other names used are, in Schneider (Theorie der Produktion 1934) (2) " Ergiebigkeitsgrad ", in Carlson (A Study on the Pure Theory of Production 1939) (3) " function coefficient ", in Schneider (Einführung in die Wirtschaftstheorie II 1948) (4) " Niveauelastizität " and in the english translation of the last work (5) " scale elasticity ". There is no reason to comment the terminology. The author of this paper only wants to point out that the " scale elasticity ", used by Schneider, should not be confused with the use of the same linguistic expression, made in this paper.

## V. Formal optimum conditions.

After this introductory discussion of terminological problems the formal treatment may commence. A firm is assumed to manufacture one product, the quantity denoted $q$, and to use $n$ different production factors, the quantities denoted $v_1, \dots, v_n$, in the process. The firm is assumed to be so small that it may not influence product price, denoted $p$, or factor prices, denoted $r_1, \dots, r_n$, by its own supply or demand. The choice of production scale and technique is assumed to be made according to a production function, expressed in explicit form as

$$q = f(v_1, \dots, v_n) \qquad [1]$$

and assumed to have derivatives at least up to second order. The firm is assumed to make its choice of production scale and production technique so as to maximize its profit. As is familiar, the maximum conditions of first and second order, the possibility that higher order conditions may be needed being ignored, are

$$p \cdot f_h - r_h = 0 \qquad h = 1, \dots, n \qquad [2]$$

(1) P. 65.
(2) P. 10.
(3) P. 17.
(4) P. 178.
(5) P. 152.

and

$$(-1)^h \cdot \begin{vmatrix} p \cdot f_{11} \cdots p \cdot f_{1h} \\ \vdots \qquad \vdots \\ p \cdot f_{h1} \cdots p \cdot f_{hh} \end{vmatrix} > 0 \qquad h = 1, \ldots, n \qquad [3]$$

Obviously, maximum profit, under free adjustment of all factor quantities, is obtained only when minimum variable costs, under restricted adjustment of factor quantities at constant scale of production, are also obtained. First and second order conditions, the higher order conditions being ignored, for minimum of variable costs at constant production are

$$\begin{aligned} r_h - \lambda \cdot f_h &= 0 \qquad h = 1, \ldots, n \\ q - f &= 0 \end{aligned} \qquad [4]$$

and

$$\begin{vmatrix} -\lambda \cdot f_{11} \cdots -\lambda \cdot f_{1h} & -f_1 \\ \vdots \qquad \vdots & \vdots \\ -\lambda \cdot f_{h1} \cdots -\lambda \cdot f_{hh} & -f_n \\ -f_1 \cdots -f_h & 0 \end{vmatrix} < 0 \qquad h = 2, \ldots, n \qquad [5]$$

These conditions contain a new symbol $\lambda$, the so called " Lagrange multiplier ", always appearing in conditions for constrained extrema. In the present context this $\lambda$ may be interpreted as marginal costs. From conditions [4] it is seen directly that $\lambda$ expresses marginal costs at partial variations of each factor. As shown by Frisch (Theory of Production 1956), all those partial marginal costs must also equal the marginal costs obtained at optimal variation of all factors simultaneously. This is the so called " indifference law " of marginal costs. Anyhow, marginal costs $\lambda$ must be equal to product price $p$. The logical connections between the conditions for profit maximum as treated in one step and the conditions for profit maximum as treated in two steps by the use of intermediary cost curves are discussed in another paper by the author already referred to.

## VI. Displacements of optimum.

For the problems discussed in the present paper a " comparative statics " analysis of the effects on factor demands and product supply caused by changes of factor prices and product price is needed. A differentiation, performed for this reason, of the system of equations [4] yields

$$\begin{cases} -\lambda \cdot \sum_{k=1}^{n} f_{hk} \cdot dv_k - f_h \cdot d\lambda = -dr_h \qquad h = 1, \ldots, n \\ -\sum_{k=1}^{n} f_k \cdot dv_k = -dq \end{cases} \tag{6}$$

In order to solve the system of equations [6] explicitely with respect to the differentials $dv_1, \ldots, dv_n$ and $d\lambda$, the following determinant is introduced.

$$D = \begin{vmatrix} -\lambda \cdot f_{11} \cdots & -\lambda \cdot f_{1n} & -f_1 \\ \vdots & \vdots & \vdots \\ -\lambda \cdot f_{n1} \cdots & -\lambda \cdot f_{nn} & -f_n \\ -f_1 \cdots & -f_n & 0 \end{vmatrix} \tag{7}$$

Its co-factors are denoted in the usual way by indices, the first of which indicates the row and the second of which indicates the column of the element whose co-factor is considered. The first $n$ rows and columns are enumerated $1, \ldots, n$, while the last ones, the border row and the border column, are identified by index $b$ on the relevant place. With the use of these conventions and by the help of " Cramer's rule " the explicit solution desired is obtained as

$$\begin{cases} dv_k = -\sum_{h=1}^{n} \frac{D_{hk}}{D} \cdot dr_h - \frac{D_{bk}}{D} \cdot dq \qquad k = 1, \ldots, n \\ d\lambda \;= -\sum_{h=1}^{n} \frac{D_{hb}}{D} \cdot dr_h - \frac{D_{bb}}{D} \cdot dq \end{cases} \tag{8}$$

Second order conditions, codified above in the formulae [3] and [5], imply that some of the quotients of a co-factor and the determinant, occurring in the system of equations [8], have definite signs. Thus it must hold that

$$\frac{D_{hh}}{D} > 0 \qquad h = 1, \ldots, n \tag{9}$$

and

$$\frac{D_{bb}}{D} < 0 \tag{10}$$

are fulfilled.

## VII. The elasticity of product supply.

It is now convenient to define a number of elasticities, the mathematical expressions of which may be directly obtained from the system of equations [8]. The elasticity of supply, denoted $\eta$, is obtained from the last equation of the system by putting $d\lambda = dp$ and all $dr_h = 0$.

$$\boxed{\eta = \frac{dq}{dp} \cdot \frac{p}{q} = -\frac{D}{D_{bb}} \cdot \frac{p}{q}} \tag{11}$$

According to [10] this elasticity of supply must be positive when second order conditions of profit maximum are fulfilled.

## VIII. Substitution elasticities of factor demands.

From the system of equations [8] may also be obtained the mathematical expressions of the elasticities of demand of one factor with respect to the price of the same or of another factor, provided that the scale of production is held constant by way of a compensatory change of product price. Those elasticities constitute the " substitution effects " mentioned above, and are to be used as a basis for the classification (at constant production) of pairs of production factors as " complements " or " substitutes ". The elasticities will be called " substitution elasticities ". As will be shown, they have a close connection with the " substitution elasticity ", defined in Hicks (Theory of Wages 1932) (1) and generalized under the name " partial elasticity of substitution " in Allen (Mathematical Analysis for Economists 1938) (2). The $i$:th equation of system [8] yields with $dq = 0$ and $dr_h = 0$ for all $h \neq j$ the substitution elasticity of the demand of the $i$:th factor with respect to the price of the :th fa ctor.

$$\epsilon_{ij} = \frac{r_j}{v_i} \cdot \frac{\partial v_i}{\partial r_j} = - \frac{D_{ji}}{D} \cdot \frac{r_j}{v_i} \qquad [12]$$

According to [9] the " direct " substitution elasticity, i.e. $\epsilon_{ij}$ when $i = j$, is always negative, provided that second order conditions for minimal costs (at constant production scale) are fulfilled. The substitution effect for a factor of production will for this reason always be negative when a rise of its own price is considered. When $i \neq j$, i.e. when the elasticities are taken " crosswise ", the factors are said to be complementary when $\epsilon_{ij}$ is negative and substitutive when $\epsilon_{ij}$ is positive. As is seen below a classification will not be altered when $\epsilon_{ji}$ instead of $\epsilon_{ij}$ is taken as a basis for it. This is so because $\epsilon_{ij}$ and $\epsilon_{ji}$ always have the same sign.

## IX. Scale elasticities.

One more type of elasticities may directly be derived from the system of equations [8]. By putting all $dr_h = 0$ in the $i$:th and [:th equations the elasticities of the demand of the two factors with respect to the quantity of product manufactured (factor prices being assumed as constant) may be obtained.

$$E_i = \frac{q}{v_i} \cdot \frac{\partial v_i}{\partial q} = - \frac{D_{bi}}{D} \cdot \frac{q}{v_i} = - \frac{D_{ib}}{D} \cdot \frac{q}{v_i} \qquad [13]$$

$$E_j = \frac{q}{v_j} \cdot \frac{\partial v_j}{\partial q} = - \frac{D_{bj}}{D} \cdot \frac{q}{v_j} = - \frac{D_{jb}}{D} \cdot \frac{q}{v_j} \qquad [14]$$

(1) P. 244.
(2) P. 504.

For later use the third members of equations [13] and [14] have been codified. This is done by use of the fact that the determinant D is symmetric, why the column and row indices may change places in any of its co-factors without affecting the value. The elasticities $E_i$ and $E_j$ are called " scale elasticities " and they will be positive, unless any factor is regressive. A regressive factor is defined by a negative scale elasticity.

### X. « Slutsky » relations.

In order to obtain the elasticities of factor demands with respect to factor prices when production is variable one may proceed in the familiar way by differentiating the system of equations [2]. However, the elasticity of the demand of the $i$:th factor with respect to the price of the $j$:th factor (at variable production), denoted $e_{ij}$, is obtained also from the $i$:th and the last equations of system [8] by putting $dr_h = 0$ for all $h \neq j$ and $d\lambda = dp = 0$. The both equations will then have the form

$$dv_i = -\frac{D_{ji}}{D} \cdot dr_j - \frac{D_{bi}}{D} \cdot dq \qquad [15]$$

$$0 = -\frac{D_{jb}}{D} \cdot dr_j - \frac{D_{bb}}{D} \cdot dq. \qquad [16]$$

Eliminating $dq$ the equations yield

$$dv_i = \left(-\frac{D_{ij}}{D}\right) \cdot dr_j - \left(-\frac{D_{bi}}{D}\right) \cdot \left(-\frac{D_{jb}}{D}\right) \cdot \left(-\frac{D}{D_{bb}}\right) \cdot dr_j \qquad [17]$$

Thus the elasticity $e_{ij}$ is easily obtained as

$$e_{ij} = \frac{dv_i}{dr_j} \cdot \frac{r_j}{v_i} = \left(-\frac{D_{ij}}{D} \cdot \frac{r_j}{v_i}\right) - \frac{r_j \cdot v_j}{p \cdot q} \cdot \left(-\frac{D_{bi}}{D} \cdot \frac{q}{v_i}\right) \cdot \left(-\frac{D_{jb}}{D} \cdot \frac{q}{v_j}\right) \cdot \left(-\frac{D}{D_{bb}} \cdot \frac{p}{q}\right). \qquad [18]$$

By using the definitions of elasticities [11], [12], [13] and [14] and the symbol

$$\boxed{a_j = \frac{r_j \cdot v_j}{p \cdot q}} \qquad [19]$$

to denote the fraction of revenue used on purchase of the $j$:th factor, all the quotients of a co-factor and the determinant may be eliminated. Thus

$$\boxed{e_{ij} = \epsilon_{ij} - a_j \cdot E_i \cdot E_j \cdot \eta} \tag{20}$$

is obtained.

This equation, valid for any $i$ and $j$, is the result of applying the splitting of effects, familiar from the theory of consumer behaviour, in the theory of the firm. The term $\epsilon_{ij}$ is the " substitution effect " and the term $-a_j \cdot E_i \cdot E_j \cdot \eta$ is the " scale effect ". When $i = j$, i.e. when a " direct " elasticity is concerned, the substitution effect will, as noticed above, be negative. Moreover the scale elasticity will be contained in a quadratic expression. As both the elasticity of supply and the fraction of revenue spent on the factor will be positive, the conclusion is that the scale effect will be negative and will reinforce the substitution effect, regardless of whether the factor considered is regressive or not. Thus the conclusion is that the elasticity of demand of a factor with respect to its own price, with production being variable, is always negative, and that it is greater in absolute value than the corresponding elasticity, defined at constant scale of production. The scale effect will obviously be greater, and so will the difference in change of factor demand be, when production is variable as compared with constant production. The scale effect will also be greater, the greater the elasticity of supply of product with respect to product price is. Thus, elastic factor demand tends to be coupled with elastic product supply.

In the case of elasticities taken crosswise, i.e. when $i \neq j$, it is generally impossible to assert anything definite about the sign or the numerical value of $e_{ij}$. It has already been noticed that the substitution effect will be negative with complementary factors and positive with substitutive factors. Obviously, with complementary factors, the scale effect will reinforce the substitution effect when none or both of the factors are regressive. Likewise, with substitutive factors, the scale effect will reinforce the substitution effect when exactly one of the factors is regressive. In all other cases the effects will have opposite directions, and the resulting net effect has an unknown direction.

In a former paper (Les effets de substitution et d'expansion dans la théorie de la production 1966) the author has used an old practice of defining all demand elasticities with an extra negative sign, so that the " direct " elasticities in normal cases will be positive. This practice has not been used in the present paper, as it seems that the benefit of positivity of certain elasticities in normal cases will not outweigh the inconvenience in mathematical and verbal argumentation of handling an extra minus sign. This change of elasticity definitions may account for some curious discrepances between the formulae of the former and the present paper.

## XI. The « partial elasticities » of Allen.

It is now convenient to demonstrate the formal connection between the substitution elasticity $\epsilon_{ij}$ introduced above and the " partial elasticity of substitution " defined in Allen (Mathematical Analysis for Economists 1938) (1) and denoted $\sigma_{ij}$. In order to do this the following determinant will be introduced

$$F = \begin{vmatrix} f_{11} \cdots f_{1n} & -f_1 \\ \vdots \quad \vdots & \vdots \\ f_{n1} \cdots f_{nn} & -f_n \\ -f_1 \cdots -f_n & 0 \end{vmatrix} \qquad [21]$$

along with its co-factors $F_{ij}$. A comparison between the determinants F and D indicates that $D = (-\lambda)^{n-1} \cdot F$ and $D_{ij} = (-\lambda)^{n-2} \cdot F_{ij}$ are true.

Thus it is also true that $F_{ij}/F = -\lambda \cdot D_{ij}/D$. According to the formal definition used by Allen, the " partial elasticity " in terms of $F_{ij}$ and F is

$$\boxed{\sigma_{ij} = \frac{\sum_{h=1}^{n} f_h \cdot v_h}{v_i \cdot v_j} \cdot \frac{F_{ij}}{F}} \qquad [22]$$

(1) P. 504.

But substitution of the expression for $F_{ij}/F$ in terms of $D_{ij}$ and D together with substitution from $r_h = \lambda \cdot f_h$ yields

$$\sigma_{ij} = \frac{\lambda \cdot \sum_{h=1}^{n} f_h \cdot v_h}{v_i \cdot v_j} \cdot \left(-\frac{D_{ij}}{D}\right) \qquad [23]$$

$$= \frac{\sum_{h=1}^{n} r_h \cdot v_h}{r_j \cdot v_j} \cdot \left(-\frac{D_{ij}}{D} \cdot \frac{r_j}{v_i}\right) \qquad [23]$$

If the fraction of total variable costs spent on the $j$:th factor is denoted by

$$\boxed{\kappa_j = \frac{r_j \cdot v_j}{\sum_{h=1}^{n} r_h \cdot v_h}} \qquad [24]$$

it is obviously true according to equation [12] that

$$\boxed{\epsilon_{ij} = \kappa_j \cdot \sigma_{ij}} \qquad [25]$$

The result is that only a multiplication with a positive fraction $\kappa_j$ is needed in order to translate the " partial elasticity " of Allen $\sigma_{ij}$ into the substitution elasticity $\epsilon_{ij}$.

It is also easy to relate the fraction of variable costs $\kappa_j$ spent on the $j$:th factor to the fraction of revenues $\alpha_j$ spent on the same factor. By this device the analogy between Allen's formula and the formula used here is brought out better. For this reason it is convenient to introduce the elasticity of product output with respect to a proportional change of all factor inputs, i.e. the " passus coefficient " of Frisch, here denoted $\Phi$. By definition

$$\Phi \cdot q = \sum_{h=1}^{n} f_h \cdot v_h$$

$$= \frac{1}{p} \cdot \sum_{h=1}^{n} r_h \cdot v_h \qquad [26]$$

Thus

$$\Phi = \frac{\sum_{h=1}^{n} r_h \cdot v_h}{p \cdot q} \qquad [27]$$

or $a_j = \Phi \cdot \kappa_j$. Equation [20] may now be written in the following form

$$e_{ij} = \kappa_j \cdot (\sigma_{ij} - \Phi \cdot \mathrm{E}_i \cdot \mathrm{E}_j \cdot \eta) \qquad [28]$$

This is of course not the formula used by Allen, as he introduces market demand of a finite elasticity. The case considered by Allen seems not to be reasonable in applications to a single firm. The same formal structure may, however, without internal inconsistencies be applied to cases with aggregated production functions. For a treatment of such cases the reader is directed to the paper by the author of these lines, referred to several times above, as only the problems of a single firm are treated at present.

## XII. Symmetry relations and summation relations.

Returning from these definitional considerations there are still several points to be discussed in connection with the elasticities introduced before the connections with Allen's partial elasticities were brought out. There are several types of relations between the elasticities defined before this was done. One type has already been formulated in equation [20]. The relations of this type may conveniently be called " Slutsky-relations ". There are two more types. They may be called " symmetry relations " and " summation relations ".

Symmetry relations are obtained by noticing the simple fact that the symmetric property of the determinant D implies $\mathrm{D}_{ij} = \mathrm{D}_{ji}$. According to equations [12] and [19] it is then obviously true that

$$a_i \cdot \epsilon_{ij} = a_j \cdot \epsilon_{ji} \qquad [29]$$

From this follows in accordance with equation [20] that

$$\boxed{a_i \cdot e_{ij} = a_j \cdot e_{ji}} \qquad [30]$$

This means that for any pair of factors the elasticity of demand of the first factor with respect to the price of the second factor has the same sign as the elasticity of demand of the second factor with respect to the price of the first factor, regardless of whether production is variable or constant.

The summation relations are obtained in the following way. By substitution of $r_j = p \cdot f_j$ into equation [12] the equation

$$\sum_{j=1}^{n} \epsilon_{ij} = \frac{p}{v_i} \cdot \frac{\sum_{j=1}^{n} (-f_j \cdot \mathrm{D}_{ij})}{\mathrm{D}} \qquad [31]$$

is obtained. Because the sum in the numerator of the right hand side is an expansion of the determinant D along the border line while the co-factors of another line, the $i$:th one, are used, the value of the sum is zero. Thus

$$\boxed{\sum_{j=1}^{n} \epsilon_{ij} = 0} \qquad [32]$$

As one of the substitution elasticities in the sum, namely the direct one (for $i = j$), is negative, the sum of the remaining elasticities, taken crosswise (for $i \neq j$), must be positive. This would be impossible if all the factors were mutually complementary, because all the elasticities of the sum would then be negative. The conclusion is that it is impossible that all the factors are complementary (at constant production scale). This implies that if there are only two factors, then complementarity is completely out of question. Equation [32] may also be interpreted as an assertion that proportional changes of all factor prices do not change the demand of the $i$:th factor, provided that production is kept constant.

By substitution from $r_j/p = f_j$ into equation [14] the equation

$$\sum_{j=1}^{n} a_j \cdot E_j = \sum_{j=1}^{n} \frac{r_j \cdot v_j}{p \cdot q} \cdot \left(-\frac{D_{bj}}{D} \cdot \frac{q}{v_j}\right) \qquad [33]$$

$$= \frac{\sum_{j=1}^{n} (-f_j \cdot D_{bj})}{D}$$

is obtained. As the numerator in the last member of this equation is a correct expansion of the determinant D along the border row, the value of the quotient will be unity. Thus

$$\boxed{\sum_{j=1}^{n} a_j \cdot E_j = 1} \qquad [34]$$

This condition implies that it is impossible that all factors are regressive. The conclusion is trivial, as no increase of output is possible when all inputs are decreased, provided that all marginal productivities are positive. If there are only two factors this implies that at most one factor may be regressive. As pointed out above, the two factors must then be substitutive. The general conclusion that the scale effect reinforces the substitution effect when exactly one of the factors is regressive will of course be applicable. Thus the existence of regressivity with two factors only means that when a price of one factor increases then the demand of the other factor must increase. If this case is regarded as unrealistic, regressivity too must be regarded as unrealistic. This is done by Hicks, as mentioned above.

From equation [20] is

$$\sum_{j=1}^{n} e_{ij} = \sum_{j=1}^{n} \epsilon_{ij} - E_i \cdot \eta \cdot \sum_{j=1}^{n} a_j \cdot E_j \qquad [35]$$

obtained. But according to equations [32] and [34] this may be written

$$\boxed{\sum_{j=1}^{n} e_{ij} = - E_i \cdot \eta} \qquad [36]$$

which means simply that a proportional change of the price of the product and the prices of all the factors will not change the demand of the $i$:th factor. As all $e_{ij}$ are negative when $i = j$, negative values for all the other $e_{ij}$ would imply positivity for all $E_i$ according to equation [36], because $\eta$ is positive. By the definition of complementarity used in some places by Hicks the condition $e_{ij} < 0$ with $i \neq j$ may be said to define complementarity at variable production scale. The assumption that all the factors constitute one complementary group (at variable production) implies that no factor may be regressive. The special case of this with two variable production factors has already been discussed.

## XIII. Elasticities taken « crosswise » between the product and the factors.

As the elasticities of factor demands with respect to factor prices and the elasticity of product supply with respect to product price have now been discussed, it may be of some interest to add a few words about two more kinds of elasticities. Those are the elasticities of product supply with respect to factor prices and the elasticities of factor demands with respect to product price. The elasticity of product supply with respect to the price of the $j$:th factor will be denoted $\eta_{*j}$, and the elasticity of the demand of the $i$:th factor with respect to product price will be denoted $\eta_{i*}$.

From equation [16]

$$\eta_{*j} = \frac{dq}{dr_j} \cdot \frac{r_j}{q} = - \frac{r_j \cdot v_j}{p \cdot q} \cdot \left( - \frac{D_{jb}}{D} \cdot \frac{q}{v_j} \right) \cdot \left( - \frac{D}{D_{bb}} \cdot \frac{p}{q} \right) \quad [37]$$

is immediately obtained. But according to equations [11], [14] and [19] this may also be written as

$$\boxed{\eta_{*j} = - a_j \cdot E_j \cdot \eta} \quad [38]$$

Equation [38] yields the simple conclusion that the supply of product is always reduced when a factor price is raised, unless the factor is regressive. In the contrary, if the price of a regressive factor is raised the supply of product is increased. This is the case referred to in the definition of regressivity by Hicks. The facts expressed by equation [38] have also been frequently used in the introductory discussion of this paper.

It is obviously true that the equation

$$\eta_{i*} = \frac{dv_i}{dp} \cdot \frac{p}{v_i} = \left(\frac{\partial v_i}{\partial q} \cdot \frac{q}{v_i}\right) \cdot \left(\frac{dq}{dp} \cdot \frac{p}{q}\right) \qquad [39]$$

holds. By way of substitution from equations (11) and (13) this may also be written as

$$\boxed{\eta_{i*} = \mathrm{E}_i \cdot \eta \, .} \qquad [40]$$

Equation [40] asserts that a product price which is raised causes the demand to increase of all non-regressive factors and the demand to decrease of all regressive factors. This is trivial, because the supply of product will always be increased when product price is raised.

## XIV. Conclusions.

The elasticity definitions introduced so far are so many that there may be some difficulties to memorize all the symbols used. For this reason, before summing up the argumentation, the elasticities will be arranged in two tables. Both tables are so framed that the rows correspond to the variables the changes of which are effects, and the columns correspond to the variables, the changes of which are causes in the definitions of the elasticities. The first table is constructed for the case where production is exogeneously fixed, so that the quantity of product together with factor prices is included among the cause variables and marginal cost together with the factor quantities is included among the effect variables. The second table is constructed for the case where production is optimally variable. Thus, in comparison to the first table, the quantity of product has to be put among the effect variables, while product price (equal to marginal cost) has to be put among the cause variables.

TABLE I. — FIXED PRODUCTION, VARIABLE MARGINAL COST.

| | $r_1$ | . | . | . | $r_n$ | $q$ |
|---|---|---|---|---|---|---|
| $v_1$ | $\epsilon_{11}$ | . | . | . | $\epsilon_{1n}$ | $E_1$ |
| . | . | | | | . | . |
| . | . | | | | . | . |
| . | . | | | | . | . |
| $v_n$ | $\epsilon_{n1}$ | . | . | . | $\epsilon_{nn}$ | $E_n$ |
| $\lambda$ | | | | | | |

TABLE II. — VARIABLE PRODUCTION, FIXED PRODUCT PRICE.

| | $r_1$ | . | . | . | $r_n$ | $p$ |
|---|---|---|---|---|---|---|
| $v_1$ | $e_{11}$ | . | . | . | $e_{1n}$ | $\eta_{1*}$ |
| . | . | | | | . | . |
| . | . | | | | . | . |
| . | . | | | | . | . |
| $v_n$ | $e_{n1}$ | . | . | . | $e_{nn}$ | $\eta_{n*}$ |
| $q$ | $\eta_{*1}$ | . | . | . | $\eta_{*n}$ | $\eta$ |

The conclusions are summarized in the six following points. But first the definitions of complementarity, substitutivity and regressivity must be recalled.

*Definitions* : The factors $i$ and $j$ are said to be complementary at constant production when $\epsilon_{ij}$ is negative and substitutive at constant production when $\epsilon_{ij}$ is positive. The factors $i$ and $j$ are said to be complementary at variable production when $e_{ij}$ is negative and substitutive at variable production when $e_{ij}$ is positive. A factor $i$ or $j$ is said to be regressive when $E_i$ or $E_j$ is negative.

*Conclusions* : 1) Both $\epsilon_{ij}$ and $e_{ij}$ are negative as $i = j$. This means that demand of a factor whose price is raised will decrease, regardless of whether production is constant or variable. Moreover the numerical value of $e_{ij}$ is greater than the numerical value of $\epsilon_{ij}$, and the difference is greater the greater $\eta$ is. This means that the demand of a factor whose price is raised is reduced by more when production is variable than when production is constant. The difference in strength of change between the cases with constant and variable production is greater the greater the elasticity of supply of product is. Thus elastic product supply tends to be coupled with elastic factor demands. 2) The sign of $\epsilon_{ij}$ is not affected when the indices are interchanged. The same is true for $e_{ij}$. Thus, for any two factors demand of the first factor is changed in the same direction when the price of the second factor rises as the demand of the second factor when the price of the first factor rises. This is true regardless of whether production is constant or variable. 3) The sign of $\eta$ is positive. Thus the supply of product is increased when its price is raised. A result from another paper by the author (1) may also be recorded here, namely that elasticity of product supply increases when the number of variable factors increases. 4) When $\epsilon_{ij}$ is negative, $e_{ij}$ is negative too, provided that $E_i$ and $E_j$ have the same sign. This means that two factors which are complementary at constant production will also be complementary at variable production, provided that none or both of the factors are regressive. When $\epsilon_{ij}$ is positive, $e_{ij}$ is positive too, provided that $E_i$ and $E_j$ have opposite signs. This means that two factors which are substitutive at constant production will also be substitutive at variable production, provided that exactly one of the factors is regressive. Thus, complementarity between factors is strengthened when they are similar with respect to regressivity, and substitutivity between factors is strengthened when they are dissimilar with respect to regressivity. 5) All factors may not be mutually complementary at constant production. Nor is it possible for all factors to be regressive. If all factors are mutually complementary at variable production, then regressivity is not possible at all. 6) the sign of $\eta_{*j}$ is opposite the sign of $E_j$. Thus product supply will be decreased when the price of a non-regressive factor is raised and increased when the price of a regressive factor is raised. The sign of $\eta_{i*}$ is the same as the sign of $E_i$. Thus a rise in the price of the product will increase the demand of all non-regressive factors and decrease the demand of all regressive factors.

(1) *Op. cit.*, p. 90.

## XV. Final remark on regressivity.

A final remark about the possibility of substitutivity (at variable production) and regressivity among factors of production, cases held highly improbable by Hicks, may now be added. As has been noticed above, no factor may be regressive, unless there is at least one pair of factors which are substitutes (defined at a variable production scale). Moreover, according to the result by Bjøntegård referred to, no such substitutivity (at variable production) is possible if there is no pair of factors such that they are substitutes in the sense used by Frisch. If the case where rises of certain factor prices at variable production may increase demands of other factors, and possibly even increase product supply, is called " abnormal ", it is true that the " abnormal " case requires that there are such factors for which increased employment of one decreases marginal productivity of another. Expressed in plain language, this means that there must be factors such that increased employment of only one of them renders a greater increase of product output than increased employment of both jointly. This seems to be incompatible with the conception of factors being co-operative in production processes. But, in such a line of argumentation it is forgotten that a production function is not definied to express a single technical process of production, but is defined as a result of a technical optimizing procedure by which, for every combination of factor quantities, one out of many different production processes is chosen according to the merit that it yields the greatest product quantity. Thus, every change in the quantities of factors employed may involve a change of technical process. Hicks asserts himself that the " abnormal " case is " a more intelligible possibility in cases of joint production " (1). The reason for this, according to his line of argumentation, is that some factors may be particularly important in the production of certain products, so that a transition from manufacturing one product to manufacturing another also involves a transition from employment of one group of factors to employment of

(1) P. 97.

another group of factors. But it seems to the author of this paper that exactly the same line of argumentation may be applied when one product is produced only, provided that there is a number of different production processes. Then some factors may be particularly important in certain processes, and a transition from one process to another may involve automatically a transition from employment of one group of factors to another. The argumentation has been made as if there were only a finite number of linear and " limitational " production processes, a case properly handled by the linear programming technique. But the case of continuous production functions may be regarded as a limiting case where the number of different processes is infinite and the differences between adjacent processes are infinitesimal. According to the usual definition of a production function it seems that such a view is much more reasonable than the view of a production function as an expression of the technique of one single process. It seems that at least a part of the scepticism as to the possibility of the " abnormal " case is dependent on a misconception of what the production function expresses. As far as the author of this paper can see, there is nothing in the general postulates of the theory of the firm to make the " abnormal " case negligeable. Nevertheless, the scepticism may be reasonable, but the final judgement on this point ought to be made by empirical test, not by theoretical argumentation.

## REFERENCES

In the preceeding text all the works referred to are attributed to the years of the appearence of the first editions. These editions, however, are in général not those to which the page indications refer. The latter are listed below.

[1] R.G.D. ALLEN, — *Mathematical Analysis for Economists*, 1956.
[2] R.G.D. ALLEN, — *Mathematical Economics*, 1957.
[3] D.T.V. BEAR, — Inferior Inputs and the Theory of the Firm, *The Journal of Political Economy*, 1965.
[4] E. BJØNTEGARD, — Etterspørsel etter produksjonsfaktorer, *Memoranda fra Sosialøkonomisk institutt*, Oslo universitet, 1965.

[5] S. Carlson, — *A Study on the Pure Theory of Production*, 1956.
[6] R. Frisch, — *Theory of Production*, 1965.
[7] J.M. Henderson and R.E. Quandt, *Microeconomic Theory*, 1958.
[8] J.R. Hicks and R.G.D. Allen, — A Reconsideration of the Theory of Value, *Economica*, 1939.
[9] J.R. Hicks, — *Theory of Wages*, 1948.
[10] J.R. Hicks, — *Value and Capital*, 1957.
[11] H. Makower and W.J. Baumol, The Analogy of Producer and Consumer Equilibrium, *Economica*, 1950.
[12] W. Pareto, *Manuel d'économie politique*, 1909.
[13] T. Puu, Les effets de substitution et d'expansion dans la théorie de la production, *Revue d'économie politique*, 1966.
[14] P.A. Samuelson, *Foundations of Economic Analysis*, 1961.
[15] E. Schneider, *Theorie der Produktion*, 1934.
[16] E. Schneider, — *Einführung in die Wirtschaftstheorie II*, 1958.
[17] E. Schneider, — *Pricing and Equilibrium*, 1962. (Translation of 16).
[18] E. Slutsky, Sulla teoria del bilancio del consumatore, *Giornale degli economisti*, 1915.
[19] H. v. Stackelberg, — Angebot und Nachfrage in der Produktionswirtschaft, *Archiv für Mathematische Wirtschafts- und Sozialforschung*, 1938.

# SOME COMMENTS ON "INFERIOR" (REGRESSIVE) INPUTS

*Tõnu Puu*

University of Uppsala, Uppsala, Sweden

Recently a special phenomenon in the theory of the firm, originally described by Hicks in *Value and Capital*, has become the subject of an intense discussion.[1] The phenomenon was originally termed regressivity, but has recently been re-baptized inferiority. As a matter of fact, it is completely analogous to inferiority of goods in the theory of consumer behaviour.

Hicks gave two accounts of this relation between product output and some factor inputs. (i) An input is regressive if demand for it decreases with increasing output (factor prices being held constant). (ii) An input is regressive if a rise in its price (other factor prices as well as product price being held constant) increases output.[2]

As a matter of fact the two formulations refer to the same phenomenon. Definition (i) displays the analogy to inferior goods, and it seems easy to accept that some inputs may be especially important for small-scale production and that the demand for them decreases with increasing output. But definition (ii) seems to be harder to digest. Starting from it many economists, among them Hicks himself, have discarded input regressivity as anomalous, improbable and perverse. Nevertheless the two definitions, one acceptable, the other improbable define the same phenomenon.

That this is so has been established by Samuelson in *Foundations of Economic Analysis*, where it is shown that a rise in the price of an input shifts the marginal cost curve upwards, if that input is not regressive, and downwards, if it is regressive.[3] Accordingly output will decrease in the former case, since the marginal cost curve then shifts up, and increase in the latter case, since the marginal cost curve then shifts down. This is a result of mathematical symmetry as may easily be seen by working out the comparative statics of the cost minimization problem for constant output.

---

[1] C. E. Ferguson, "Inferior Factors" and the Theories of Production and Input Demand, *Economica*, 1968, R. D. Portes, Input Demand Functions for the Profit-Constrained Sales-Maximizer: Income Effects in the Theory of the Firm, *Economica*, 1968, L. R. Bassett and T. E. Borcherding, "Inferior Factors" and the Theories of Production and Input Demand: Comment, *Economica*, 1969.

[2] J. R. Hicks, *Value and Capital*, Oxford, 1957, pp. 93–96.

[3] P. A. Samuelson, *Foundations of Economic Analysis*, Cambridge, Mass., 1961, p. 67.

Why is regressivity still difficult to accept, although (i) seems possible and (ii) obviously refers to the same case? The answer is probably that there has not been given any explanation according to which (ii) is *itself* easy to accept. I suggest the following explanation.

Assume that the price of a regressive input (i.e. one suited for small-scale production) increases. At constant output there would be a substitution away from this input and from the other regressive inputs, which probably form a cooperative group of inputs suitable for small-scale production, in favour of non-regressive or normal inputs. Thus, the small-scale inputs would be replaced by large-scale inputs, which would mean that the resulting production process would be adjusted towards large-scale production.

But, the characteristic for a large-scale process is that the bulk of costs are incurred even at small outputs, whereas the additional costs for an increase are relatively small. Thus, a shift downwards of the *marginal* cost curve is not difficult to understand. And, because of this, the fall in profits caused by the increase in an input price might be reduced by expanding output.

## Regressivity and Giffen's Paradox

It has been observed that, in contrast to the case of the theory of consumer behaviour, it is not possible for demand curves for inputs to have positive slope—even in case of regressivity.

This can be explained in several ways. Anyhow, it is useful to split the effect of an increase in the price of an input on the demand for that input into two parts, one due to substitution between inputs at constant output and the other due to the actual variation of output.

Substitution will, of course, be away from the more expensive input. It is a characteristic of the theory of the firm that the residual effect via the change of output reinforces the substitution.

The reason for this has already been given above. If the input is not regressive the rise of its price will shift the marginal cost curve up, and output will be decreased. But the demand of a normal input decreases with decreasing output. On the other hand, if instead the input is regressive, then the rise of its price shifts the marginal cost curve down, and output will be increased. But the demand of a regressive input decreases with increasing output.

Thus, the effect of the adjustment of output to an increase in the price of an input will be a decrease in demand for that input, regardless of whether output is increased or decreased. This means that the substitution effect will be reinforced, and so this accounts for the fact that the total effect is always adverse to the input which has become more expensive.

Another way of seeing this is provided by the formal derivation of a counterpart to the "Slutsky relation" in the theory of the firm that I have suggested elsewhere.[1] There, the elasticity, the sign of which classifies an input as normal or regressive, is contained in a quadratic expression, thus making the sign unimportant for he direction of the effect.

## Special Reasons for Neglecting Regressivity

Special reasons have been offered as to why regressivity should be regarded as exceptional. One is that regressivity is impossible with homogeneous production functions. However, this seems to be a rather weak reason, as homogeneity is assumed for mathematical simplicity in exemplifications and in econometric applications.

Another reason offered is that regressivity is not possible when all second order cross derivatives of output with respect to any pair of inputs are positive. The belief that these derivatives ought to be positive probably rests upon a misconception of the production function, according to which it is thought that the production function expresses one technical process, and not the choice among an infinity of technical processes according to the criterion that output be maximal with each input combination. According to the latter conception, a change of an input combination implies a change of technical process, and then there are no foundations at all for belief in the positivity of the cross derivatives.

Both of these two arguments against regressivity have been suggested, but neither of them seems to be convincing. However, it is true that there are some limits to the possibility for regressivity, namely the following. (i) It is not possible for all inputs to be regressive at a certain output. If they were, then an increase in output would be obtained by a decrease in all inputs. With positive marginal products this would lead to a contradiction. (ii) It is not possible for any input to be regressive for all outputs. The reason is simply that the amount of an input must be increased above zero before it can be reduced. Aside from these trivial restrictions, which would apply for inferior consumer goods as well, I cannot see anything to make the case unlikely.

As to the presence of factor inferiority in reality, the phenomenon probably may be encountered when a firm operates several plants simultaneously. Usually it will be profitable to operate a modern plant, designed for large-scale production, side by side with an older plant, designed for small-scale production, for some interval of total output. It may then be possible that one of the plants is operated at a level where marginal cost is decreasing. An increase of total output will in such a case be combined with a decrease of production in the plant with decreasing marginal cost. If there is some factor which

---

[1] T. Puu, Les effets de substitution et d'expansion dans la théorie de la production, *Revue d'Economie Politique*, 1966, *id.*, Complementarity, Substitutivity and Regressivity in the Theory of Production, Published in *Recherches récents sur la Fonction de Production.* Namur, 1968.

is employed especially intensively in this plant, it is reasonable to expect that total demand for that factor will decrease as total production is increased. Thus, labour may be inferior as may any physical type of factor input. The theory of parallel operation of several plants or "machines" employed in the example has been developed by Skogh in this journal.[1]

## Graphical Analysis of the Two-input Case

After this summary discussion of the general case, I am going to discuss these matters for the special two-input case in some detail with the aid of "iso-marginal-physical-productivity curves", abbreviated iso-MPP curves. I think these curves provide a very helpful tool for many purposes.[2]

In an ordinary factor diagram, with the familiar isoquants and isocost lines, it is not possible to follow more than the substitution effects for changes of input prices on the demand for inputs. The substitution effect is visualized by "rolling" the isocost tangency line along an isoquant. But, as far as the effect due to output variation is concerned, we do not even know whether the isocost line, which has been "rolled" to obtain its new slope, has to be shifted outwards or inwards in the factor diagram, i.e. we do not know whether output will be increased or decreased. Even less can we identify the new isoquant by graphical means.

However, we know that the marginal productivities at optimum have to equal the ratios of factor prices to product price. Thus, if only one factor price is changed (the other factor price as well as the product price being held constant), then only one marginal productivity has to be changed, while the other must be held constant. Now, marginal productivities depend only upon the combination of factor inputs used, which means that for a given production function there are two families of iso-marginal-physical-productivity curves in the factor diagram, one for each factor. They are called iso-$MPP_1$ curves and iso-$MPP_2$ curves respectively. In order to trace the effects of a change in the price of a factor, we have only to follow a curve belonging to the family of iso-MPP curves for the factor whose price has remained constant in the direction where the MPP for the other factor changes appropriately.

Let the production function be:

$$q = f(v_1, v_2)$$

An iso-$MPP_i$ curve for $i = 1, 2$ is defined by the implicit function:

$$\frac{\partial q}{\partial v_i} = f_i = \text{constant} \quad i = 1, 2$$

[1] S. Skogh, Cost Minimization and Profit Maximization, *Ekonomisk Tidskrift* 1964, pp. 186–202.

[2] These curves were devised by Professor Tord Palander and have been presented in seminar discussions during 1965 at Uppsala University.

We now have to discuss the characteristics in some respects of these curves in the region where second-order conditions for profit maximization are fulfilled. The derivatives of the first order, indicating the slopes of iso-$MPP_i$ curves are obtained from:

$$df_i = f_{i1} \cdot dv_1 + f_{i2} \cdot dv_2 = 0 \quad i = 1, 2$$

which yield:

$$\left(\frac{dv_2}{dv_1}\right)_{f_i} = -\frac{f_{i1}}{f_{i2}} \quad i = 1, 2$$

where the index $f_i$ identifies the factor whose marginal productivity is held constant. This index is necessary in order to distinguish the slopes of the two kinds of iso-MPP curves from each other and from the slope of the isoquant

$$(dv_2/dv_1) = -(f_1/f_2).$$

Second-order conditions for profit maximum require:

$$f_{11} < 0; \; f_{22} < 0$$

and

$$f_{11} \cdot f_{22} > f_{12} \cdot f_{21}$$

to be fulfilled, where of course $f_{12} = f_{21}$. Immediately we find that, if second-order conditions are fulfilled, then the slopes of both iso-MPP curves are either positive or negative according to whether $f_{12} = f_{21}$ is positive or negative. Thus, both curves, in a certain point $(v_1, v_2)$, have either positive or negative slope. Moreover, it is true according to second-order conditions that:

$$\frac{\left(\frac{dv_2}{dv_1}\right)_{f_1}}{\left(\frac{dv_2}{dv_1}\right)_{f_2}} = \frac{f_{11} \cdot f_{22}}{f_{12} \cdot f_{21}} > 1$$

This implies that in a certain point the slope of the iso-$MPP_1$ curve is steeper than the slope of the iso-$MPP_2$ curve, regardless of whether they are both positively sloped or both negatively sloped, provided that we measure $v_1$ along the horizontal and $v_2$ along the vertical axis. This yields two possibilities for the region where a profit maximum may be located. They are illustrated in Figs. 1*a* and 1*b*, the difference between the cases being due to the sign of the cross derivatives.

Next we have to find out how one marginal productivity changes as we move along the iso-curve for the other marginal productivity. The result, indicated by arrows indicating the direction in which the other marginal productivity *increases* as we move along one iso-MPP curve, is depicted in the figures.

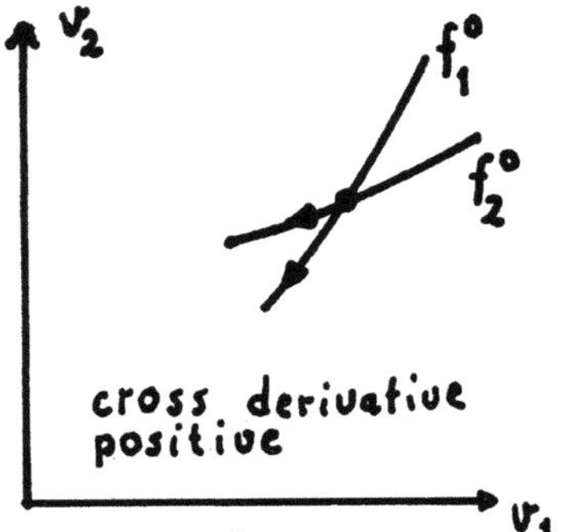

Fig. 1a

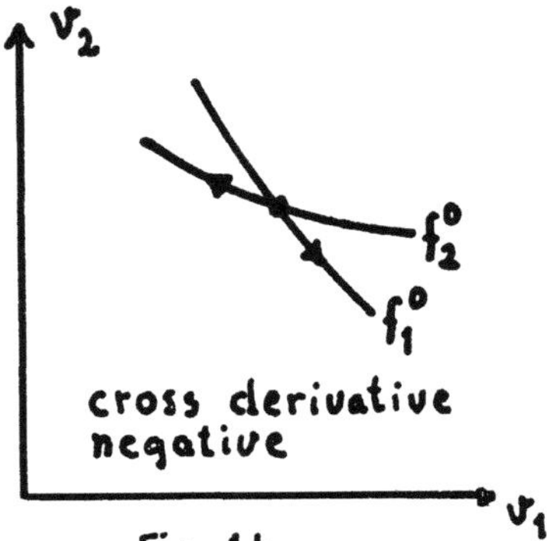

Fig. 1b

In order to obtain the result indicated we take the derivative of $f_1$ with respect to $v_1$, but in such a way that $v_2$ is also changed in order to keep $f_2$ constant. Thus:

$$\left(\frac{df_1}{dv_1}\right)_{f_2} = f_{11} + f_{12} \cdot \left(\frac{dv_2}{dv_1}\right)_{f_2}$$

$$= \frac{f_{11} \cdot f_{22} - f_{12} \cdot f_{21}}{f_{22}} < 0$$

If second-order conditions are fulfilled, this expression is negative as indicated, which means that $f_1$ increases as we move *to the left* along the curve for $f_2^0$. Accordingly the arrows point to the left on the curves for $f_2^0$ in Fig. 1(*a–b*).

Likewise, we may take the derivative of $f_2$ with respect to $v_2$, while $f_1$ is being held constant by an appropriate variation of $v_1$. This yields:

$$\left(\frac{df_2}{dv_2}\right)_{f_1} = f_{21} \cdot \left(\frac{dv_2}{dv_1}\right)_{f_1}^{-1} + f_{22}$$

$$= \frac{f_{11} \cdot f_{22} - f_{12} \cdot f_{21}}{f_{11}} < 0$$

Again, if second-order conditions are fulfilled, this expression is negative, which means that $f_2$ increases as we move *downwards* along the curve for $f_1^0$. Accordingly the arrows point downwards on the curves for $f_1^0$ in Fig. 1(*a–b*).

Now we are able to combine the iso-MPP curves with an isoquant—the dashed curve in diagrams 2*a–d*. There are in all four different possibilities.

The diagram 2*a* is drawn for the case where the cross-derivatives $f_{12} = f_{21}$ are positive. Then both iso-MPP curves are positively sloped, while the isoquant is negatively sloped, as is usual when marginal productivities are positive.

Obviously the arrows point towards lower-level iso-quants, which means that an increase in the price for either factor decreases optimum output, i.e. both factors are normal. In this case it can also be seen that both factors are

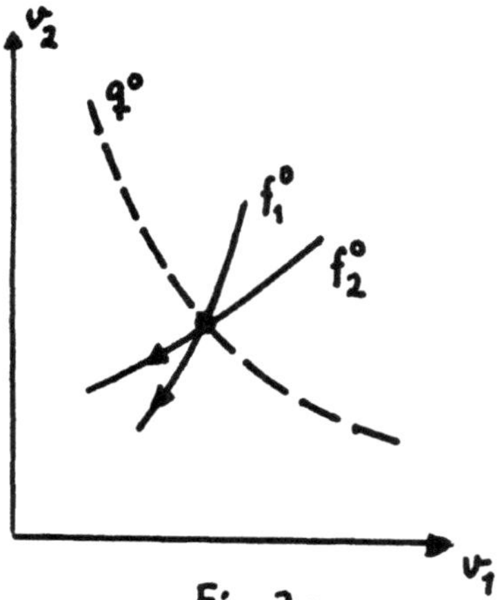


Fig. 2a

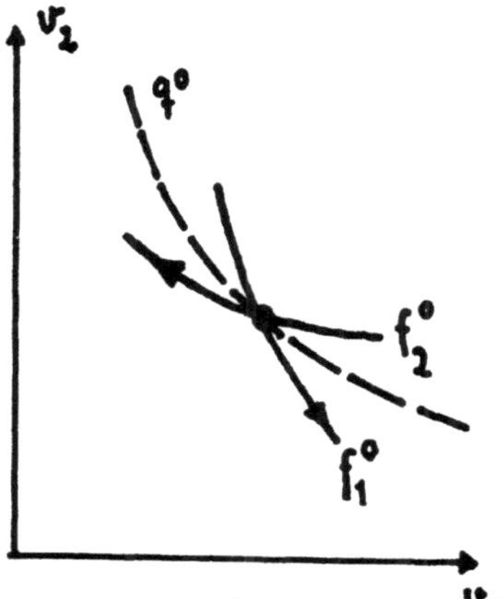


Fig. 2b

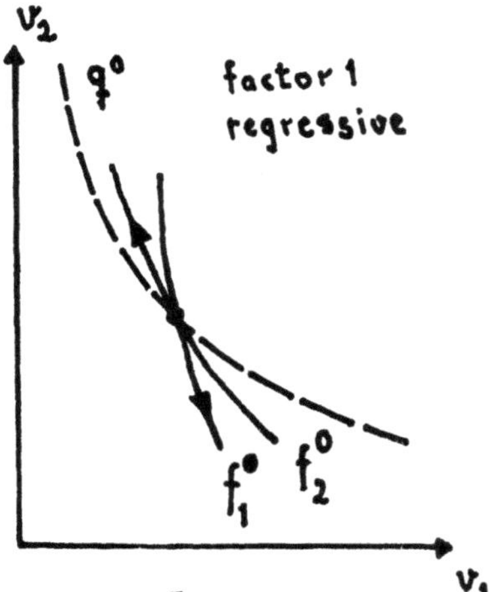


Fig. 2c

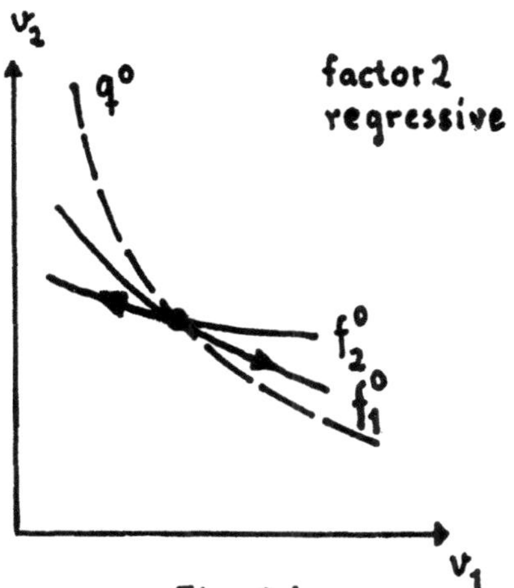


Fig. 2d

complementary (for variable production), i.e. optimal demand is decreased for both factors when the price of one of them rises.[1]

Even if the cross derivative $f_{12}=f_{21}$ is negative, it is possible for both factors to be normal. This case is depicted in Fig. 2*b*, where both arrows still point towards lower-level isoquants. An increase in either factor price thus leads to lower optimum output, but now decreased demand for the relatively more expensive factor is always accompanied by increased demand for the other factor, even though this increase does not outweigh the effect of the decrease in the factor whose price has risen, so that output is still decreased.

---

[1] At constant production the inputs must, of course, always be substitutes when there are only two of them exactly as in the theory of consumer behaviour.

This means, technically speaking, that both factors are normal, but are substitutes for variable production.

There remain two possible cases where one factor is regressive in each case. In Fig. 2*c* factor $v_1$ is regressive, as the arrow along $f_2^0$ points towards higher-level isoquants. Likewise, in Fig. 2*d* factor $v_2$ is regressive, as the arrow along $f_1^0$ points towards higher-level isoquants. In each case the other factor is, of course, normal. As in the case illustrated by Fig. 2*b*, the factors are substitutes for variable production.

These four cases exhaust all possibilities for intersections between the three curves, provided that the second-order conditions are fulfilled.[1]

In other regions than where possible profit maxima may be located, there are naturally other possibilities for intersections between the iso-MPP curves. In order to complete the picture of these iso-MPP curves, I am going to illustrate these curves for some analytical production functions over the whole positive quadrant.

## Illustrations Using Analytical Production Functions

Assume a traditional Cobb-Douglas production function with constant returns to scale and symmetric positions for both factors in the productive process:

$$q = 0.1 \cdot v_1^{0.5} \cdot v_2^{0.5}$$

That the isoquants are hyperbolas is well known. The iso-MPP curves are positively sloped straight lines through the origin, illustrated in Fig. 3*a–b*. As the factors are symmetric, the iso-$MPP_2$ curves may be obtained from the iso-$MPP_1$ curves by rotation of the diagram in such a way that the axes are interchanged, and *vice versa*.

The character of the iso-MPP curves means that a pair of curves, one from each family, either have only the origin in common, or coincide everywhere. This illustrates the well-known fact that with a linearly homogeneous production function no definite optimum may be determined by the first-order conditions for profit maximum, provided that we are dealing with a competitive firm.

[1] This graphical technique has been devised for the case of a competitive firm. It may, however, easily be extended to deal with pure monopoly, which is discussed as the main case in some of the papers listed in note 1, p. 241. Assuming product price to be—not a constant any longer—but a function of output, we obtain total revenue as a function of the two inputs. The partial derivatives of this total revenue function with respect to the inputs, i.e. the marginal value productivities ($MVP_i$ and $MVP_2$) too will be functions of $v_1$ and $v_2$ only. Thus, two maps of iso-$MVP_1$ curves may be depicted in the factor diagram. They will, of course, be distortions of the iso-$MPP_i$ curve maps—the distortion being due to the demand function for ouput. As the $MVP_i$ have to equal input prices in optimum, and as the intersection of the iso-$MVP_i$ curves with each other and with the isoquants are relevant for second order optimum conditions and for the existence of inferior inputs, all the previous discussion may be applied to pure monopoly if MPP is replaced by MVP.

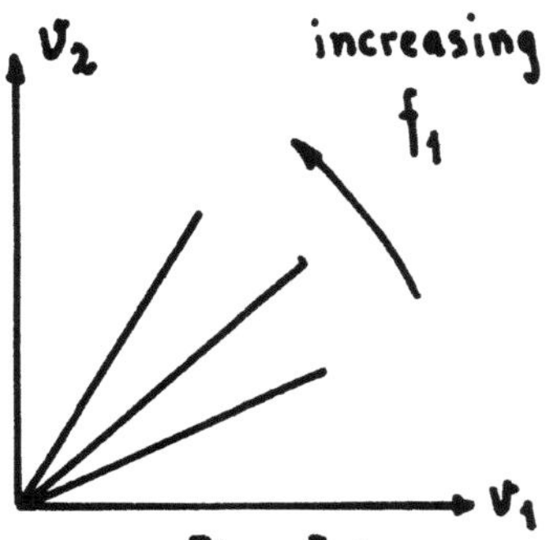


Fig. 3a

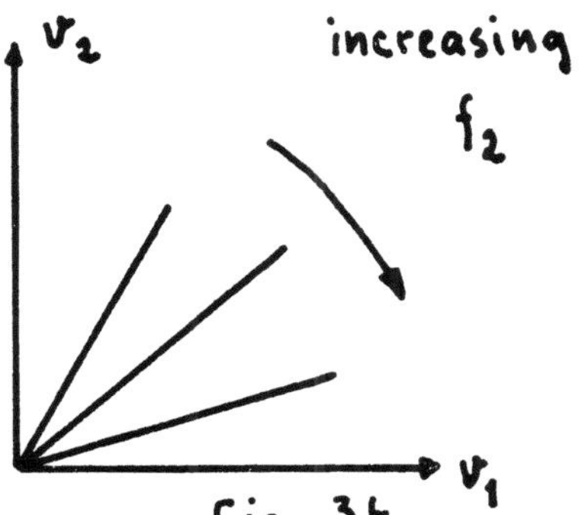


Fig. 3b

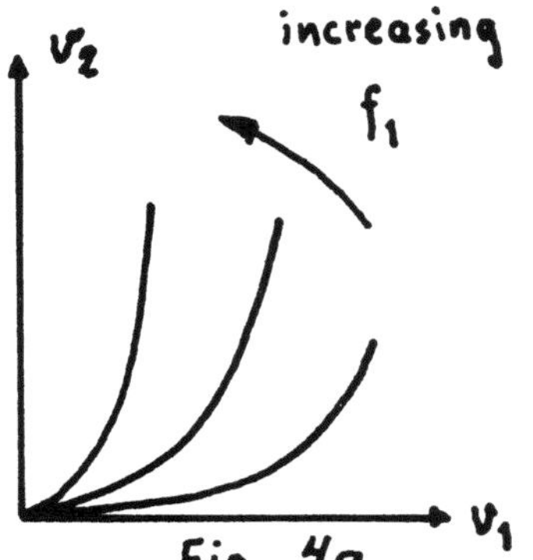


Fig. 4a

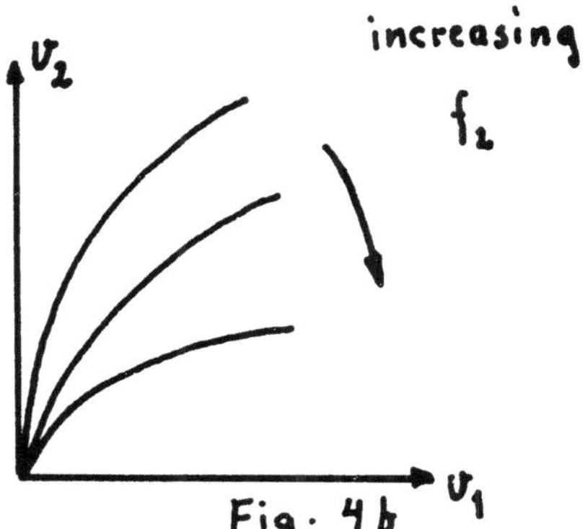


Fig. 4b

Obviously second-order conditions may not be satisfied anywhere in the positive quadrant. As we have seen, they require that iso-MPP$_1$ curves cut iso-MPP$_2$ curves in such a way that the former is steeper. But this is not possible when the "curves" coincide.

It would be a mistake to believe that the linearity is due to the symmetrical form of the production function. The linearity would result from any combination of values of the exponents, provided that their sum equals unity.

Assume next that the Cobb-Douglas function is changed in such a way that the sum of the exponents is less than unity, i.e. there are decreasing returns to scale, but the elasticity of output with respect to a proportional increase of all inputs is still a constant (though now less than unity). Say:

$$q = 0.1 \cdot v_1^{0.4} \cdot v_2^{0.4}$$

It is easily seen that $f_1 = 0.04 \cdot (v_2^{0.4}/v_1^{0.6})$. Along an iso-MPP$_1$ curve we have $v_2 = c_1 \cdot v_1^{1.5}$, where $c_1$ is a positive constant increasing with increasing $f_1^0$. Thus, because the exponent 1.5 is greater than unity, the iso-MPP$_1$ curves are con-

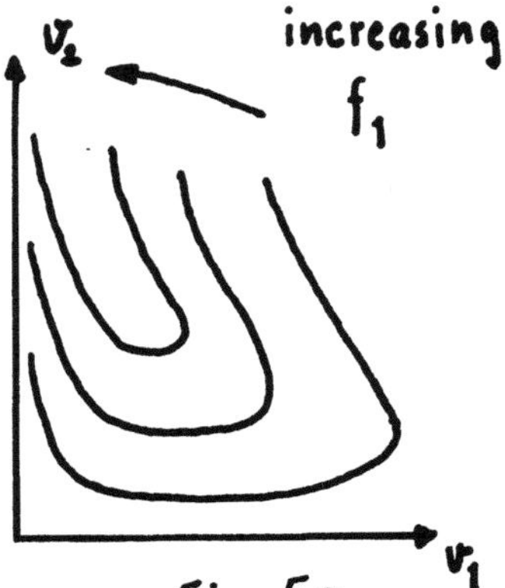


Fig. 5a

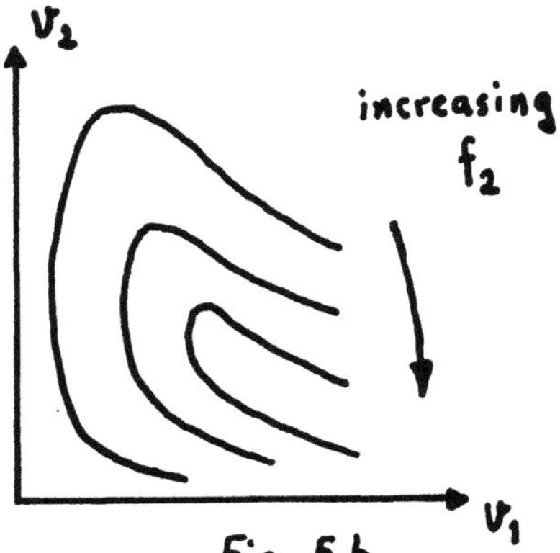


Fig. 5b

cave from above, as shown in Fig. 4*a*. In the same manner we obtain $f_2 = 0.04 \cdot (v_1^{0.4}/v_2^{0.6})$, which gives for an iso-MPP$_2$ curve approximately $v_2 = c_2 \cdot v_1^{0.67}$. As the exponent 0.67 is smaller than unity, the iso-MPP$_2$ curves will be convex from above, as shown in Fig. 4*b*. The constant $c_2$ decreases with increasing $f_2^0$, which implies that the iso-MPP$_2$ curves lie lower the higher marginal productivity of this factor is, just as indicated in Fig. 4*b*.

But as the factors are symmetric, as in the previous case, the map of iso-MPP$_2$ curves might also be obtained from the map of iso-MPP$_1$ curves by such a rotation of the diagram as was mentioned in the previous case, and *vice versa*. From the Figs. 4*a* and 4*b* it is easily seen that the iso-MPP$_1$ curves would be steeper than the iso-MPP$_2$ curves at all interesection points. Thus second-order conditions would be fulfilled everywhere.[1]

In the present case, as contrasted to the previous one, the marginal cost is no longer constant. With decreasing returns the marginal cost curve will be uniformly increasing. However, it would be of some interest to study the iso-MPP curves of some analytical production function which exhibits a region of increasing returns to scale as well as a region of decreasing returns to scale, so that it yields a U-shaped marginal cost curve, familiar from all elementary textbooks on the theory of the firm, and strictly defined by Frisch in his "regular ultra-passum law".[2] This is not possible with the usual Cobb-Douglas function.

Such a function is, however, yielded by the following transformation of the Cobb-Douglas function first introduced. Put:

---

[1] If the sum of coefficients in the analytical function were greater than unity, then the characters of the two diagrams as regards concavity and convexity would be reversed. Then the iso-MPP$_2$ curves would be steeper than the iso-MPP$_1$ curves. Thus, second-order conditions would not be fulfilled anywhere with this alternative.

[2] R. Frisch, *Theory of Production*, Dordrecht, 1965, Chapter 8.

$$x = 0.1 \cdot v_1^{0.5} \cdot v_2^{0.5}$$

and

$$q = 200 \cdot e^{-(1/x)}$$

The iso-$MPP_1$ curves are depicted in Fig. 5*a* and the iso-$MPP_2$ curves in Fig. 5*b*. As before, with symmetrical factors, the diagrams may be obtained from each other by rotation.

Second-order conditions will be fulfilled only in limited regions of these diagrams, namely to the right of and above a certain isoquant. The isoquants look exactly like those of the two previous examples, i.e. they are hyperbolas but if they are drawn for equal increases in product output, then the map will show a region of increasing density of iso-quants first, and then a region of decreasing density of iso-quants as we move outward from the origin.[1]

[1] This function has been used in econometric research in V. Ringstad, Econometric Analyses Based on a Production Function with Neutrally Variable Scale Elasticity, *The Swedish Journal of Economics*, 1967, pp. 115 ff. Details about the mathematical properties of this function may be found in a mimeographed paper: T. Puu and S. Skogh, *An Analytical Production Function*, Uppsala, 1968. Marginal costs for this function are:

$$C'(q) = \frac{20 \cdot (r_1 \cdot r_2)^{0.5}}{q \cdot (\ln 200 - \ln q)^2}$$

It is easy to show that this curve has a unique minimum at $q = 200 \cdot e^{-2}$ and that it is strictly convex from below for all positive outputs. (I would like to complete the picture by exemplifying with a production function showing regressivity, but unfortunately there is no reasonable analytical function available with such characteristics.)

# FREE ENTRY AND EFFICIENT DISTRIBUTION OF INPUTS IN A ONE-PRODUCT INDUSTRY

by Tönu Puu

It is a well known fact that with a *fixed* set of active firms in an industry the distribution of aggregate input quantities between individual firms, obtained with profit-maximizing firms (that regard factor prices and product price as independent of their own decisions), is such that aggregate output is maximized (1). Thus, perfect competition within a fixed set of active firms would seem to be efficient according to Paretian optimality criteria.

The reason for this is simple. Competitive firms maximizing their profits would equalize marginal productivity of each factor to the ratio of its price and product price. But — as product price and factor prices are the same for all competitive firms — marginal productivity of any factor would be the same in all firms. And this would exactly constitute the conditions that indicate impossibility of increasing aggregate output of the industry by marginal redistributions of inputs among the firms, as the transference of a unit of any input from one firm to another would decrease the output of the former exactly as much as it would increase the output of the latter. It may also be seen that the marginal conditions indicate a maximum of aggregate output — and not a minimum (or a point of inflection) — provided that they indicate maximal profits for the individual firms.

But what about free entry and free exit, i.e. the case where the assumption, that the set of active firms is fixed, is relaxed? It is usually assumed that firms stay active (in the short run) as long as their revenues at least cover their variable costs. Would the entry and exit of firms according to this principle still indicate that the distribution of inputs is efficient? The aim of this paper is to try to answer this question.

The case of free entry and free exit has been sufficiently discussed under the assumption that all firms have identical techniques.

---

(1) L. R. Klein, *Macroeconomics and the Theory of Rational Behaviour*, K. May, *The Aggregation Problem for a One-Industry Model*, and S. S. Pu, *A Note on Aggregation*, all in « Econometrica » 1946 and 1947 provide the classical treatment of aggregation. As to the efficiency of competitive equilibrium, see any standard work on Welfare economics.

Metroeconomica (1972) Vol. XXIV:70-85

This, however, is only a special case. At least equally interesting is the case where firms with decreasing technical efficiency turn active as the industry expands. I am going to discuss this as the general case.

Moreover, the formal discussion would be little informative, unless it is accompanied by examplifications. I have chosen a transformation of the Cobb-Douglas function — such that it satisfies the Frischian « regular ultra passum law » — for the job, as the usual functions in the theory of production with fixed elasticity of output with respect to proportional input variations for obvious reasons would not do.

EFFICIENT DISTRIBUTION OF AGGREGATE INPUTS: GENERAL CASE

Assume that there is a continuum of firms, identified by a variable $t$ in the interval $(0, T)$. For each firm the production function is

$$q = f(v_1, \dots, v_n; t) \tag{1}$$

where $q$ denotes the quantity of output and $v_1, \dots, v_n$ denote the quantities of inputs. Thus, $t$ changes the form of the relation between output and a vector of inputs. It may be assumed, that, as the identification variable $t$ increases from 0 to $T$, it decreases the technical efficiency of production. What this means exactly will be seen in the sequel. Such an assumption is necessary in order that the question of which firms will be active in any case may be dealt with in terms of the upper bound $T$ only. If there may be « gaps » in the interval the problem becomes more complicated. Aggregate output is defined by

$$Q = \int_0^T q \, dt \tag{2}$$

and aggregate inputs by

$$V_i = \int_0^T v_i \, dt \qquad i = 1, \dots, n \tag{3}$$

Now, the efficiency problem may be solved by answering the following question: Given a vector of aggregate input quantities $V_1, \dots, V_n$, which are the distribution functions

$$v_i = g_i(t) \qquad i = 1, \dots, n \tag{4}$$

satisfying conditions (3) and making $Q$ according to (1) and (2) maximal? If the optimal distribution functions have been found, then any deformation of these functions by changing the variables $k_1, \dots, k_n$ from their zero values in equations

$$v_i = g_i(t) + k_i \cdot h_i(t) \qquad i = 1, \dots, n \tag{5}$$

must decrease aggregate output, whatever the functions $h_1(t), \dots, h_n(t)$ are. This mathematical problem may be dealt with by a standard device from the calculus of variations.

This requires that the following Lagrangean expression be formulated:

$$L = \int_0^T f(g_1(t) + k_1 \cdot h_1(t), \dots, g_n(t) + k_n \cdot h_n(t); t)\, dt + \qquad (6)$$
$$+ \sum_{i=1}^{n} \mu_i \cdot \left(V_i - \int_0^T g_i(t)\, dt - k_i \cdot \int_0^T h_i(t)\, dt\right)$$

It is formed by adding to the aggregate output the constraints multiplied by yet undetermined Lagrangean multipliers. In order that $Q$ be maximal at given $V_1, \dots, V_n$ with the distribution functions $g_1(t), \dots, g_n(t)$ it is necessary that the partial derivatives of $L$ with respect to $k_1, \dots, k_n$ and $\mu_1, \dots, \mu_n$ be zero as $k_1, \dots, k_n$ assume zero values. Thus:

$$\frac{\partial L}{\partial k_i} = \int_0^T (f_i - \mu_i) \cdot h_i(t)\, dt = 0 \qquad i = 1, \dots, n \qquad (7)$$

$$\frac{\partial L}{\partial \mu_i} = V_i - \int_0^T g_i(t)\, dt = 0 \qquad i = 1, \dots, n \qquad (8)$$

where $f_i$ denotes the marginal productivity of the $i$ : th input. Equations (7) must be fulfilled, whichever the deformation functions $h_i(t)$ are. Obviously this is true provided that

$$\mu_i = f_i(g_1(t), \dots, g_n(t); t) \qquad i = 1, \dots, n \qquad (9)$$

hold for any value of $t$.

If one assumes a vector of values for the Lagrangean multipliers, which now have turned out to denote marginal productivities — equal for any factor in all the firms —, then equations (9) furnish $n$ equations in the variables $v_1 = g_1(t), \dots, v_n = g_n(t)$ for each value of $t$.

Thus, assuming values of marginal productivities we may compute the inputs used by each firm, i.e. derive the distribution functions $g_i(t)$. Integrating over $t$ from 0 to $T$, we may next obtain the values of $V_1, \dots, V_n$ according to equations (3) above. Thus, aggregate inputs are obtained at an assumed combination of marginal productivites.

By carrying through this procedure for all conceivable vectors of the marginal productivities, we obtain aggregate inputs — $n$ in number — as functions of the $n$ marginal productivities. Inverting this system of equations we obtain the $n$ marginal productivities $\mu_1, \dots, \mu_n$ as functions of the aggregate input quantities $V_1, \dots, V_n$ in stead.

But, as the distribution functions $g_i(t)$ may be solved as soon as a vector of marginal productivities is assumed, we may as well say that the distribution functions may be derived once a vector of aggregate input quantities is assumed. Hence, according to equations (1), (2) and (4), aggregate output may be computed. If the procedure is carried out for different vectors of aggregate inputs, then the aggregate production function may be obtained, giving

$$Q = F(V_1, \dots, V_n; T) \tag{10}$$

which is derived under the assumption of efficient distribution of the aggregate input quantities among the firms in such a way that aggregate output is maximized. This relation in general depends upon the upper bound $T$ of the interval of firms assumed to be active. I am going to discuss the influence on $Q$ by variations of $T$, but there are some matters which must be dealt with before this is done.

* * *

Up to now nothing has been said about other conditions than the marginal ones for the efficient distribution problem. As to second order conditions it is obviously sufficient for the marginal ones to give a maximum if the quadratic form:

$$d^2Q = \sum_{i=1}^{n} \sum_{j=1}^{n} \left(\int_0^T f_{ij} \cdot h_i(t) \cdot h_j(t)\, dt\right) \cdot dk_i \cdot dk_j \tag{11}$$

is negative definite for any deformation functions $h_1(t), \dots, h_n(t)$. If the integration sign is moved outside the summation signs, it is seen that $d^2Q$ becomes an integral of the quadratic forms on the matrices of second order derivatives $[f_{ij}]$ written in the variables $h_1(t) \cdot dk_1, \dots, h_n(t) \cdot dk_n$. Provided that all these quadratic forms are negative definite — something which must hold if the profits of all firms are maximal — then the definite integral $d^2Q$ has to be negative definite too. Actually, we would only need to discuss constrained variations, but as definite negativity may be ensured for unrestricted variations it must also hold for more restricted classes of variations. Thus profit maximization in competitive firms implies efficient distribution as far as second order conditions are concerned. As to the first order conditions, the problem was already discussed verbally in the introduction, i.e. that profit maximization of competitive firms equalizes marginal productivities for any factor among all firms — something which constitutes the first order conditions for efficient distribution according to equations (9) above.

* * *

But this discussion, amounting to the conclusion that competition entails efficient distribution of inputs, has been limited to the case where the set of active firms is fixed, i.e. the upper bound $T$ is fixed.

Next we have to find out how $T$ has to be chosen in order that $Q$ be maximal according to (10), and to see whether this value of $T$ is the one obtained by the rule that firms actually remain in business as long as their revenues cover variable costs. If the answer is affirmative, then it is obvious that with free entry (and free exit) efficient distribution of inputs is still obtained with competitive firms maximizing their profits.

In order to find out these things we have to investigate the derivatives of first and second order of $Q$ with respect to $T$. If the first order derivative is zero and the second order derivative is negative for a certain value of $T$, then this value is obviously chosen so as to make $Q$ maximal. According to equations (1) and (2) above the first order derivative is:

$$\frac{dQ}{dT} = \int_0^T \sum_{i=1}^n f_i \cdot \frac{dv_i}{dT} dt + \hat{q} \tag{12}$$

$$= \sum_{i=1}^n \int_0^T f_i \cdot \frac{dv_i}{dT} dt + \hat{q}$$

where $\hat{q}$ denotes the output of the marginal firm, i.e. the one with $t = T$. Now, according to equations (9) above the marginal productivities $f_i$ are equal to the Lagrangean multipliers $\mu_i$, which are the same for all firms — or (technically expressed) independent of the integration variable $t$ — and may thus be moved outside the integration sign. Thus

$$\frac{dQ}{dT} = \sum_{i=1}^n \mu_i \cdot \int_0^T \frac{dv_i}{dT} dt + \hat{q} \tag{13}$$

But the definite integrals of $dv_i/dT$ may be easily obtained by differentiating equations (3) with respect to $T$ and remembering that aggregate input quantities are not changed, i.e. $dV_i/dT = 0$. This yields:

$$\frac{dV_i}{dT} = \int_0^T \frac{dv_i}{dT} dt + \hat{v}_i = 0 \qquad i = 1, \ldots, n \tag{14}$$

where $\hat{v}_i$ denotes the quantity of the $i:th$ input employed by the marginal firm, i.e. the one for which $t = T$. Thus, substitution from equations (14) into equation (13) gives:

$$\frac{dQ}{dT} = \hat{q} - \sum_{i=1}^n \mu_i \cdot \hat{v}_i \tag{15}$$

Now it is true according to definition that the « passus coefficient » — or the elasticity of output with respect to a proportional increase of all inputs — is the sum of all the « marginal elasticities » — or the marginal productivities transformed into elasticities (2). Thus, the

(2) This terminology is borrowed from R. Frisch, « Theory of Production », 1965.

passus coefficient, denoted $\varepsilon$, equals the sum over $i$ of $f_i \cdot (v_i/q)$. But, as the $\mu_i$ are equal to the marginal productivities $f_i$ for all firms, we obtain for the marginal firm that

$$\hat{\varepsilon} \cdot \hat{q} = \sum_{i=1}^{n} \mu_i \cdot \hat{v}_i \qquad (16)$$

Substitution from equation (16) into equation (15) finally yields:

$$\frac{dQ}{dT} = \hat{q} \cdot (1 - \hat{\varepsilon}) \qquad (17)$$

Thus it is true that aggregate output may not be increased by marginal changes of the upper bound of the interval of active firms, provided that the passus coefficient of the marginal firm equals unity. An entry or an exit of firms (on the production activity margin) does not affect aggregate output when the marginal firm produces with a passus coefficient equal to unity.

But, it is easily seen from equation (16) that the product $\hat{\varepsilon} \cdot \hat{q}$ equals total variables costs (computed in units of the product) for the marginal firm, as $\mu_i$ is equal to the ratio of the $i$ : *th* factor price to product price in a competitive industry. Accordingly, the right hand member of equation (17) expresses the excess of revenues above variable costs in the marginal firm. If we assume, that the firms are active whenever at least variable costs are covered, and inactive otherwise, then that firm will be marginal (according to this rule for entry and exit of firms) that has a passus coefficient equal to unity. Thus, marginal conditions for the choice of $T$ are the same in a competitive industry with free entry and free exit as they are in the solution of the efficiency problem regarding the distribution of aggregate inputs. Consequently, free entry and free exit in a competitive market entail efficient distribution of inputs as far as marginal conditions are concerned. (As a matter of fact the marginal change of aggregate output, due to the entry or exit of a marginal firm, always equals the excess of revenue above variable costs for this firm, of course computed in units of the product).

It should be noticed that the distribution of inputs will be efficient even if all individual firms, except the marginal one, have positive profits. Free entry (in this case with firms with different techniques) will not eliminate profits (in the more efficient firms), but it nevertheless entails an allocation of resources that maximizes total output.

* * *

From equation (17) we can immediately see that for $\varepsilon = 1$

$$\frac{d^2Q}{dT^2} = -\hat{q} \cdot \frac{d\hat{\varepsilon}}{dT} \qquad (18)$$

i.e. that the second order derivative is negative if the passus coefficient of the marginal firm rises when the interval of active firms is augmented. The meaning of this condition, however, is a little complicaded, because we would have to discuss first how the passus coefficient varies with $t$ in a given interval of active firms $(0, T)$ and then how the whole structure of passus coefficients for different firms is shifted when the interval itself is changed. But, tentatively we might say, as the passus coefficient of a certain firm denotes the proportion of its revenue spent as variable costs, that $\varepsilon$ increases with $t$ when the firms are ordered according to decreasing profit margins. This seems to be a reasonable assumption if it is wished that the firm with the highest value of the identification variable, i.e. the one with $t = T$, be the marginal one. Moreover, when the interval of active firms is augmented, it seems probable that the profit margins of all formerly active firms are reduced, i.e. that the curve showing $\varepsilon$ as dependent upon $t$ shifts upwards when the upper bound $T$ is pushed to the right. Thus, the passus coefficient of the marginal firm would increase, because the augmentation of the interval of active firms would decrease profit margins for all firms already in business, when new competitors are admitted, *and* because the firm, which will be marginal after the augmentation, is another one with still smaller profit margin. Accordingly, the stationary value of $Q$ would be a maximum with respect to variations of $T$ when the latter is chosen so that $\hat{\varepsilon} = 1$, and this maximum would be unique. This means that the solution of the efficiency problem for distribution of aggregate inputs would require that, for all vectors of aggregate inputs in equation (10) above, $T$ is chosen so that $\hat{\varepsilon} = 1$, and this would be the case with free entry and free exit in a competitive industry. The resulting production function for the whole industry would then be an envelope to the functions for different values of $T$ in equation (10). This envelope will be encountered further in the example below.

Now it has to be admitted that the reasoning is based upon the assumption that the ordering according to decreasing profit margins among the firms is the same for all vectors of aggregate inputs, and that this assumption is a very weak point. Therefore, I am going to give another expression for $d^2Q/dT^2$ which will throw some further light upon the problem, but it will be seen that neither this formulation ascertains negativity of the derivative for all reasonable cases. However, it is at least in the example.

In order to find the second formula for $d^2Q/dT^2$, let us differentiate equation (12) once more with respect to $T$. Thus:

$$\frac{d^2Q}{dT^2} = \int_0^T \sum_{i=1}^n \sum_{j=1}^n f_{ij} \cdot \frac{dv_i}{dT} \cdot \frac{dv_j}{dT} \, dt \tag{19}$$

$$+ \int_0^T \sum_{i=1}^n f_i \cdot \frac{d^2 v_i}{dT^2} \, dt + 2 \cdot \frac{d\hat{q}}{dT}$$

where we get one $d\hat{q}/dT$ by differentiating $\hat{q}$ in equation (12) and the second one from the integration border in the first term of (12). Next, let us differentiate (14) with respect to $T$, whereby we obtain:

$$\frac{d^2V_i}{dT^2} = \int_0^T \frac{d^2v_i}{dT^2}\, dt + 2\cdot\frac{d\hat{v}_i}{dT} = 0 \qquad i = 1, \dots, n \qquad (20)$$

In the first term of the second row of (19) we may move the summation sign outside the integration sign, then substitute $\mu_i$ (which is independent of the integration variable) in stead of $f_i$ and move it outside the integration sign, and finally substitute from equation (20). This yields:

$$\frac{d^2Q}{dT^2} = \int_0^T \sum_{i=1}^{n} \sum_{j=1}^{n} f_{ij}\cdot\frac{dv_i}{dT}\,\frac{dv_j}{dT}\, dt - \qquad (21)$$

$$- 2\cdot\sum_{i=1}^{n} \mu_i\cdot\frac{d\hat{v}_i}{dT} + 2\cdot\frac{d\hat{q}}{dT}$$

But, according to equation (1), it will be true for the marginal firm that $\hat{q} = f(\hat{v}_1, \dots, \hat{v}_n;\ T)$. Thus:

$$\frac{d\hat{q}}{dT} = \sum_{i=1}^{n} \mu_i\cdot\frac{d\hat{v}_i}{dT} + \frac{\partial\hat{q}}{\partial T} \qquad (22)$$

as the $\mu_i$ equal the marginal productivities of all active firms. Substitution from (22) into (21) gives the final formula:

$$\frac{d^2Q}{dT^2} = \int_0^T \sum_{i=1}^{n} \sum_{j=1}^{n} f_{ij}\cdot\frac{dv_i}{dT}\cdot\frac{dv_j}{dT}\, dt + 2\cdot\frac{\partial\hat{q}}{\partial T} \qquad (23)$$

The first term is an integral of quadratic forms, which are all negative as the firms maximize their profits, and the second term is a partial derivative whose sign tells us whether the output will be increased or decreased if the vector of inputs used by the marginal firm is transferred to another firm, lying just outside the activity frontier. If this would increase output it would increase aggregate output to make a gap in the active interval and thus the whole discussion — carried through under the assumption that all firms in the interval $(0, T)$ are active — would be meaningless. Thus, in order that the whole discussion be meaningful, we have to assume that $\partial\hat{q}/\partial T$ is negative. If this is true, it is also true that both terms in equation (23) are negative. The assumption, sufficient but not necessary for negativity of $d^2Q/dT^2$, means that we may arrange the firms in an absolute order of technical efficiency independently of which combination of input quantities is considered. This is equivalent to saying that, if one firm may obtain a greater output from one vector of inputs than another firm using the same vector, then the former one will obtain a greater output from every other conceivable input vectcr too. Obviously, problems arise when some firms are more efficient than others at small scale but less efficient at large scale. The whole discussion would then have to be formulated so that there is a sequence of intervals of active firms — instead of just one interval —, but even though the discussion is not much complicated by this modification, the formulas will become so awkward that *I* have omitted the complication.

## THE SPECIAL CASE OF IDENTICAL FIRMS

The discussion is considerably simplified if we assume that all firms have identical production functions, i.e. if we delete the variable $t$ in equation (1) above. This is the traditional case of free entry. Omitting $t$, we obtain the equations, corresponding to (9) above, and stating that the marginal productivity of each input be the same in all firms, as:

$$\mu_i = f_i\,(g_1\,(t)\,,\,\dots\,,\,g_n\,(t)\,) \qquad i = 1\,,\,\dots\,,\,n \qquad (24)$$

With given marginal productivities $\mu_1\,,\,\dots\,,\,\mu_n$ we will obtain constant values independent of $t$ for all the arguments of the marginal productivity functions by solving equations (24). Thus:

$$v^0{}_i = g_i\,(t) \qquad i = 1\,,\,\dots\,,\,n \qquad (25)$$

which means that all active firms will use the same quantities of all inputs. Accordingly, it will be seen from equations (3) above that

$$V_i = v^0{}_i \cdot \int_0^T dt = T \cdot v^0{}_i \qquad i = 1\,,\,\dots\,,\,n \qquad (26)$$

which means that $T$ will for the special case denote the number of active firms. As to the output, it is true for all firms, that

$$q^0 = f\,(v^0{}_1\,,\,\dots\,,\,v^0{}_n) \qquad (27)$$

and, according to equation (2), the aggregate output

$$Q = q^0 \cdot \int_0^T dt = T \cdot q^0 \qquad (28)$$

simply equals the number of firms multiplied by the output produced by a single active firm.

As to the derivatives of the aggregate production functions, we might make the derivations by the help of equantions (26)-(28), but it is simpler to start from the general formulas (17) and (23) respectively. For the derivative $dQ/dT$ equation (17) is still valid — it ought only be noticed that the output quantity and the passus coefficient, which above referred to the marginal firm only, now are the same for all individual firms. Thus, aggregate output may not be increased by any marginal entry or exit of firms, provided that the passus coefficients equal unity in the active firms. As to the derivative $d^2Q/dT^2$, we must put $\partial\hat{q}/\partial T$ equal to zero in equation (23), because the variable $t$ no longer enters into the production function. Thus the second order derivative is negative in this special case and the stationary point will be a maximum.

The aggregate production function will in this case be linearly homogeneous depending upon adjustments in the number of active firms which lead to proportional changes of output and all inputs according to equations (26) and (28) taken as aggregates for the whole industry, whereas the corresponding quantities for the single firms are unchanged. This characteristic of aggregate production functions under free entry and identical firms has been noticed in the literature (3).

The derivation of the aggregate production function is quite straight-forward in the special case of identical firms. From equation (16) above we see that, if the passus coefficient is equal to unity, then the sum of all marginal productivities, multiplied by the amounts of inputs used, is equal to output for each individual firm. Now, marginal productivities are given as functions of $v^0_1, \dots, v^0_n$ by equations (24). But according to equations (26) it is true that $v^0_i = V_i/T$. Thus, $\mu_i = f_i(V_1/T, \dots, V_n/T)$. As $q^0 = Q/T$, a unitary passus coefficient implies that:

$$\frac{Q}{T} = \sum_{i=1}^{n} f_i\left(\frac{V_1}{T}, \dots, \frac{V_n}{T}\right) \cdot \frac{V_i}{T} \tag{29}$$

Moreover, substitution from (26) and (28) into (27) yields:

$$\frac{Q}{T} = f\left(\frac{V_1}{T}, \dots, \frac{V_n}{T}\right) \tag{30}$$

The last two equations show that with a given vector of aggregate inputs $V_1, \dots, V_n$ the values of $T$ and $Q$ — i.e. the number of active firms and aggregate output — are determined. We can also see immediately that any proportional increase of all aggregate inputs according to these equations is consistent with an increase of the number of firms and of aggregate output by the same proportion — leaving the optima of individual firms unchanged.

(3) See R. Bentzel and O. Johansson, *Om homogenitet i produktionsfunktioner*, « Ekonomisk Tidskrift », 1959.

AN EXAMPLE

I am now going to clarify the general discussion of free entry above by the help of a set of analytical production functions, which are different for different firms. Let us first find out the characteristics of the analytical functions. Put

$$q = \frac{10}{(1+t)} \cdot e^{-x} \tag{31}$$

where $x$ is the inverse of the common Cobb-Douglas expression, i.e.

$$x = \frac{1}{v_1^{a_1} \dots v_n^{a_n}} \tag{32}$$

and $a_1 + \dots + a_n = 1$. These functions are monotonic transformations of the traditional Cobb-Douglas functions [4]. For a certain firm the iso-quants look exactly like those of non-transformed Cobb-Douglas production functions with the Hicks-Allen elasticity of substitution equal to unity for any pair of inputs. The transformation, however, changes the map of isoquants — if drawn for equal changes of output —, so that the density of iso-quants first increases and then decreases with increasing output. Thus, there is a region of increasing returns as well as a region of decreasing returns. The passus coefficient decreases monotonically with increasing output, so that the transformed function obeyes the Frischian « regular ultra passum law ». That this is so may be easily seen as the marginal productivities are

$$f_i = a_i \cdot \frac{q \cdot x}{v_i} \qquad i = 1, \dots, n \tag{33}$$

The « marginal elasticities » are $f_i \cdot (v_i/q) = a_i \cdot x$, and the passus coefficient, which is the sum of all marginal elasticities, is obtained as $\varepsilon = x$ — because the sum $a_1 + \dots + a_n$ equals unity. Accordingly, the passus coefficient, which equals $x$, will be the inverse of the common Cobb-Douglas expression, as is seen from equation (32). Hence the decrease of the passus coefficient with increasing output.

The characteristics of the transformation are confirmed by the shapes of avarage and marginal cost functions. They are, derivations being deleted, $AVC = k \cdot q^{-1} \cdot (ln\ 10 - ln\ (1+t) - ln\ q)^{-1}$ with a minimum at $q = (10/(1+t)) \cdot e^{-1}$ and $MC = k \cdot q^{-1} \cdot (ln\ 10 - ln\ (1+t) - ln\ q)^{-2}$ with a minimum at $q = (10/(1+t)) \cdot e^{-2}$. Both curves are $U$-shaped, convex from below, they have unique

---

(4) This function has been introduced in V. RINGSTAD, *Econometric Analyses Based on a Production Function with Neutrally variable Scale Elasticity*, « The Swedish Journal of Economics », 1967. Details about the mathematical properties may be found in a mimeographed paper: T. PUU, « An Analytical Production Function », Uppsala, 1968.

minima at the indicated points and the *AVC*-curve is cut by the *MC*-curve in its minimum — everything exactly as in microeconomic text-books. (In these cost functions $k$ denotes a constant solely dependent upon the exponents of the Cobb-Douglas function and upon the prices of inputs).

* * *

As the supply functions of the individual firms begin at the *AVC*-minima it will be of some interest to find out how these minima are distributed within the continuum of firms. We have already seen that at the *AVC*-minima $q = (10/(1 + t))\cdot e^{-2}$, and by substitution we see that at this point $MC = AVC = k/q$. Accordingly, the cost functions are shifted to the left and upwards as the identification variable $t$ increases. With a given output price the optimal outputs decrease with increasing $t$, as do the profit margins until, for a certain $t = T$, variable costs are exactly covered by revenues. For higher values of $t$ the firms non longer remain in business. This may also be seen from the fact that the excess of revenues above variable costs equals $q\cdot(1 - x)$, (because $x$ now denotes the passus coefficient), if computed in units of output as always in this paper. It will be seen that $x$ increases with increasing $t$, and thus the profit margins decrease as $t$ increases. — We can also see directly from equations (31)-(32) that the output obtained from a given vector of inputs is smaller the higher the value of $t$ is.

According to equation (33) the system of equations (9) — stating that marginal productivities be equal in all individual firms which are active — takes the form:

$$\mu_i = a_i\cdot\frac{q\cdot x}{v_i} \qquad i = 1, \dots, n \tag{34}$$

Solving for $v_i$ we obtain:

$$v_i = \frac{a_i}{\mu_i}\cdot q\cdot x \qquad i = 1, \dots, n \tag{35}$$

and integrating:

$$V_i = \frac{a_i}{\mu_i}\cdot \int_0^T q\cdot x\, dt \qquad i = 1, \dots, n \tag{36}$$

As $q\cdot x$ expresses the remuneration of inputs — computed in units of output — in the individual firm, it is true that the definite integral of (36) denotes the aggregate remuneration of inputs in the whole industry. For this magnitude, which is of course given for a fixed interval $(0, T)$, we may as well introduce the following notation

$$R = \int_0^T q\cdot x\, dt = \sum_{i=l}^{n} \mu_i\cdot V_i \tag{37}$$

Eliminating $a_i/\mu_i$ from (35)-(36) and using the notation introduced in (37) we obtain:

$$v_i = V_i \cdot \frac{q \cdot x}{R} \qquad i = 1 , \ldots , n \tag{38}$$

Next, substitution into (32) yields:

$$\frac{1}{x} = V_1^{a_1} \cdot \ldots \cdot V_n^{a_n} \cdot \frac{q \cdot x}{R} \tag{39}$$

Taking the definite integral of $1/x$ according to (39) we obtain

$$\int_0^T \frac{1}{x} dt = V_1^{a_1} \cdot \ldots \cdot V_n^{a_n} \tag{40}$$

because, according to (37), the definite integral of $(q \cdot x)/R$ equals unity.

In order to compute the definite integral of (40) we may change integration variable. For this procedure we first substitute the expression for $q$ from (31) into (39) and obtain

$$x^2 \cdot e^{-x} = K \cdot (1 + t) \tag{41}$$

where $K$ equals $R/(10 \cdot V_1^{a_1} \ldots V_n^{a_n})$ , which is a constant for a given integration interval $(0 , T)$ . Differentiating (41) we obtain

$$(2 - x) \cdot x \cdot e^{-x} \, dx = K \, dt \tag{42}$$

If we *define* $x_1$ as the value of $x$ with $t = 0$ and $x_2$ as the value of $x$ with $t = T$ , we have according to (41):

$$x_1^2 \cdot e^{-x_1} = K \tag{43}$$

and

$$x_2^2 \cdot e^{-x_2} = K \cdot (1 + T) \tag{44}$$

From (42) we see that $x$ must be an increasing function of $t$ when $x$ is positive but less than two. Now, it was stated in the introduction that this condition is fulfilled when marginal costs have begun to increase beyond the $MC$-minimum; and this must be the relevant part of the $MC$-curve when second order conditions for profit maximum are fulfilled. With a given $K$ , each value of $t$ would give two solutions for the passus coefficient according to equation (41), but one of them would correspond to the pessimal situation instead of the optimal one. Thus, as we are only concerned with the rising branches of marginal cost curves, the passus coefficient $x$ decreases with increasing $t$ . Accordingly, $x_1$ is the smallest value of $x$ and $x_2$ is the largest one.

In order to obtain the definite integral of (40) we may exchange the integration variable $t$ against the variable $x$, and the interval $(0, T)$ against $(x_1, x_2)$. From (42) we get

$$\frac{1}{x} dt = \frac{1}{K} \cdot (2 - x) \cdot e^{-x} dx \tag{45}$$

which yields

$$\int_0^T \frac{1}{x} dt = \frac{1}{K} \cdot \int_{x_1}^{x_2} (2 - x) \cdot e^{-x} dx \tag{46}$$

Now, the indefinite integral of $(2 - x) \cdot e^{-x}$ is $-(1 - x) \cdot e^{-x}$. Using this and substituting from equations (43)-(44) we get

$$\int_0^T \frac{1}{x} dt = \frac{(1 - x_1)}{x_1^2} - (1 + T) \cdot \frac{(1 - x_2)}{x_2^2} \tag{47}$$

Thus, equations (40) and (47) together yield

$$\frac{(1 - x_1)}{x_1^2} - (1 + T) \cdot \frac{(1 - x_2)}{x_2^2} = V_1^{a_1} \cdot \ldots \cdot V_n^{a_n} \tag{48}$$

Likewise, equations (43)-(44) together yield

$$x_1^2 \cdot e^{-x_1} - \frac{1}{(1 + T)} \cdot x_2^2 \cdot e^{-x_2} = 0 \tag{49}$$

We see that equations (48) and (49) give a solution $(x_1, x_2)$ as soon as values of $T$ and $V_1, \ldots, V_n$ are assumed; i.e. as soon as we fix the interval of active firms and the vector of aggregate inputs to be distributed the integration borders for integration in the variable $x$ will be obtained. These integration borders denote — in this special case — the passus coefficients of the most efficient and the least efficient firms respectively.

Now, the integration borders $x_1$ and $x_2$ provide everything we need in order to compute aggregate output. According to (2) and (31) it is true that

$$Q = 10 \cdot \int_0^T \frac{e^{-x}}{(1 + t)} dt \tag{50}$$

Here too we must change integration variable. From equations (41) and (42) we obtain:

$$\frac{e^{-x}}{(1 + t)} dt = \frac{(2 - x)}{x} \cdot e^{-x} dx \tag{51}$$

Thus:

$$Q = 10 \cdot \int_{x_1}^{x_2} \left( \frac{2}{x} \cdot e^{-x} - e^{-x} \right) dx \qquad (52)$$

Now, there is no simple integral to the expression $(2/x) \cdot e^{-x}$. However, if $e^{-x}$ is expanded, each term in the expansion may be integrated separately. Accordingly, we have

$$Q = 20 \cdot \left( ln\, x_2 - ln\, x_1 + \sum_{s=1}^{\infty} \frac{(-x_2)^s}{s \cdot s\,!} - \sum_{s=1}^{\infty} \frac{(-x_1)^s}{s \cdot s\,!} \right) + \\ + 10 \cdot (e^{-x_2} - e^{-x_1}) \qquad (53)$$

For computational purposes it is perfectly sufficient to take for example five terms in the interminable series. In order to obtain the aggregate output $Q$ from a sequence of aggregate inputs $V_1, \ldots, V_n$ the procedure to be followed is: i) assuming a value of $T$ compute $x_1$ and $x_2$ from equations (48)-(49), then ii) insert these values into (53) obtaining the desired accuracy by taking the desiered number of terms in the sums. The case considered is simple, as the only characteristic of the vector of aggregate inputs which is relevant is the expression $V_1^{a_1} \ldots V_n^{a_n}$. In the diagram we may therefore plot $Q$ as a function of this Cobb-Douglas expression. In the diagram two different values of $T$ have been assumed, yielding two different curves.

The diagram also contains a curve which is an envelope to the two curves discussed above. This curve is obtained by putting $x_2 = 1$, i.e. by putting the passus coefficient of the marginal firm equal to unity. Then equation (48) is transformed into $(1 - x_1)/x_1^2 = V_1^{a_1} \cdot \ldots \cdot V_n^{a_n}$. Thus, $x_1$ is determined once a vector of aggregate inputs is fixed. Equation (49), which is transformed to $x_1^2 \cdot e^{-x_1} = 1/(e \cdot (1 + T))$, next assigns a value for $T$ to every $x_1$, i.e. to every vector of aggregate inputs. This means that the interval of active firms is changed every time the vector of aggregate inputs is changed, according to the rule that the interval be augmented or diminished in such a way that the passus coefficient of the marginal firm $x_2$ always equals unity. This adjustment via entry and exit of firms obviously reassures that aggregate output is maximized, as the curve obtained for the case of free entry and free exit is an envelope to the curves for fixed intervals of active firms. We might also derive the expressions for $dQ/dT$ and $d^2Q/dT^2$, but the procedure is complicated. However, in carrying out the procedure we would see that the first order derivative is zero only when $x_2 = 1$, and that the second order derivative is negative for $x_2 = 1$. This would only give a mathematical proof of what we can see from the diagram.

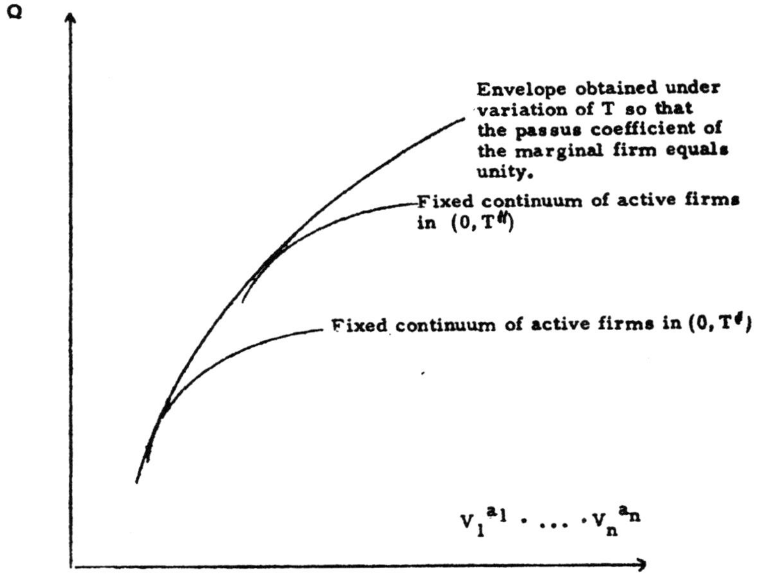
Q
Envelope obtained under variation of T so that the passus coefficient of the marginal firm equals unity.
Fixed continuum of active firms in (0, T##)
Fixed continuum of active firms in (0, T#)
V1a1 · ... · Vnan

Figure 1.

JOURNAL OF ENVIRONMENTAL ECONOMICS AND MANAGEMENT 4, 185–199 (1977)

# On the Profitability of Exhausting Natural Resources

TÖNU PUU

*Department of Economics, Umeå University, S-901 87, Umeå, Sweden*

Received November 10, 1975

Two models are treated. One deals with a mineral deposit, the other with a biological substance. It is assumed that in the deposit there exist all grades of ore, and that the biological substance grows as long as a positive quantity is left. The course of investment and production decisions is derived when capital is expressly built up for the purpose of exploitation of the specific resource. Within the simple linear control problem it is concluded that exhaustion is never profitable. The steady state in the biological case is discussed and compared to maximum sustainable yield.

This paper deals with the question of whether it is profitable from the narrowly selfish point of view of an individual profit-maximizing firm to exhaust a natural resource completely. Two cases will be treated, first the case of a mineral deposit of given size, and then the case of a growing biological substance (like fish).

The conclusions are fairly optimistic. It is demonstrated that *under the assumptions of the model* it never pays to exhaust a resource completely. The assumptions are that any mineral deposit contains ore of every grade, and that a biological substance continues to grow as long as a positive quantity of it is left. I am well aware of the fact that several important minerals occur in concentrated high-grade deposits only, and hence fail to satisfy the so called A/G rule used by geologists, as well as of the fact that a certain minimum population of a species might be necessary for its survival. Nevertheless, I think it is worth the effort to analyze the cases where increasing costs of working low-grade ores or harvesting dispersed specimens of fish always puts an end to exploitation before the resource is exhausted—unless, of course, product price rises beyond any limit.

Not even the point made for the limited field of application is, however, new. For the case of fishery it was made by Colin Clark, and the case of mining could seem quite obvious. What distinguishes this paper from previous discussions is that the production decision is treated together with the decision to build up a capacity for working the resource, the capital being completely tied to the activity for which it was created and being useless for other purposes. The non-exhaustion conclusion remains in spite of this and in spite of an assumption that capacity once bult up never wears out completely but decays like a radioactive substance as long as it is used.





ISSN 0095-0696

## A. THE EXPLOITATION OF A MINERAL DEPOSIT

*The Dynamic System*

Assume that a mining enterprise has at its disposal an ore deposit, such that the positive, continuous function

$$f(h)$$

defined on the interval (0, 1) gives the frequency of ore containing the grade $h$. This means that there is some ore of every grade from pure metal to completely worthless material. The A/G rule, meaning that the quantity of ore increases geometrically as the grade decreases arithmetically, would correspond to the special case of an exponential form of the function postulated. This rule is frequently used by geologists (see [5, 9]).

Next, the function

$$X(H) = \int_0^H h \cdot f(h) dh$$

gives the quantity of pure metal remaining in the deposit and obtainable from grades less than the marginal one, denoted $H$. It is implicitly supposed that the firm first works better grades before turning to worse ones. For notational convenience we let the quantity of raw material contained in the whole deposit be one unit. (Otherwise $X$ would not be a quantity but a proportion.)

The inverse of the last function

$$H(X) \tag{1}$$

then gives the marginal grade when the quantity of pure metal remaining in the deposit is given. Its derivative $H'(X) = 1/[H \cdot f(H)]$, which is positive, tells to what extent the marginal grade decreases as more of the deposit is extracted.

Now, denote the maximum amount of ore which can be mined at any instant by $Y$ and the fraction of $Y$ actually mined by $U$. Accordingly, the quantity of ore worked at time $t$ is $U \cdot Y$, and the quantity of pure metal produced is $H(X) \cdot U \cdot Y$. But this is also the rate at which the quantity of pure metal remaining in the deposit is reduced. We hence get the differential equation

$$\dot{X} = -H(X) \cdot U \cdot Y. \tag{2}$$

$U$ being a fraction of capacity used, its value must be in the closed real interval (0, 1).

The capacity $Y$ depends on the previous investments and on depreciation. Investments are denoted by $V$, and give the gross increase of capacity at $t$. Capital, i.e., capacity, is depreciating (in the sense of physical wear) at a constant exponential rate $s$—much like the decay of a radioactive substance. Moreover, it is assumed that capital wears out only when it is used in production. Hence, the depreciation of capital to be deducted from gross investments is $s \cdot U \cdot Y$, and the net change in the stock of capital (or capacity) is $V - s \cdot U \cdot Y$. This yields another differential equation

$$\dot{Y} = V - s \cdot U \cdot Y. \tag{3}$$

The gross investments can, of course, not be negative. In addition, there must be an upper limit to the capacity increase that may be carried out at each point of time. This is due to delivery and installation capacity constraints. For simplicity I assume this upper bound to be constant over time. In addition one unit of capacity is defined to equal this maximum possible increase of it at an instant of time. The only consequence of this assumption is to fix the units in which both $X$ and $Y$ are measured. The benefit is that the value of $V$ too is constrained to the closed interval (0, 1).

Assume now that at time $t = 0$, the deposit contains a given amount of metal, denoted $\bar{X}$ and that there is no initial capacity so that $Y$ is zero when exploitation starts.

What has been formulated is a complete dynamic system for the development of the state variables $X$ and $Y$. The trajectories are determined by the differential equations (2) and (3) and the initial conditions just specified. The trajectories may be influenced by the entrepreneur by the choice of the control variables $U$ and $V$ subject to the constraint that $U$ and $V$ lie within the unit interval.

In order to determine what values of the control variables the entrepreneur should choose at each point of time, we now have to formulate a target function.

*The Target Function*

The quite natural assumption to make is that the entrepreneur maximizes the present value of all his profits over the period of existence of the firm as an active unit.

According to assumptions $U \cdot Y$ is the quantity of ore processed. Multiplication by $H(X)$ yields the quantity of metal produced, and multiplication by the current price of the product, denoted $P$, yields the revenue, which hence is $P \cdot H(X) \cdot U \cdot Y$.

For simplicity it is assumed that the cost of converting one unit of ore into whatever quantity of pure metal it contains is constant. This constant cost is denoted $c$. Observe that this does not mean that the cost of producing one unit of pure metal is constant. The latter, which equals $c/H(X)$, increases as the marginal grade decreases with continuing exploitation. What has been said is that the processing cost is $c \cdot U \cdot Y$.

In addition there is the cost for investments in capacity. Denoting the current price of equipment by $R$, we can write investment cost as $R \cdot V$.

Profits at a point of time may now be calculated as

$$P \cdot H(X) \cdot U \cdot Y - c \cdot U \cdot Y - R \cdot V.$$

A typical development of this expression over time would be that revenue above working cost first increases as capacity is built up and production is increased until the decreasing grade (and the consequently decreasing revenue above working cost *per unit*) reverses the process. The whole expression would probably be negative in the beginning as capacity is built up and become positive first when the revenue over working cost has become large enough to offset investment cost. When investments are no longer considered profitable the last term disappears and production goes on until working costs are no longer covered.

To get the target function we only have to discount current profits at a rate of interest $r$ and integrate with respect to time over the period of activity. This yields

$$\int_0^T [P \cdot H(X) \cdot U \cdot Y - c \cdot U \cdot Y - R \cdot V] \cdot e^{-rt} dt. \tag{4}$$

I propose that the entrepreneur would steer the dynamic system, described by (2) and (3) so that (4) is maximized. Doing this the entrepreneur has to choose values of $U$ and $V$ in the unit interval permitted, and has to take in account the initial conditions specificed above, i.e., that at $t = 0$ the equations $X = \bar{X}$ and $Y = 0$ hold. In addition, there is a terminal inequality constraint, namely, that at $t = T$ the relation $X \geq 0$ holds. No constraint is placed on the terminal value of $Y$, and the choice of the time for closing down, $T$, is free.

For the sake of simplicity I suppose that the prices, $P$ and $R$, as well as the rate of interest, $r$, stay constant over time. It is not difficult to change the assumptions in this respect, but the results are much more ambiguous and not very interesting in view of the main theme of this paper. That a resource might be exhausted if product price goes to infinity is not an interesting conclusion, and the complex changes over time of entrepreneurial behavior when prices change cyclically is not very illuminating for the question of resource exhaustion.

*On Optimum*

We now have a simple and well-defined problem of optimal control that may be treated by Pontryagin's "Maximum Principle." To state the optimality conditions we have to define the Hamiltonian for the problem by taking the momentary increment to the integral target function and adding the right hand members of the differential equations (2) and (3), each multiplied by an undetermined multiplier. This yields

$$L = [P \cdot H(X) \cdot U \cdot Y - c \cdot U \cdot Y - R \cdot V] \cdot e^{-rt} - \lambda \cdot H(X) \cdot U \cdot Y + \mu \cdot (V - s \cdot U \cdot Y). \quad (5)$$

In order that (4) be maximized Pontryagin's principle requires that: (1) The Hamiltonian (5) be maximal with respect to the control variables $U$ and $V$ at each point of time. (Of course their values must be chosen according to the constraints.) (2) The "costate variables" $\lambda$ and $\mu$ satisfy the differential equations $\dot{\lambda} = -\partial L/\partial X$ and $\dot{\mu} = -\partial L/\partial Y$. Pontryagin's theorem ensures the existence of differentiable $\lambda$ and $\mu$ functions of time that satisfy these equations. (3) At the terminal point of time $T$ it holds that $\lambda \geq 0$, with $\lambda = 0$ if the resource $X$ left unexploited is still positive. Likewise, it is required that at $T$ we have $\mu = 0$.

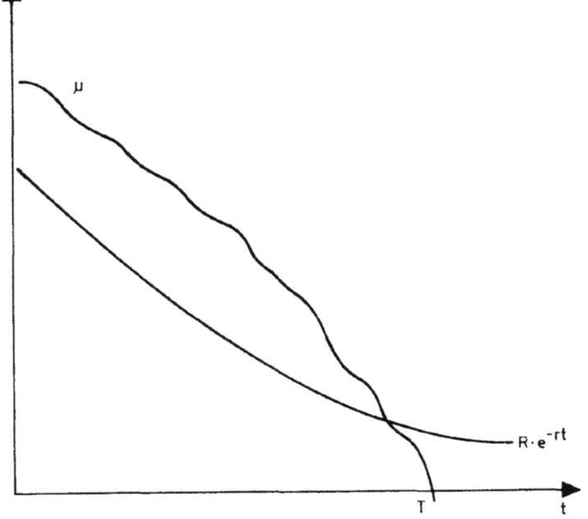


FIGURE 1

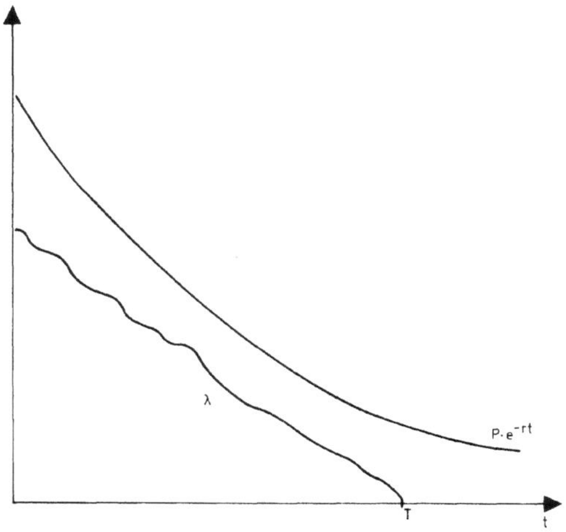


FIGURE 2

These are the so-called transversality conditions connected with the terminal conditions (or rather lack of terminal conditions) for the state variables. (4) When the choice of the terminal point $T$ is free the value of the Hamiltonian $L$ must be zero at that point of time.

The further discussion would benefit from introducing some abbreviating symbols. Define

$$A = [P \cdot H(X) - c] \cdot e^{-rt} - \lambda \cdot H(X) - \mu \cdot s, \tag{6}$$

$$B = \mu - R \cdot e^{-rt}. \tag{7}$$

Using these symbols we may write

$$L = A \cdot U \cdot Y + B \cdot V. \tag{8}$$

Obviously, the Hamiltonian is maximal with respect to $U$ and $V$ if $U$ is put equal to zero or unity depending on whether $A$ is negative or positive, and $V$ is put equal to zero or unity depending on whether $B$ is negative or positive.

Hence, there are in all only four policies to consider, namely: doing nothing, building up a plant without producing for the moment, producing without making anything to increase or replace worn equipment, and finally, using maximum capacity for both plant construction and production. In the sequel we are going to see that one of the possibilities may be ruled out as suboptimal in all situations, namely, construction without simultaneous production. We will also see that the other policies follow in a certain sequence. First the plant is constructed at maximum speed with production going on with full capacity all the time. Then all investment ceases and capital is permitted to decay, whereas production is still going on for some time. Finally production is finished once and for all (provided that product price does not rise).

In the derivation of these conclusions we will see how the costate variables $\lambda$ and $\mu$, which not unexpectedly turn out to be shadow prices for metal contained in the deposit and for production equipment, respectively, develop over time. We will also find out that it will never be profitable to let production go on until the whole deposit is exhausted in finite time.

*Development of the Shadow Prices*

Consider the differential equation $\dot{\mu} = -\partial L/\partial Y$. As $A$ according to (6) is independent of $Y$, we easily obtain $\partial L/\partial Y = A \cdot U$ from (8). Hence

$$\dot{\mu} = -A \cdot U. \tag{9}$$

But, we have seen that the sign of $A$ determines the choice of $U$. If $A$ is negative $U$ is put equal to zero. This implies that (9) must be nonpositive, i.e., that $\mu$ is a nonincreasing function of time. The curve representing its development in Fig. 1 is always falling, unless it has horizontal segments at times when production is discontinued. (Later on we will find out that this latter possibility can never be optimal before production is definitely finished off. Hence we depict the curve as falling.)

As $\mu$ is a nonincreasing function of time ending up with zero value at $T$ it must be nonnegative on the time interval (0, $T$), i.e., the shadow price for productive capacity has to be nonnegative during the active period. Actually, we can show that it has to be positive.

This can be seen in Fig. 1 where the $\mu$ curve is depicted together with the curve for $R \cdot e^{-rt}$. According to (7) the criterion for deciding whether capacity will be increased (or maintained) or not depends on the sign of $B = \mu - R \cdot e^{-rt}$. If production will at all be started, $B$ must initially be positive. This is so because there is no initial capacity at all, so that it must be built up by investments from the very beginning. But $R \cdot e^{-rt} = R$ at $t = 0$. It is hence positive and $\mu$ must then be even greater if $B$ be positive. As $\mu$ starts at a positive value, is continuously falling over time and ends up at zero only at closing time, we can conclude that it is positive as claimed.

From the diagram we also see another thing. As the exponential curve starts below the curve for the shadow price, and always remains positive in finite time, whereas the curve for the shadow price comes down to the axis at $T$, the curves must intersect some time before $T$. Hence, investments cease—at the intersection where the criterion $B$ reverses sign—some time before production is finished.

We next consider the differential equation for $\lambda$. It reads $\dot{\lambda} = -\partial L/\partial X$. The partial derivative is easily obtained from (5) so that

$$\dot{\lambda} = -(P \cdot e^{-rt} - \lambda) \cdot H'(X) \cdot U \cdot Y. \tag{10}$$

In this expression $Y$ is positive because there always remains some capacity if any has ever been installed. The derivative $H'(X)$ is positive as the marginal grade is higher the greater the ore remaining in the deposit. $U$ is either zero or unity, depending on the sign of $A$. Inspection of the expression (6) shows that, due to the positivity of $c$, $s$, and $\mu$, $A$ must be negative whenever $(P \cdot e^{-rt} - \lambda)$ is negative. Hence, in (10) $U$ would be zero whenever the expression in parentheses was negative. This implies that $\lambda$ as well as $\mu$ is a nonincreasing function of time. As it ends up with zero value at $T$, we can also conclude that it is nonnegative on the interval (0, $T$), as is $\mu$.

Figure 2 is a diagram analogous to the preceding one, where the path of $\lambda$ is plotted along with the path of $P \cdot e^{-rt}$. In this case there is no intersection. The $\lambda$ curve always has to be below the exponential. The reason has already been stated. If the shadow price of the resource exceeds the discounted market price for metal, $U$ is put equal to zero. But then, due to (10), $\lambda$ would remain constant, lying above the falling exponential function for ever. Hence, $\lambda$ could never attain the zero value at $T$ prescribed by the optimality conditions. (This holds for the case where the deposit is not exhausted, which will be seen to be the relevant case.)

### *The Unprofitability of Exhausting the Resource*

We can now see why it is unprofitable to exhaust the whole deposit in finite time. According to the optimality conditions, the value of the Hamiltonian (5) must be zero when the choice of the terminal moment $T$ is free. We have also seen that $\mu$ must be zero at the same moment. Moreover, it was demonstrated above that a period with $V$ zero would precede the closing down of all activity. Hence, $V$ as well as $\mu$ and $L$ are zero at $T$.

On the other hand $U$ must equal unity, because if it were zero every activity would have been closed down and $T$ already passed. Finally, $Y$ is, as always, positive.

Putting all these values into (5) we obtain the equation

$$[P \cdot H(X) - c] \cdot e^{-rT} - \lambda \cdot H(X) = 0. \tag{11}$$

This can never be fulfilled with $H(X) = 0$. But, due to assumptions, the marginal grade $H$ can only be positive if the quantity $X$ of ore left is positive as well.

At $T < \infty$ it thus holds that $X$ is still positive. This, in turn, implies (due to the Pontryagin conditions) that $\lambda$ has to be zero at $T$. This result was employed in the discussion of the preceding paragraph. (Of course, it was not used in a way to make the reasoning circular.) We can also use the result in (11) to see that at $T$

$$P \cdot H(X) = c \tag{12}$$

must hold. This means that production is finished when the marginal grade equals the ratio of processing cost to product price.

### *Output Policy*

We are now going to see how output policy, i.e., the choice of value for $U$, varies in time. In order to find this out we have to see how its choice criterion $A$ changes during the period of activity.

Differentiating (6) with respect to time and substituting from (9) and (10) we get

$$\dot{A} = -r \cdot [P \cdot H(X) - c] \cdot e^{-rt} + s \cdot A \cdot U. \tag{13}$$

Now, suppose $A$ is negative. As we have seen, $U$ is then put equal to zero, and only the first term of (13) remains. It must be negative as $H(X)$ comes down to the ratio $c/P$ only at $T$. Hence, if $A$ is negative, $\dot{A}$ is negative as well. If the criterion makes it unprofitable to keep production going at any time before $T$, the situation remains unchanged, the reasons for putting $U$ equal to zero being strengthened.

Thus, production will be cut off definitely at one moment, and will not be resumed unless prices change.

### *Investment Policy*

It is a bit harder to find out the optimal investment policy, i.e., the develop-

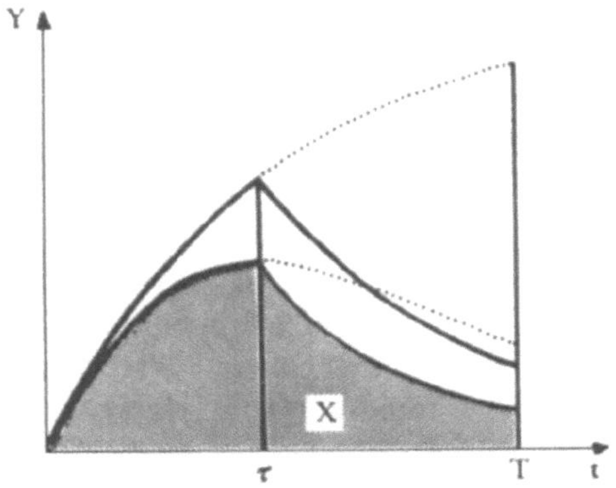


FIGURE 3

ment of $V$ over time. As in the preceding case we can differentiate its criterion function (7) with respect to time getting

$$\dot{B} = \dot{\mu} + r \cdot R \cdot e^{-rt}.$$

But we do not get much out of this expression.

I have constructed a formal proof that investment, like production, is finished at one point of time, never being resumed again. As, however, the proof is very long, I shall only outline it here, leaving the proof for the Appendix. The reasoning is as follows.

First, I make sure that the $B$ function possesses derivatives up to the third order at least. Next, knowing that $B$ is positive when production starts and negative when it finishes, it is seen that $B$ must have an odd number of zeros. Due to the existence of derivatives the $B$ curve must then have a point of inflection while it is rising, followed by a maximum when it is positive—no matter whether the number of zeros is three, five, seven, or any greater odd integer. This is shown to be possible only if the marginal grade of the ore is greater at the maximum than at the point of inflection. This, however, contradicts that the marginal grade decreases over time as more of the resource is used up. Hence, only one zero for the criterion function $B$ is possible, and this means that investments are terminated at one single point of time. This time, denoted $\tau$, was seen to occur before $T$.

*Change of Capacity and Production over Time*

We are now able to solve the differential equation (3). $U$ is always unity from time 0 to time $T$, whereas $V$ is unity from time 0 to time $\tau$ and zero from then on until $T$. Using this information and the initial condition that there is no capacity at time 0, we get

$$Y = (1 - e^{-st})/s$$

for $t$ in the interval $(0, \tau)$ and

$$Y = e^{-st}(e^{s\tau} - 1)/s$$

for $t$ in the interval $(\tau, T)$.

$U$ being unity, production equals $Y$ in terms of the quantity of ore processed.

The quantity of pure metal produced is obtained after multiplication with the marginal grade.

In Fig. 3 it is shown how capacity (and production) change over time. The shaded area equals the quantity of metal extracted. Observe that this quantity is completely determined by the ratio $c/P$. Hence, with given processing cost and product price a certain quantity of metal is always extracted independently of investment policy. This means that if the period of construction is prolonged due to lower investment costs, so that a greater maximum capacity is attained, the quantity to be worked will be extracted earlier.

The dashed curves depict the development if plant construction is not finished during the period illustrated. As is seen, capacity approaches a certain level asymptotically. This is a joint effect of depreciation and of the limited maximum speed of plant construction. One could ask if the nonexhaustion result does not depend on this capacity limit. The answer is already given: The quantity of metal extracted is fixed, independently of this. Hence, investments and production would only be finished earlier if the constraint was relaxed.

*Interpretation of the Shadow Prices*

Until now we have simply identified the costate variables $\lambda$ and $\mu$ as shadow prices for metal in the deposit and for productive capacity. It may be seen that this is reasonable by formal analysis.

Putting $U = 1$, as we are justified to do now, we get from (10)

$$\dot{\lambda} - H'(X)\cdot Y\cdot\lambda = -P\cdot Y\cdot H'(X)\cdot e^{-rt}, \tag{14}$$

which is a linear, first-order differential equation in $\lambda$. Its solution is readily obtained as

$$\lambda\cdot H(X) = -P\cdot\int H'(X)\cdot H(X)\cdot Y\cdot e^{-rt}dt + \text{constant}.$$

We see that $\dot{H} = H'(X)\cdot\dot{X} = -H'(X)\cdot H(X)\cdot Y$. Using this abbreviation, and taking the difference of the equations above for time points $t'$ and $T$, so that the arbitrary constant is removed, we get (remembering that at $T$, $\lambda = 0$)

$$\lambda\cdot H(X) = -P\cdot\int_{t'}^{T}\dot{H}\cdot e^{-rt}dt, \tag{15}$$

the values of $\lambda$ and $H(X)$ being those at $t'$ in the left-hand member. In the right-hand member the time derivative $\dot{H}$ is, of course, a function of the integration variable.

$P\cdot e^{-rt}$ in the right-hand member is the discounted value of one additional unit of metal available at $t$. Having an extra unit of ore of the marginal grade added to the deposit of given composition actually pushes the whole curve showing the marginal grade as a decreasing function of time to the right as exploitation of the remaining grades will be postponed when working capacity is limited. This explains the appearance of $\dot{H}$. Integration gives the present value of all increased revenues in the future.

The appearance of $H(X)$ in the left-hand member might seem hard to explain if $\lambda$ were the shadow price of unworked *metal* and not ore. But, as capacity is related to working of ore, the time for which exploitation of poorer grades will be postponed due to an additional unit of metal of the marginal grade is inversely related to this marginal grade—the poorer it is, the longer will it take to extract it.

We now turn to the interpretation of $\mu$. Due to (6) and (9) we have

$$\dot{\mu} - s\cdot\mu = -[P\cdot H(X) - c]\cdot e^{-rt} + \lambda\cdot H(X) \tag{16}$$

which too is a first-order linear equation. Its solution is

$$\mu\cdot e^{-st} = -\int [P\cdot H(X) - c]\cdot e^{-(r+s)t}dt + \int \lambda\cdot H(X)\cdot e^{-st}dt + \text{constant.}$$

By exactly the same procedure as with $\lambda$ we obtain for some point of time $t'$

$$\mu = \int_{t'}^{T} [P\cdot H(X) - c]\cdot e^{-s(t-t')}\cdot e^{-rt}dt - \int_{t'}^{T} \lambda\cdot H(X)\cdot e^{-s(t-t')}dt. \tag{17}$$

Hence, $\mu$ is the difference of two positive terms, of which the first must predominate, as we have seen. Assume that at $t'$ an additional unit of capacity is added. At any later point of time $t$ the piece of capacity has worn down to $e^{-s(t-t')}$. As capacity is always fully utilized we obtain the proceeds from the piece of capital by multiplying what remains of it by the excess of revenues over costs $[P\cdot H(X) - c]$. Multiplication by the discount factor $e^{-rt}$ and integration gives all benefits from the additional capacity. This explains the first term of (17).

But, the increase of capital also means that the deposit is exploited at a faster rate. The additional capacity remaining at $t$, i.e., $e^{-s(t-t')}$, multiplied by the grade that then is marginal $H(X)$, gives the decrease of the resource at that moment due to the additional capacity. We already have identified $\lambda$ as the value of the resource. Hence, multiplication by $\lambda$ and integration gives what is a cost of extra capacity. This explains the second term, and makes it possible to formally identify $\mu$ as the imputed value of capacity.

## B. THE EXPLOITATION OF A BIOLOGICAL SUBSTANCE

The model discussed can with a very small alteration be adjusted to the case of the exploitation of a biological (i.e., growing) substance, as in hunting and fishing.

The simple change is that the quantity of resource is no longer constant, but grows according to some rule, as

$$\dot{X} = G(X). \tag{18}$$

The function might be zero if the argument were zero, then increase with the argument to reach a maximum and then decrease toward zero. The reason for this would be that more fish produce more fish until the ecological limits are reached and lack of food or natural enemies put an end to the growth. In the absence of economic exploitation the population would settle down at the maximum quantity it can attain, i.e., where $G(X)$ is zero. About such growth functions see [2, 3, 6].

At economic exploitation the population would be reduced below this maximum permitted by the natural conditions. If all economic factors (cost of harvesting and capital equipment) are disregarded it would seem optimal to keep the population constantly at a size where $G'(X)$ is zero, by harvesting the "interest" without touching the "capital." This harvest is usually called the maximum sustainable yield, and scientists used to think it self-evident that this is the best situation obtainable.

*The Formal System*

Of course the different symbols and relations have to be reinterpreted. So $X$ will be the weight of the biomass of fish and $Y$ will be the capacity of harvesting in terms of the maximum acreage that can be "beaten" at a moment of time. The function $H(X)$ indicates the average tonnage of fish caught per acre beaten. The positivity of its derivative indicates that the greater the population of fish is, the greater is the yield from a certain fishing activity. After normalization of the units of measurement as in the preceding case we can again constrain $U$ and $V$ to the closed interval (0, 1).

The differential equation (2) will be changed to

$$\dot{X} = G(X) - H(X)\cdot U\cdot Y, \tag{19}$$

whereas the equation (3) is still valid.

The target function (4) is also valid and so are the initial and terminal conditions.

So, we have a new optimal control problem. If we still use the abbreviating symbols (6) and (7) we may write down the Hamiltonian as

$$L = A\cdot U\cdot Y + B\cdot V + \lambda\cdot G(X). \tag{20}$$

All the optimality conditions according to Pontryagin's theorem still apply. We conclude that this implies that $U$, $V$ are zero or unity depending on whether $A$, $B$ are negative or positive, but do not repeat the other conclusions.

*Unprofitability of Extinction*

We will now see whether it may be profitable to extinguish a whole population.

As the terminal value of $Y$ is free, $\mu$ must still be zero at the point of finishing the activity. With finite $T$ this according to (7) implies that $B$ is then negative, and hence $V$ must be zero.

Substituting these zeros and putting $U$ equal to unity (as otherwise the activity would already be finished) in the Hamiltonian (20), and using the knowledge that we must have $L$ equal to zero as the entrepreneur himself chooses the terminal time, we get

$$[P\cdot H(X) - c]\cdot Y\cdot e^{-rT} + \lambda\cdot[G(X) - H(X)\cdot Y] = 0. \tag{21}$$

Now, if the species is exterminated at $T$, we have $X = 0$ and, according to assumptions, $H(X) = G(X) = 0$. But because $Y$ is positive this is impossible with finite $T$. It will thus not be profitable to exhaust the resource in finite time.

We can even strengthen the conclusion and see that it cannot be profitable to terminate the activity at any finite point of time, leaving a positive amount of the resource for the future. If $X$ is positive at $T$, then we have seen that $\lambda$ must be zero. Hence from (21) $H(X) = c/P$ must hold at $T$. But, this situation cannot last, because with a positive $X$ the population continues to grow and $H(X)$ will increase immediately after $T$, so that it exceeds the ratio $c/P$. This, however, means that production again becomes profitable. Hence, the activity will continue forever.

The fact that production again becomes profitable immediately after a moment when it might be cut off indicates that a policy which runs the population down to a very small size and then resumes fishing after a break is an unlikely solution. The most probable hypothesis is that some steady state is approached.

*An Optimal Steady State*

Let us see which characteristics a steady state would have, and whether the optimality conditions would be fulfilled when it is attained.

First, the population of fish and the capital equipment should be constant, i.e., $\dot{X} = \dot{Y} = 0$. Moreover, it is obvious that only capital equipment that is used at full capacity would be maintained. Hence, $U = 1$. These values inserted into (3) and (19) yield

$$Y = G(X)/H(X) \tag{22}$$

and

$$V = s \cdot Y. \tag{23}$$

Now, this may seem odd as $V$ was assumed to take on only zero and unitary values in optimum. If, however, the criterion $B$ is zero, any value of $V$ may be chosen. And this is exactly what we will require. (The only trouble that may arise in this connection would be if (23) prescribed a value of $V$ that was greater than unity. But this may be identified as a complication arising when capital depreciates so fast that the optimal capacity needed cannot be built up in view of the constraints on capital delivery and installation.)

According to (7) $B$ is zero when

$$\mu = R \cdot e^{-rt}. \tag{24}$$

This must hold in the steady state. The differential equation for $\mu$ (16) still holds. Differentiating (24) we obtain $\dot{\mu} = -r \cdot R \cdot e^{-rt}$. If we substitute this into (16) we get a constraint on $\lambda$, that may be solved as

$$\lambda \cdot H(X) = [P \cdot H(X) - c - (r + s) \cdot R] \cdot e^{-rt}. \tag{25}$$

As everything in the right-hand member, except $t$, is constant we conclude that $\lambda$ like $\mu$ (as is seen from (24)) asymptotically approaches zero at the exponential rate $r$.

But, among the optimality conditions we have a differential equation for $\lambda$, and we must check that it does not contradict (25). Observe that the corresponding equation for $\mu$ has already been checked, as the expression (25) just expresses the constraint on $\lambda$ that makes the expression (16) true.

Unlike the case for $\mu$, where the differential equation (16) was still true, the equation (14) for $\lambda$ is slightly altered. This is due to the $G(X)$ function introduced in the fishery case. The differential equation that is relevant for the present case reads, $\dot{\lambda} + G'(X) \cdot \lambda - H'(X) \cdot Y \cdot \lambda = -P \cdot Y \cdot H'(X) \cdot e^{-rt}$. We immediately see that in the steady state everything, except, of course, $\dot{\lambda}$, $\lambda$, and $t$ is constant. Obviously, an exponential solution curve for $\lambda$ with the rate of decrease $r$ is a solution to the differential equation. And this demonstrates that the expression (25) satisfies the differential equation. The conclusion is that in the steady state described above the differential equations for the costate variables, required for optimality, are fulfilled.

If we now substitute from (24) and (25) into (6) we get

$$A = r \cdot R \cdot e^{-rt}. \tag{26}$$

This is positive in finite time and hence the choice of $U$ equal to unity is optimal.

We have thus shown the existence of a steady state where the controls are optimally chosen with respect to their criteria functions, where the optimal differential equations for the costate variables are fulfilled, and where the values of these latter variables asymptotically go to zero as time goes to infinity. This fulfils the transversality conditions in the asymptotic form at infinite time horizon when the values of the state variables are deliberately chosen to be positive. The conclusion is that the steady state is optimal, and that a path in time converging to it (due to a well-known theorem by Arrow) is optimal too.

*The Size of Population in the Steady State*

We are now going to discuss the quantity of $X$ in the steady state.

If we take $\lambda$ and its derivative according to (25) and substitute them into the optimal differential equation for $\lambda$ just discussed, we get after some simplifications

$$[r - G'(X)] \cdot [P \cdot H(X) - c - (r + s) \cdot R] = [c + (r + s) \cdot R] \cdot H'(X) \cdot Y. \tag{27}$$

We can conclude from this equation only that $G'(X)$ must be smaller than $r$. As $G(X)$ was supposed to have a maximum, we can imagine that its derivative is continuously decreasing with $X$. Hence, an upper bound on its derivative implies a lower bound on the steady state population $X$. But this lower bound on the population varies with the economic circumstances. The population may be smaller or greater than that corresponding to maximum sustainable yield. Only very specific constellations of prices, cost, and interest rate, together with the characters of the $H$ and $G$ functions, would solve the system of equations (22) and (27) for an $X$ at which $G'(X)$ happens to be zero.

But is this so odd? It is, of course, at first sight appealing to maintain a population that yields a maximum quantity of "interest" leaving the capital intact forever. But, the "maximum yield" does not automatically fall in the arms of the fishermen. It might be better to reduce the stock of fish below maximum yield, because, even though a smaller population is more difficult to harvest, the greater capital equipment used to keep the population down may nevertheless yield more fish *captured* than would be the case with a maximum yield population.

## APPENDIX: FORMAL PROOF THAT RESUMED INVESTMENT IS SUBOPTIMAL

Let us write down the first two derivatives of $B$ with respect to time. According to (7)

$$\dot{B} = \dot{\mu} + R \cdot e^{-rt} \cdot r$$

and

$$\ddot{B} = \ddot{\mu} - R \cdot e^{-rt} \cdot r^2,$$

where according to (6), (9), and (13)

$$\dot{\mu} = -[P \cdot H(X) - c] \cdot e^{-rt} + \lambda \cdot H(X) + \mu \cdot s,$$

$$\ddot{\mu} = [P \cdot H(X) - c] \cdot e^{-rt} + \dot{\mu} \cdot s.$$

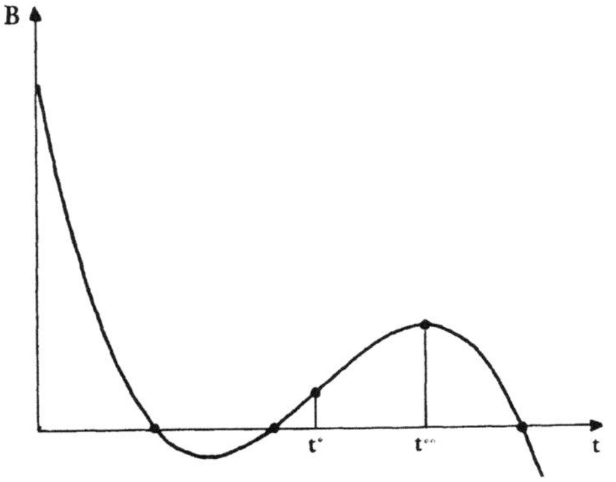


FIGURE 4

The last expression is obtained by putting $A \cdot U = \dot{\mu}$ in (13).

On inspection of these conditions, taking into consideration that $H'(X) = 1/H \cdot f(H)$ is a continuous function when $H \neq 0$, it is seen that $B$ has derivatives up to the third order.

It was seen above that $V$ is first unity and finally zero, i.e., its criterion $B$ is first positive at $t = 0$ and finally negative at $t = T$. In the passage from a positive to a negative value on the interval $(0, T)$, $B$ must pass zero an odd number of times. In order that this number be greater than one, it is necessary that $B$ decreases to zero, has a maximum at a positive $B$, decreases to zero again and finally stays negative up to $T$. In the passage from the minimum to the maximum there must be a point of inflection while the curve is rising (by virtue of the mean value theorem) as the derivatives of the two lowest orders are continuous. Moreover, the point of inflection must be followed by a positive maximum for $B$. The case is outlined in Fig. 4. This is the simplest way in which $B$ may be zero before $T$ more than once. The development of $B$ described yields three roots to the equation $B(t) = 0$, all less than $T$. The number of roots may, as said above, also be five or seven or nine, etc. But in all these more complicated cases it must still be true that $B$ has a point of inflection while rising, followed by a maximum at a positive value of $B$. Formally, there are $t^*$ and $t^{**}$ in the interval $(0, T)$, with $t^* < t^{**}$, such that $\ddot{B}(t^*) = 0$ together with $\dot{B}(t^*) > 0$, and $\dot{B}(t^{**}) = 0$ together with $B(t^{**}) > 0$ hold.

Using these conditions

$$[P \cdot H(X^*) - c] \cdot e^{-rt} \cdot r + \dot{\mu}(t^*) \cdot s = R \cdot e^{-rt^*} \cdot r^2$$

is obtained at the point of inflection. As $\dot{B}$ is then positive $\dot{\mu} > -R \cdot e^{-rt} \cdot r$ holds, i.e.,

$$-\dot{\mu}(t^*) \cdot s < R \cdot e^{-rt^*} \cdot r \cdot s.$$

Adding the left- and right-hand members of these expressions and multiplying by $e^{rt^*}/r$ yields

$$[P \cdot H(X^*) - c] < (r + s) \cdot R. \tag{i}$$

The interpretation of this condition is that at $t^*$ the marginal grade must have decreased so much that the current profit obtainable by an additional unit of capital is smaller than the yearly sum of interest and depreciation.

Let us next look at the conditions assumed to apply at $t^{**}$. At this time point $B$ has a maximum with a positive maximum value. Thus,

$$-[P \cdot H(X^{**}) - c] \cdot e^{-rt^{**}} + \lambda(t^{**}) \cdot H(X^{**}) + \mu(t^{**}) \cdot s = -R \cdot e^{-rt^{**}} \cdot r$$

must be fulfilled in order that $B$ be maximal.

This may be written

$$[P \cdot H(X^{**}) - c] \cdot e^{-rt^{**}} - \mu(t^{**})s > R \cdot e^{-rt^{**}} \cdot r$$

in view of the fact that $\lambda(t^{**}) \cdot H(X^{**}) > 0$. On the other hand, positivity of $B$ means that $\mu(t^{**}) > R \cdot e^{-rt^{**}}$ or

$$\mu(t^{**}) \cdot s > R \cdot e^{-rt^{**}} \cdot s$$

must be true. Adding left- and right-hand members of these two expressions and multiplying by $e^{rt^{**}}$ yields

$$[P \cdot H(X^{**}) - c] > (r + s) \cdot R, \tag{ii}$$

i.e., that the current profit at $t^{**}$ from an additional capital unit is greater than the sum of interest and depreciation. It is now obvious that (i) and (ii) may both hold, only provided that

$$H(X^{**}) > H(X^{*}). \tag{iii}$$

But with $U = 1$,

$$\begin{aligned} \dot{H} &= H'(X) \cdot \dot{X} \\ &= -H'(X) \cdot H(X) \cdot Y \end{aligned}$$

is always negative. As $t^{*} < t^{**}$, it must then be true that

$$H(X^{**}) < H(X^{*}), \tag{iv}$$

which contradicts (iii). Accordingly the case discussed is impossible, which means that $B(t) = 0$ has exactly one root in the interval $(0, T)$.

Hence $B$ decreases from a positive value to zero and becomes negative, and once it has become negative it stays negative. This means that investments are started at maximum rate ($V = 1$) at $t = 0$, and are switched off definitely at some moment after which only production is going on for some time until it is switched off too at $T$.

## REFERENCES


1. W. Beckerman, "Two Cheers for the Affluent Society," St. Martin, New York (1974).
2. R. J. H. Beverton and M. B. Schaefer, Fishery dynamics, *in* "The Sea," Vol. 2 (1962).
3. C. Clark, The economics of overexploitation, *Science* **181** (1973).
4. P. R. Ehrlich and A. H. Ehrlich, "Population, Resources, Environment," W. H. Freeman, San Francisco (1970).
5. J. Gilluly, A. C. Waters, and A. O. Woodford, "Principles of Geology," Chapt. 12, W. H. Freeman, San Francisco (1968).
6. R. Hannesson, "Economics of Fisheries" (1974).
7. O. C. Herfindahl and A. V. Kneese, "Economic Theory of Natural Resources" (1974).
8. H. Hotelling, The economics of exhaustible resources, *J. Political Econ.* **39** (1931).
9. S. G. Lasky, How tonnage and grade relations help predict ore reserves, *Eng. Min. J.* (1950).

# PART II

# Spatial Economics

Regional Science and Urban Economics 8 (1978) 225–248. © North-Holland

# TOWARDS A THEORY OF OPTIMAL ROADS*

Tönu PUU

*Umeå University, Umeå, Sweden*

Received June 1977

The purpose is to find an allocation of a given total amount of road capital in two-dimensional space such that total transportation costs for a region are minimized. A continuous model in analogy to hydrodynamics is used. Transports are supposed to be generated by the gravity hypothesis. It is discussed how transportation paths are optimally adjusted to a given distribution of road capital, and how road capital should be distributed at a given traffic distribution. It is also discussed how the latter problem should be solved when it is taken into account that the distribution of roads affects the choice of paths.

## 1. Introduction

The purpose of the present paper is to discuss how fixed transportation capital of a given total quantity (like roads of a given aggregate length) ought to be allocated in two-dimensional space in order that reasonable requirements for economic efficiency be met. With efficiency is meant that the yearly costs for fuel, wear of vehicles and travelling time for all transportation needed in a geographical region is minimized.

At the present level of abstraction travelling costs are taken as proportional to travel time. We even disregard congestion, so that travel cost and time are proportional to travel distance. This latter assumption seems hard to define in view of the host of literature in the 'New Urban Economics' expressly devoted to congestion. Congestion, however, is a highly *local* phenomenon. What I have in mind is a region like a whole country and not a small urban area. Deviations of e.g. optimal paths or routes to avoid congestion centers then count relatively little in relation to the whole extensions of most paths, and so congestion costs are limited enough in comparison to the total cost of transportation to make the last abstraction defendable. The decisive reason for this choice, however, is that otherwise certain variational problems become mathematically insoluble at the very outset.

*The project is financially supported by the Swedish Social Science Research Council. For comments on earlier versions of this work the author is indebted to Åke Andersson, Göteborg, Alan Ingham, Southampton, and Urs Schweizer, Bonn, as well as to members of the Economics Departments at the Universities of København, Münster and Oslo. A special thanks is due to the physicist Anders Bårány, Uppsala.

Optimality of a road capital distribution can only be given a complete treatment provided that another optimization problem is solved. Given a distribution of road capital, i.e. a network of roads, the individual transporters have to find the path for each single transport that makes its cost as small as possible. The solutions for the individual cases are independent if there are no externalities, i.e. congestion costs. Otherwise, they are parts of a simultaneous equilibrium solution. Such equilibria for some special cases have been discussed by Lam and Newell and by Williams and Ortuzar Salas.

In the absence of externalities the independent actions of the individual transporters automatically lead to minimization of total transportation costs, whereas otherwise the fact that congestion forces some traffic out from the congested area may not be sufficient for a minimum to be attained. In addition specific tolls might be required to force the transporters to choose paths, even more deflected from congestion centers, that are individually suboptimal but socially optimal. As was already said, this complication forces me to abstract from congestion.

Up to now the discussion has concerned the partial minimization of transportation costs by adjusting the paths at a given spatial allocation of roads. Associated with the solution to this problem is a distribution of traffic on the region.

There is also another partial minimization that is the concern of the authorities responsible for the construction of roads which is the converse of the preceding one. If, instead, the distribution of traffic is a given datum, a spatial allocation of roads of given aggregate length, minimizing total transportation costs, might be sought.

When both partial optimizations are simultaneously solved a kind of equilibrium, resembling Cournot's duopoly solution, is attained. The roads are then so arranged in space that the free choice of paths by the individuals leads to a traffic distribution, such that the best solution for the authorities is to put the roads where they actually are. Underlying this is that the optimizers of one group regard the actions of those belonging to the other as given.

An overall optimum is now, returning to the analogy with duopoly theory, a Stackelberg solution where the road administration is the 'leader' and the individual commuters are the 'followers'. This means that the authorities expressly take in consideration that changing the allocation of roads changes the choices of paths and hence the distribution of traffic.

In contrast to duopoly, however, the authorities on one hand and the individual transporters on the other do not have any conflicting interests. All strive at the common goal of minimizing total transportation costs. As reductions of transportation costs achieved by individual transporters choosing better paths are in aggregate not overthrown by an improved allocation of roads, and as an improved road allocation in its turn leads to a further reduction of total costs that is not overthrown by the search of still better paths, it is likely that a process of successive adjustments leads to an equilibrium in the Cournot sense (if it exists and the process is stable) which at the same time is a local minimum in the Stackelberg sense. Provided that sufficient convexity is introduced in the mathematical problem, the equilibrium-optimum could be expected to be global.

As the problem has now been formulated, I have to say something about the choice of model. There exist several analogies from other sciences that have been fruitfully employed for transportation problems. In the main there are two different approaches. The most popular one is a discontinuous programming approach, where individuals are located at a finite number of 'nodes' and where roads are 'arcs' connecting the nodes. This makes the theory for flows in electrical networks applicable. Due to the possibility of employing mathematical programming and computers, the method is powerful for solving problems of a partial and applied character.

When, as in the present paper, the main interest is to obtain general conclusions, then the discontinuous approach becomes awkward. It is then better to regard the region as a connected portion of the plane, delimited by smooth arcs, and population as distributed by a continuous density function. It is not feasible in this model to regard roads as arc segments. Rather the distribution of roads would be represented by a continuous scalar point function, defined on the region and expressing the cost of transfer or traversability at each point. The scalar property implies that traversability is the same in each direction across a given point, hence abstracting from real networks. In such a transfer cost field the problem of finding an optimal path becomes a variational problem having analogies from many branches of physics. The paradigm was introduced in transportation studies in some very elegant papers by Beckmann. More recently it has been employed in works by Wardrop and by Angel and Hyman.

Another feature of Beckmann's analysis, lost in the more recent works mentioned, that is maintained in the following, is the analogy to hydrodynamics where transport origins are treated as continuously distributed point sources and transport destinations as likewise continuously distributed point sinks. As will be seen, this provides a measure of traffic with conservation or 'incompressibility' properties. With fixed origins or fixed destinations transportation structure is represented by vector fields whose directions are directions of paths chosen and whose moduli represent traffic. Unlike the fully analysed basic Beckmann case, where the movement of one merchandise from excess supply sources to excess demand sinks is studied, and hence may be studied in terms of one vector field, we presently deal with a non-denumerable infinity of vector fields. As the fields do not interfere with each other to merge into a resultant field, but have moduli that aggregate to total traffic, no analogy to physical phenomena exists. Part of the way we are, however, still aided by hydrodynamics and its mathematical tools, viz. vector analysis and complex calculus.

We have now outlined the problem and the methods used. We can also specify the given data, namely the geometrical shape of the region and the population density function.

What is needed more are two substantial hypotheses about how transports or trips are generated and distributed and about how transfer cost is related to the quantity of road capital invested in each point.

As to the first one, there is an empirically well established hypothesis available from geography, supported by ample evidence for aviation traffic, telephone calls, etc. It is the gravity hypothesis for 'interaction', borrowed from Newtonian mechanics and introduced in the field by Stewart. According to this, interaction (number of transports) between two locations in space is supposed to be proportional to the product of population densities at the two locations and reciprocally proportional to their distance or some power of it.

In spite of the empirical support and of the intuitive appeal of the idea that every two persons at the same distance need one communication each standard time period, the theory has been severely criticized. It has been demonstrated to have inherent contradictions in application to some problems, like trips to work, where a doubling of employees and working places would lead to a quadrupling of trips, which is absurd. Hence a specific calibration procedure in terms of 'balancing factors' was called for. Economists have also criticized the lack of an underpinning in terms of a behavioural theory of utility maximization type.

It is not my intention to comment on the many, more or less appealing, theoretical underpinnings offered. One of the most successful and interesting models is the statistical, or rather thermodynamic, entropy model offered by Wilson. As, however, the gravity model has empirical support and as the later work is concerned just with finding theoretical support for this and the similar entropy model, it seems justified to take it as a building block for the following discussion.

We presently take a very crude version of the gravity (or entropy) hypothesis, treating the need for transportation as proportional to the product of population densities and disregarding the dependence on distance altogether. This, naturally, is the analytically simplest case.

Knowing the transfer cost function we may, within the model chosen, determine the optimal paths between any two locations of the region by variational calculus. Knowing in addition how population is distributed and how, due to hypothesis, transports are generated and distributed, we may by the hydrodynamic methods also derive a measure of traffic for each point of the region.

But this solves only the first one of the partial minimization problems. In order to solve the second one, i.e. find out the optimal distribution of roads with a given traffic distribution, we have to relate the abstract concept of transfer cost to road capital by a specified mathematical relation.

The general characteristics of such a relation are not difficult to find out. Obviously, a lot of road capital invested in a point means low transfer cost. In the continuous model we may imagine roads to be represented by a network that is 'microscopic', or rather in the limiting continuous case even vanishes in mesh. If the magnified picture of the microscopic network contained in a 'point' is not completely filled with roads going everywhere in every imaginable direction, then it is in general not possible to take a straight line path between any two nodes of the network. The linear distance has to be augmented by detours. Increasing road capital by adding new shortcuts to the existing network reduces these detours, but on average the reductions display 'decreasing returns' as in aggregate a new shortcut saves less detours the more ramified the network already is.

The simplest way of formalizing these ideas would be to let transfer cost be a sum of two terms, one constant 'linear cost', and one 'detour cost' reciprocally proportional to road capital invested. It can be explicitly shown that such a hyperbola holds in the limiting case for a regular triangular network vanishing in mesh size, or for any conformal transformation of the network. Intuitively, however, a relation at least resembling the one postulated seems reasonable to adopt for more irregular networks as soon as one adopts the continuous idealization with its transfer cost concept (at least in the scalar form).

With this last building block the second partial optimization problem too can be solved, provided that a given amount of road capital to be allocated is specified as a constraint. Such a single constraint, of course, only makes sense if the whole region is supposed to be uniformly suitable for the building of roads and ground prices are supposed to be equal everywhere. These are further idealizations necessary in order to make the task tractable.

With the assumed relation between transfer cost and road capital, the optimal distribution of road capital at a given distribution of traffic is solved by the second optimization to prescribe that road capital be distributed in proportion to the square root of traffic.

I have included a section where data for Sweden in 1973, concerning transportation work and road networks for a subdivision into local subregions, are used to estimate a power curve for the relation between road capital and traffic (obtained from the primary data after division by areas). The fit is relatively good and the square root rule within quite safe confidence limits. The value of this should of course not be overrated, but supposing that the Swedish road administration had been reasonably successful in planning the network of roads (by its proper planning instruments) then the empirical data would give some indirect confirmation to the continuous model in general and to the relation between transfer cost and road capital postulated in particular.

We can now pass to the formal development of the complete model.

## 2. Transportation costs and the intensity of traffic

We denote the region by $S$ and its border by $G$. The border is assumed to be positively oriented, so that moving along it in the positive direction means having the interior of the region on the left-hand side. $G$ is, of course, a closed curve.

On $S$ is defined a continuous population density function $p(x, y)$. Total population, i.e. the surface integral of this function over the region is denoted $P$.

According to assumptions the number of transports from a point $\xi, \eta$ to a point $x, y$ is $p(\xi, \eta)p(x, y)$. When only transports started at a fixed point are considered this product is written $\bar{p}p$, where $\bar{p}$ is population at the fixed point of origin $\xi, \eta$.

Assume now that transportation facilities are given. According to the assumptions they are represented by a continuous transfer cost function, denoted $f(x, y)$ and likewise defined on $S$.

A certain transportation path is given parametrically by $x(\tau)$ and $y(\tau)$, where $\tau$ is the length of arc along the path, measured from the point of origin $\xi, \eta$. The cost for a certain transport is then given by the definite integral

$$I(t) = \int_0^t f \mathrm{d}\tau. \tag{1}$$

If we only consider transports flowing out from one single fixed point $\xi, \eta$, then it is obvious that the optimal path to any intermediate point, lying on a longer path, has to coincide with the relevant part of the latter. It follows from the definition (1), according to which transportation costs are 'additive', i.e. obtainable by integration, that such a policy must be followed if the paths be candidates for optimality. The result is then that there is only *one* path going through each point of $S$, except the singular point $\xi, \eta$, to which all the paths converge. They hence constitute a set of field lines.

Let us further associate with each point of the region (except the singular $\xi, \eta$) a scalar quantity denoting the intensity of traffic, or rather the *partial* intensity of traffic flowing in a certain direction and having the given point $\xi, \eta$ as origin. Later on we will define the *total* intensity of traffic flowing across the point in all directions and starting at all the points of the region.

But for a given point of origin we have only one set of field lines, and we may therefore with each point – still excepting $\xi, \eta$ – associate a vector field whose direction is the direction of the path and whose modulus is the partial intensity of traffic. Denote the vector field $\boldsymbol{v}$. The partial intensity of traffic is hence $|\boldsymbol{v}|$, and the direction taken by it is given by the unit vector $\boldsymbol{v}/|\boldsymbol{v}| = (\cos\theta, \sin\theta)$. Accordingly, $\boldsymbol{v}$ is a field, defined everywhere on $S$, except at $\xi, \eta$ where there is a singularity.

With a certain field $\boldsymbol{v}$ we may also associate a scalar function $I(x, y)$ defined on $S$ and expressing the cost of transportation from $\xi, \eta$ to the point $x$, $y$ according to (1) when the field lines of $\boldsymbol{v}$ are used as transportation paths.

Until now, we have not said anything about how the modulus of $\boldsymbol{v}$ is determined, only about its direction, which is the direction of a system of arbitrary transportation paths. The modulus must be determined by two things, namely how many transports end in each point of the region and how many transports flow across its border.

We know from vector analysis that the divergence of a vector field tells how many elements are added to a flow in each point. In the present case there is a 'sink' or a negative 'source' in each point, as $\bar{p}p$ transports are delivered there. Accordingly the divergence of $\boldsymbol{v}$ equals $-\bar{p}p$, i.e.,

$$\nabla \cdot \boldsymbol{v} = -\bar{p}p. \tag{2}$$

This poses one constraint on $\boldsymbol{v}$. The other constraint is that no transports go across the boundary $G$ to the exterior of the region, i.e., $\boldsymbol{v} \cdot \boldsymbol{n} = 0$ on $G$ where $\boldsymbol{n}$ is the unit outward normal to the boundary curve.

The conditions together with the field lines determine the field $\boldsymbol{v}$ everywhere, except at the singular point of origin.

Let us next compute the cost for all transports originating at $\xi, \eta$, denoted $C(\xi, \eta)$. As $I$, according to (1), is the cost of transportation from the point of origin to an arbitrary point $x, y$, and as $\bar{p}p$ is the number of transports ending there, the whole cost incurred is

$$C(\xi, \eta) = \iint_S I\bar{p}p \, \mathrm{d}x \, \mathrm{d}y. \tag{3}$$

We are now going to transform this expression into another one, in terms of the transfer cost $f$ and the partial intensity of traffic $|\boldsymbol{v}|$. First, we notice from (2) that we may write

$$C(\xi, \eta) = -\iint_S I\nabla \cdot \boldsymbol{v} \, \mathrm{d}x \, \mathrm{d}y. \tag{4}$$

Next, we see that, according to a standard formula in vector analysis,

$$\nabla \cdot (I\boldsymbol{v}) = \nabla I \cdot \boldsymbol{v} + I\nabla \cdot \boldsymbol{v}. \tag{5}$$

Now, according to Gauss' divergence theorem for two-dimensional space, the surface integral of the divergence of a vector field over a region equals the line integral of the outward normal component of the vector taken along the boundary. The requirement for this to be applicable is that the region be delimited by a closed boundary curve (as assumed) and that the vector field be regular everywhere.

There is a problem, namely the singularity at the point $\xi, \eta$, which prevents the last condition from being fulfilled for the region $S$ itself. We may, however, easily handle this difficulty by surrounding the singular point by a second boundary curve and excluding the portion of $S$ inside this curve. The new region is denoted $S'$ and the curve that delimits the excluded part is denoted $\Gamma$. It is assumed that $\Gamma$, like $G$, is positively oriented. For $\Gamma$ we take a niveau curve for $I = \text{constant}$. Hence, we may decrease the excluded portion indefinitely by taking smaller and smaller values of $I$. In the limit, as $I$ goes to zero, $S'$ goes to $S$.

For all $S'$, no matter how small $I$ is, Gauss' theorem is applicable. Hence

$$\iint_{S'} \nabla \cdot (I\boldsymbol{v}) \, \mathrm{d}x \, \mathrm{d}y = \int_{\Gamma} I\boldsymbol{v} \cdot \boldsymbol{n} \, \mathrm{d}s, \tag{6}$$

as we do not need to write down the line integral along $G$ because the normal component of $\boldsymbol{v}$ vanishes (due to the assumption that no transports cross the boundary $G$). As before, the vector $\boldsymbol{n}$ is the outward normal, in eq. (6) to the boundary $\Gamma$.

As, however, $I$ is constant along $\Gamma$, we may move it outside the integration sign in the right-hand member of (6).

Next, we apply Gauss' theorem to $\nabla \cdot \boldsymbol{v} = -\bar{p}p$ for the same region $S'$. This yields

$$\int_{\Gamma} \boldsymbol{v} \cdot \boldsymbol{n} \, \mathrm{d}s = -\bar{p} \iint_{S'} p \, \mathrm{d}x \, \mathrm{d}y, \tag{7}$$

as again the line integral along $G$ vanishes for the same reason as in (6). (The factor $\bar{p}$ has been moved outside the integration signs as it denotes population at the fixed point of origin and is hence independent of the space coordinates $x, y$ of the variable endpoint.)

In the limit, as $I$ goes to zero, the right-hand member of (7) approaches $-\bar{p}P$, where, as before, $P$ is total population of the region.

What has been said is that the right-hand member of (6) in the limit is the product of two factors, namely $I$ which goes to zero and the integral (7) which goes to the finite number $-\bar{p}P$. Hence, the right-hand member of (6) goes to zero, whereas the region of integration in the left-hand member of (6) goes to the whole region $S$. This means that the improper integral

$$\iint_{S} \nabla \cdot (I\boldsymbol{v}) \, \mathrm{d}x \, \mathrm{d}y = 0. \tag{8}$$

Application of this to (5) and using expression (4) yields

$$C(\xi,\eta) = \iint_S \nabla I \cdot \boldsymbol{v}\, dx\, dy. \tag{9}$$

But, as $\boldsymbol{v}/|\boldsymbol{v}|$ is a unit vector in the direction of the transportation path, we see that $dI/dt = \nabla I \cdot \boldsymbol{v}/|\boldsymbol{v}|$ and this, according to (1) equals $f$. Hence $\nabla I \cdot \boldsymbol{v} = f|\boldsymbol{v}|$ and

$$C(\xi,\eta) = \iint_S f|\boldsymbol{v}|\, dx\, dy. \tag{10}$$

This is the final transformation of (3). The total cost for all transports originating at $\xi,\eta$, initially expressed in terms of the transportation cost to each point $I$ and the number $\bar{p}p$ of transports ending there, is now obtained in terms of the transfer cost across a point $f$ and the partial intensity of traffic there $|\boldsymbol{v}|$. The expressions (3) and (10) tell us how much all transportation costs for individuals situated at $\xi,\mu$. The expressions may be used to find out how profitable different points are for individuals from the point of view of centrality of location.

But, in order to discuss equilibrium and optimality for the whole region, we need the cost of transportation for all individuals, living in all the points of the region. This latter cost is

$$\iint_S C(\xi,\eta)\, d\xi\, d\eta, \tag{11}$$

or, if we define the *total* intensity of traffic

$$i(x,y) = \iint_S |\boldsymbol{v}|\, d\xi\, d\eta, \tag{12}$$

we get total cost according to (10) and (11) as

$$\iint_S f(x,y) i(x,y)\, dx\, dy. \tag{13}$$

This is the expression that the roadbuilding authorities will attempt to minimize.

## 3. Optimal paths

In order to be able to use the expressions for the costs (10) and (13) we have to see how the partial intensity of traffic $|\boldsymbol{v}|$ and the total intensity of traffic $i$ are distributed on the region, and for this we must know the optimal paths for the individual transports. We might determine each optimal path individually, but it is better to find out in one step which traffic vector field over the whole region minimizes total cost for all the transports originating at a certain point. That is, we try to find out which vector field $\boldsymbol{v}$ minimizes the expression (10) under the constraint (2) and the boundary condition that $\boldsymbol{v}\cdot\boldsymbol{n}$ be zero on the boundary $G$. This problem is nearly identical with one solved by Martin Beckmann, the only difference being that, whereas in his transportation model there is no net outflow from singular points, in the present case all the transports flow out from the singular point $\xi, \eta$.

The constrained minimization problem may be transformed into minimizing the following Lagrange expression

$$\iint_S (f|\boldsymbol{v}| + \lambda(\bar{p}p + \nabla\cdot\boldsymbol{v}))\,\mathrm{d}x\,\mathrm{d}y, \tag{14}$$

where $\lambda$ is a continuous function of the space coordinates $x, y$, not yet determined.

The Euler equation for minimization of (14) is

$$f\boldsymbol{v}/|\boldsymbol{v}| = \nabla\lambda, \tag{15}$$

which means that the vector field $f\boldsymbol{v}/|\boldsymbol{v}|$ is the gradient of a potential function $\lambda$. The field lines of $\boldsymbol{v}$ coincide with the field lines of $\nabla\lambda$, even though the two fields are by no means identical, the difference being a scalar factor $f/|\boldsymbol{v}|$.

It is easily seen that the line integral of (15) taken along an *optimal* transportation path is

$$\int_0^t f\,\mathrm{d}\tau = \int_0^t \nabla\lambda\cdot\boldsymbol{v}/|\boldsymbol{v}|\,\mathrm{d}\tau, \tag{16}$$

because $(\boldsymbol{v}/|\boldsymbol{v}|)^2 = 1$. But, $\nabla\lambda\cdot\boldsymbol{v}/|\boldsymbol{v}|\mathrm{d}\tau = \mathrm{d}\lambda$ is an exact differential, and hence the line integral (16) is independent of the integration path. The value of (16) only depends upon the endpoint. Provided that we arbitrarily put the potential $\lambda$ equal to zero in $\xi$, $\eta$, the right-hand member of (16) equals $\lambda$. The left-hand side, according to (1), equals $I$. Hence, we may write

$$\lambda = I. \tag{17}$$

The field (15) turns out to be the gradient of $I$, and this in turn means that the field lines of $\boldsymbol{v}$ cut the isopotential curves for $I$ orthogonally.

We are now going to see how (15) determines the field lines for $\boldsymbol{v}$.

As the curl of a gradient is always zero, we know that $\nabla\times\nabla\lambda = 0$. From (15),

$$\nabla\times(f\boldsymbol{v}/|\boldsymbol{v}|) = 0. \tag{18}$$

But, according to a formula for the curl, analogous to the formula (5) for the divergence, it is true that

$$\nabla f \times \mathbf{v}/|\mathbf{v}| + f\nabla \times (\mathbf{v}/|\mathbf{v}|) = 0. \tag{19}$$

As now $\mathbf{v}/|\mathbf{v}|$ is a unit vector, the first term, according to the definition of a 'cross' product, equals the *sine* of the angle between the gradient of $f$ and the vector $\mathbf{v}$, multiplied by the modulus of the gradient. Denote the angle of the gradient by $\omega$ and the angle of the vector $\mathbf{v}$ by $\theta$. The angle in question is then $\theta-\omega$. From the definition of the 'dot' product we, on the other hand, know that the first term with the cross replaced by a dot equals the *cosine* of $\theta-\omega$, multiplied by the modulus of the gradient. Hence

$$(\nabla f \times \mathbf{v}/|\mathbf{v}|)/(\nabla f \cdot \mathbf{v}/|\mathbf{v}|) = \sin(\theta-\omega)/\cos(\theta-\omega).$$

But,

$$\nabla f \cdot \mathbf{v}/|\mathbf{v}| = \mathrm{d}f/\mathrm{d}\tau.$$

Using these results in (19) and multiplying by $\cos(\theta-\omega)$ we obtain

$$\mathrm{d}f/\mathrm{d}\tau \sin(\theta-\omega) + f\nabla \times (\mathbf{v}/|\mathbf{v}|)\cos(\theta-\omega) = 0. \tag{20}$$

As $\mathbf{v}/|\mathbf{v}|$ equals the vector $(\cos\theta, \sin\theta)$, we see that, according to the definition of a curl,

$$\nabla \times (\mathbf{v}/|\mathbf{v}|) = \cos\theta\,\partial\theta/\partial x + \sin\theta\ \partial\theta/\partial y.$$

As, moreover, the vector $(\cos\theta, \sin\theta)$ is of unit length and points in the direction of the transportation path, we find that $\cos\theta = \partial x/\partial\tau$ and that $\sin\theta = \partial y/\partial\tau$. Collecting these results we obtain

$$\nabla \times (\mathbf{v}/|\mathbf{v}|) = \mathrm{d}\theta/\mathrm{d}\tau. \tag{21}$$

If we now substitute this into (20) we see that

$$\mathrm{d}f/\mathrm{d}\tau\ \ \sin(\theta-\omega) + f\cos(\theta-\omega)\,\mathrm{d}\theta/\mathrm{d}\tau = 0. \tag{22}$$

If $\omega$ is constant, i.e. the gradient of $f$ always points in the same direction, we obtain

$$\mathrm{d}/\mathrm{d}\tau(f\sin(\theta-\omega)) = 0, \tag{23}$$

or

$$f\sin(\theta-\omega) = c, \tag{24}$$

where $c$ is a constant. Equation (24) tells that the angle which the transportation path makes with the direction of the steepest increase of transfer cost increases along the path if transfer cost increases along it. Hence, the path is deflected from the direction of steepest decrease of $f$ if the path goes in the direction of increasing $f$. In the same way the path is attracted toward the direction of steepest increase of $f$ if the path goes in the direction of decreasing $f$.

The result is analogous to that for the problem of finding the paths of light rays in an isotropic medium. In the case where the medium consists of two layers of different homogeneous media, (24) gives Snell's law for the refraction of light in a separation point between the two layers. We notice that this law for the analogous case of transportation over two media, such as by land and by sea, was given by Tord Palander.

Suppose now that we may specify the transfer cost function so that it only depends upon the distance $r$ of the point from the origin of the coordinate system, i.e. $f(x,y)=f(r)$, where $r=\sqrt{(x^2+y^2)}$. The reason for this is that we later on are going to specify the region $S$ as a unit disk with a uniform distribution of population. Now, we may, without further analysis, state that the transfer cost function for such a region must have circular symmetry in order to be a candidate for an equilibrium or an optimum. If we put the origin in the center of the disk, we obtain the formula $f(r)$. For such a transfer cost function the eq. (22) may be expressed in a simpler way. [It should be noticed that (24) is not valid for the present case, as the angle of the gradient of $f$ changes when one moves from one point to another.]

As $\omega$ is the angle of the gradient, we obtain by differentiation that

$$\nabla f = f'(x/r, y/r) = f'(\cos\omega, \sin\omega).$$

This immediately gives $x = r\cos\omega$ and $y = r\sin\omega$. Hence, $r$ and $\omega$ (fortunately) turn out to be polar coordinates for $x, y$.

Differentiating the expressions for $x, y$ in polar coordinates with respect to arc length $\tau$, measured along the transportation path, we obtain

$$\dot{x} = \dot{r}\cos\omega - r\dot{\omega}\sin\omega, \qquad \dot{y} = \dot{r}\sin\omega + r\dot{\omega}\cos\omega,$$

where the dot above the variables indicates differentiation with respect to arc length.

But as $\theta$ is the angle of the transportation path we have

$$\dot{x} = \cos\theta, \qquad \dot{y} = \sin\theta.$$

We substitute these in the former equations and solve for $\dot{r}$ and $r\dot{\omega}$.

Then, employing the formulae for the cosine and the sine of a difference, we obtain

$$\cos(\theta-\omega) = \dot{r}, \qquad \sin(\theta-\omega) = r\dot{\omega}.$$

Eq. (22) may hence be written

$$\mathrm{d}/\mathrm{d}\tau(fr\dot{\omega})+f\dot{r}\dot{\omega} = 0, \tag{25}$$

or

$$\mathrm{d}/\mathrm{d}\tau(fr^2\dot{\omega}) = 0. \tag{26}$$

This, however, implies that

$$fr^2\dot{\omega} = c, \tag{27}$$

where $c$ is a constant. Now the infinitesimal arc $\mathrm{d}\tau$, expressed in polar coordinates, is $\sqrt{(r^2+r'^2)}\,\mathrm{d}\omega$ where $r' = \mathrm{d}r/\mathrm{d}\omega$. Thus we obtain $\dot{\omega} = 1/\sqrt{(r^2+r'^2)}$, which substituted into (27) yields

$$fr^2 = c\sqrt{(r^2+r'^2)}. \tag{28}$$

This is a differential equation for the optimal path in terms of polar coordinates $r$ and $\omega$. We observe that this equation may also be derived directly as the Euler equation for minimization of the expression

$$\int f\mathrm{d}\tau = \int f(r)\sqrt{(r^2+r'^2)}\,\mathrm{d}\omega.$$

Let us now, as an illustration, specify the transfer cost function even more. Let $f(r) = r^n$. If $n$ is positive it is cheapest to travel in the central parts of the region; if $n$ is negative it is cheapest to travel in the peripheral parts. The costs that may be saved by travelling in the low-cost part of the region are larger, the larger the absolute value of $n$ is. It is to be expected that with $n$ different from zero the paths deviate from straight line segments so that they are convex to the origin if $n$ is positive and concave to the origin if $n$ is negative. If $n = 0$ transfer cost is the same everywhere and it is to be expected that the optimal paths are straight line segments.

This is verified by the formal solutions. If $f = r^n$, (28) becomes

$$r^{n+2} = c\sqrt{(r^2+r'^2)}, \tag{29}$$

or

$$rr'' = (n+2)r'^2+(n+1)r^2. \tag{30}$$

This second-order differential equation has a solution in terms of elementary functions. The general solution may be written

$$R\cos(\Omega+b)=a, \tag{31}$$

where, for convergence, we have defined two intermediate variables $R=r^{n+1}$ and $\Omega=(n+1)\omega$.

The solution (31) has two parameters to be determined by the endpoints. Hence, (31) may provide a solution curve that passes through any two points, provided that the acute angle between the endpoints does not exceed $\pi/(n+1)$. If the angle does exceed this critical value, then the optimal paths are *radial*, i.e. they go right in to the center from one endpoint and right out to the other endpoint.

In fig. 1 are illustrated the solution curves (with $n$ equal to 1 and 2 respectively) for a fixed point of origin. Fixing the point removes one degree of freedom so that a one-parameter family of curves results. Hence, the pictures show sets of field lines of the type meant in the verbal discussion under section 2.

We may also easily obtain the iso-potential curves for $I$ (or $\lambda$). Where the solution (31) is relevant we have the relation

$$(n+1)I=\surd(R_0^2+R_1^2-2R_0R_1\cos(\Omega_1-\Omega_0)). \tag{32}$$

The indices 0 and 1 indicate the two endpoints. This expression is again relevant if the acute angle between the endpoints does not exceed $\pi/(n+1)$.

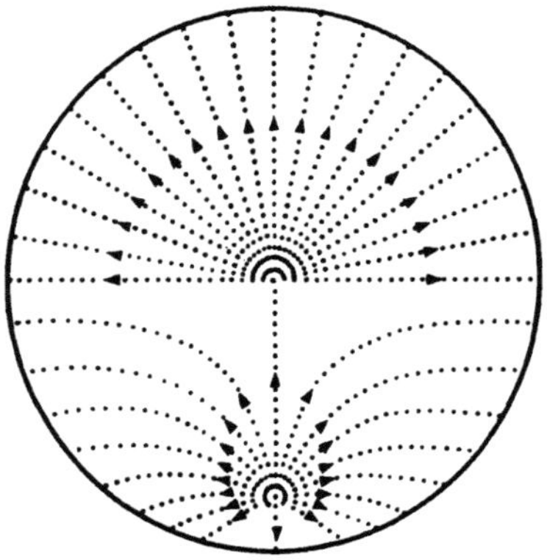


Fig. 1a

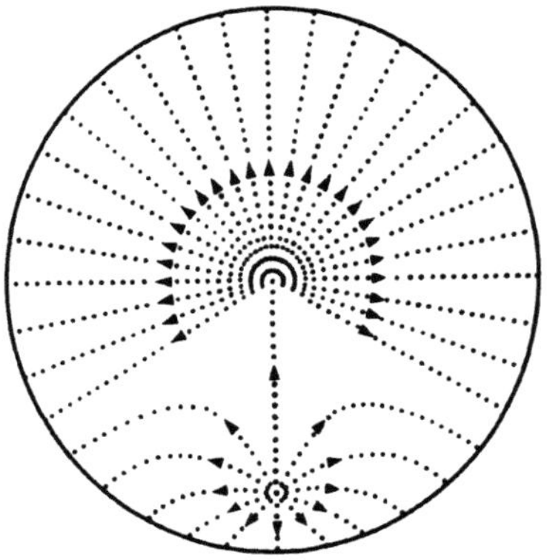


Fig. 1b

For larger angles we have

$$(n+1)I = R_0 + R_1. \tag{33}$$

Fig. 2 shows the sets of iso-potential curves together with the corresponding optimal paths, for the cases already illustrated. It is seen that the paths cut the iso-curves for constant $I$ orthogonally, as stated above.

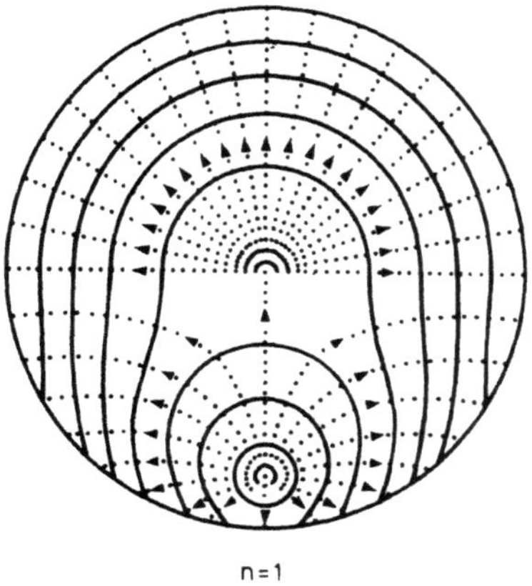


Fig. 2a

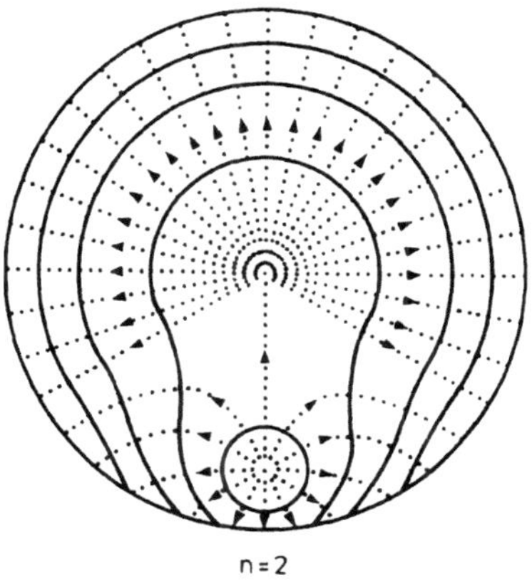


Fig. 2b

There is, however, another way of representing these solutions. If we namely regard $R$ and $\Omega$ as polar coordinates for *new* rectangular coordinates $X$ and $Y$, so that $X = R\cos\Omega$ and $Y = R\sin\Omega$, we obtain a quite interesting mapping from $x$ and $y$ to $X$ and $Y$.

In order to characterize this mapping we may see how single points, curves and the whole region are affected by it. As regards the individual points we see that they are moved by both rotation and radial projection, as the angle $\omega$ is changed to the angle $\Omega = (n+1)\omega$ and the radius vector $r$ is changed to the radius vector $R = r^{n+1}$.

Assuming $n$ to be non-negative (i.e. assuming that the concentration of road capital – if there is any – is to the central part of the region), we see that the angles rotate counter-clockwise and that the points of the unit disk are projected towards the center.

If we imagine that each point represents one 'person' in the population, so that population is uniformly distributed on the original disk, then the uniformity is obviously distorted by the mapping. The exact extent of this distortion is given by the Jacobian of the mapping, which equals

$$\partial(X, Y)/\partial(x, y) = ((n+1)r^n)^2. \tag{34}$$

Hence, if $dx\,dy$ people live in the infinitesimal rectangle of area $dx\,dy$ of the original disk, it follows that $dX\,dY/((n+1)r^n)^2$ people live in the rectangle of area $dX\,dY$ of the transformed region. As $n$ is non-negative, this means a concentration of population to the central parts, or possibly that its distribution is left unchanged in the limiting case.

The next question is: What happens to curves? The curves of special interest are the solution curves for transportation paths. We have seen that they are of two different kinds. In the sector where the solution (31) is relevant the paths are curved, whereas they are radial outside the sector. The remarkable thing now is that the curved paths are mapped onto straight line segments, whereas the radial paths are left radial.

Hence, a situation with a uniform distribution of population and curved transportation paths is translatable to an imaginary situation where population is clustered but transportation paths are linear. If $n$ is positive, so that transfer is cheapest in the central parts and the optimal paths deviate from the straight line by being convex to the origin, the clustering of population is to the central parts. Both agglomeration of people and cheapness of transfer cause traffic to be most intense in the central parts of the region.

The third characterization of the mapping concerns the transformation of the shape of the region, i.e. the unit disk. From one point of view it is not changed at all. Every point of the original unit disk is mapped into a new unit disk, and there is some point of the original disk that corresponds to every point of the new one – even though, as we have seen, the density of points is altered.

But, the correspondence is not one-to-one. By the rotation the new disk is covered $(n+1)$-ply. The wedge of the original disk, where the paths were curved, is magnified to a whole disk itself, and the rest of the original disk, where the paths were radial, makes $n$ additional disks.

We may therefore think of the new region as made up of $(n+1)$ identical disk-shaped sheets, slit up along the positive real axis and joined together in a kind of 'spiral'. This is a so-called Riemann-surface, well known from the study of mappings.

Calculation shows that

$$\begin{aligned} \partial X/\partial x &= (n+1)r^n \cos n\omega = \partial Y/\partial y, \\ -\partial X/\partial y &= (n+1)r^n \sin n\omega = \partial Y/\partial x. \end{aligned} \tag{35}$$

Hence, the Cauchy–Riemann differential equations are fulfilled and the mapping is *conformal*. This implies that it may be represented by an *analytical* complex function of a complex variable. Let us define the complex variables $z = x + iy$ and $Z = X + iY$. The function is then simply

$$Z = z^{n+1}. \tag{36}$$

Wardrop has most elegantly employed complex functions in this context.

## 4. The partial and the total intensity of traffic

We are now going to discuss the distribution of traffic on the unit disk. We start with the simplest case, namely with $f = 1$. As is immediately seen from eq. (31), all paths become linear (in $x, y$-space) and hence we may write the parametrical equations for a solution curve in terms of arc length $\tau$ as

$$x = \xi + \tau\cos\theta, \qquad y = \eta + \tau\sin\theta,$$

where $\theta$ is a constant for each path.

We see that $\tau$ equals $\sqrt{((x-\xi)^2 + (y-\eta)^2)}$ and that hence $\nabla\tau = (\cos\theta, \sin\theta) = \boldsymbol{v}/|\boldsymbol{v}|$. This means that

$$\boldsymbol{v} = |\boldsymbol{v}|\nabla\tau. \tag{37}$$

In order to determine $\boldsymbol{v}$ we must take into consideration eq. (2), stating that $\nabla\cdot\boldsymbol{v} = -\bar{p}p$, and the boundary condition, stating that $\boldsymbol{v}\cdot\boldsymbol{n} = 0$ on $G$. Assume for simplicity that the population is equally distributed on the region, i.e. that $p(x, y) = 1$ everywhere. Hence, we have $\nabla\cdot\boldsymbol{v} = -1$, and this applied to (37) yields [according to the same relation that was used in (5) above] $\nabla|\boldsymbol{v}|\cdot\nabla\tau + |\boldsymbol{v}|\nabla^2\tau = -1$. Computing the Laplacian $\nabla^2\tau$ to equal $1/\tau$, we get the partial differential equation

$$\nabla|\boldsymbol{v}|\cdot\nabla\tau + |\boldsymbol{v}|/\tau + 1 = 0. \tag{38}$$

This is easily solved and yields

$$|\boldsymbol{v}| = \tfrac{1}{2}(T^2 - \tau^2)/\tau, \tag{39}$$

where $T$ depends only upon the starting point $\xi, \eta$ and upon the slope $\theta$ of the transportation path. When the boundary condition is taken into consideration we see that, according to (37), $|\boldsymbol{v}|$ has to be zero on the boundary. Hence, $T$ becomes the distance from $\xi, \eta$ to the boundary in the direction $\theta$.

We have now arrived at an expression for the *partial* intensity of traffic. The total intensity may be obtained from (39) according to (12), but the calculation is in general very complicated. For the simple case considered, and if we in addition assume the region to be the unit disk with its center in the origin, we can, however, quite easily obtain the solution

$$i(x, y) = 4(1 - r^2)E(r), \tag{40}$$

where $E(r)$ is the complete elliptic integral of the second kind, and where, as before, $r = \sqrt{(x^2 + y^2)}$. We see that $i$ is a uniformly decreasing function of the distance from the origin.

From expression (40) we can also calculate the 'total traffic' on the region, or the total transportation work done, as

$$\iint_S i(x, y)\,\mathrm{d}x\,\mathrm{d}y = 128\pi/45,$$

which approximately equals 8.94.

Hence, with an equal distribution of population on the unit disk and with a constant transfer cost function (leading to linear paths) the total intensity of traffic always *increases as we move towards the center of the disk*. This may be interpreted as a *pure* influence of the two-dimensional region, causing the most intense communications to take place in the central parts, as this occurs in the absence of the two factors that might otherwise cause the same, namely concentration of population and concentration of traffic due to lower transfer cost.

For one more case we may solve the problem completely, namely for the case of radial transports. Say that population is still equally distributed, but that the transports are all radial instead of linear, i.e. they go from one end-point right into the center and right out again to the other end-point.

We have already seen that some of the transports generated at the function $f = r^n$ are of this kind. The radial transports radiating *out from* the center go in the direction of the gradient of $r$. Hence, $\boldsymbol{v} = |\boldsymbol{v}|\nabla r$ and the differential equation, corresponding to (38) above, is

$$\nabla|\boldsymbol{v}| \cdot \nabla r + |\boldsymbol{v}|/r + 1 = 0. \tag{41}$$

Its solution is

$$|\boldsymbol{v}| = \tfrac{1}{2}(1 - r^2)/r. \tag{42}$$

This time it is very easy to obtain the total intensity according to (12). We see that the partial intensity is independent of the point of origin. Identical transports, in quantity and direction, radiate from the center for all $\xi, \eta$. Hence, $i$ would simply be the product of the expression (42) and the area of the disk, which is $\pi$. But, we have only considered transports radiating out from the center. There are as many transports that radiate *into* the center, and thus we have to multiply the number obtained by 2. We have

$$i(x, y) = \pi(1 - r^2)/r. \tag{43}$$

Total traffic in this case is

$$\iint_S i(x, y)\,\mathrm{d}x\,\mathrm{d}y = 4\pi^2/3,$$

which approximately equals 13.16. This means that with radial paths 47%

more traffic is created than with linear paths (which represent the case of minimum possible total traffic).

As compared with (40) this gives a distribution where the tendency for traffic to increase in intensity towards the center of the region is still more pronounced. In the computer diagrams (figs. 3 and 4) are shown the traffic distributions with linear and radial paths.

Moreover, we saw in the preceding paragraph that, with $f = r^n$, the transports in a sector $n/(n+1)$ of the unit disk are radial. As $n$ increases, the portion of the disk where the paths are not radial rapidly approaches zero, and we see that the case with only radial transportation is the limiting case as $n$ goes to infinity.

A moment of reflection reveals that radial transportation is a limiting case not only for this special type of transfer cost function. It represents in general the case of the 'convexest possible' paths for a transfer cost function with circular symmetry $f(r)$ *provided that the paths be optimal*. This is so because, as is easily seen, each path, which is not wholly contained in the acute angle formed by joining the endpoints to the center, is both longer and more expensive than the path formed by segments of the lines defining this angle.

## 5. Optimally allocated road capital

Up to now, we have been discussing only the choice of optimal transportation paths, and the distribution of traffic, associated with the solution, *when the transfer cost function is a given datum.*

It is now time to turn to the distribution of roads, i.e. to make the transfer cost function a *variable* in optimization. It is natural to start with the partial problem of finding the allocation of roads that minimizes total transportation costs when instead the distribution of traffic is a given datum.

The minimand is given by eq. (13) above, stated once more for convenience,

$$\iint_S f(x, y)i(x, y)\,\mathrm{d}x\,\mathrm{d}y. \tag{13}$$

This is to be minimized by variation of $f$, regarding $i$ as given.

Above we argued, that a hyperbolic relation between transfer cost and road capital invested would be reasonable. If we denote road capital by $l$, we can formalize the relation as

$$f(x, y) = a + b/l(x, y), \tag{44}$$

where $a$ and $b$ are some constants.

The constraint that a given total amount of road capital is to be

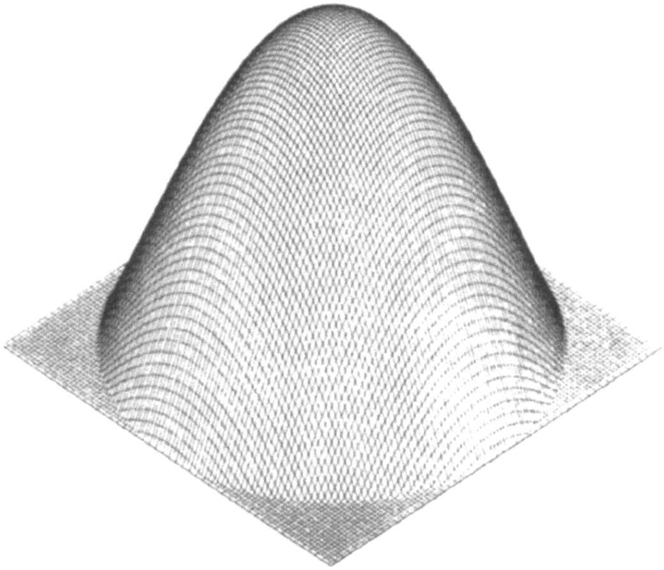

Fig. 3. Linear paths.

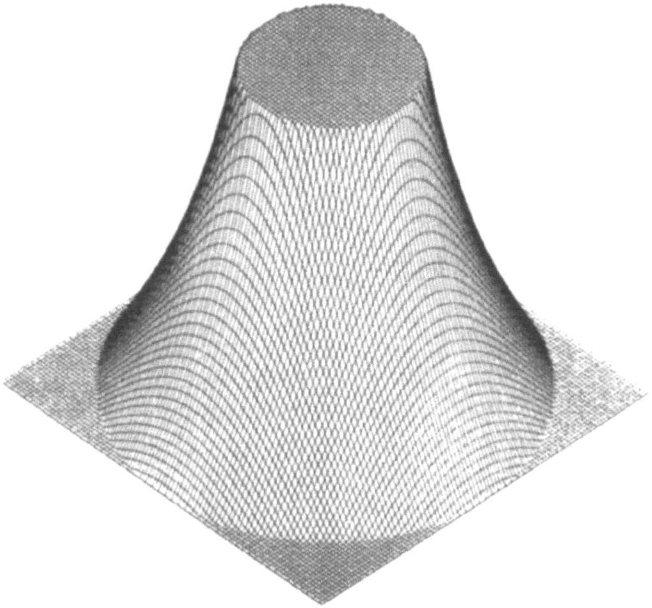

Fig. 4. Radial paths.

distributed reads

$$\iint_S l(x, y)\,\mathrm{d}x\,\mathrm{d}y = \pi\bar{l}, \tag{45}$$

where $\bar{l}$ denotes the average road capital invested in the region (which for simplicity is taken as the unit disk, even if this part of the discussion is applicable to more general shapes).

Minimization of (13) subject to the constraints (44) and (45) obviously yields the first-order condition

$$l(x, y) = \gamma\sqrt{i(x, y)}, \tag{46}$$

where $\gamma$ is a constant whose value may be calculated to equal $\pi\bar{l}/\iint\sqrt{i}\,\mathrm{d}x\,\mathrm{d}y$.

This means that road capital ought to be distributed *in proportion to the square root of traffic*. The character of the transfer cost function (44) provides for such convexity that condition (46) really renders a local minimum. As was said in the introduction this first-order condition for the partially optimal distribution of roads at given distribution of traffic is necessary in all kinds of optima and equilibria, no matter whether they are of the Cournot or the Stackelberg type.

In the next section we will see that data for Sweden in 1973 are in quite good agreement with the square root rule, something which gives indirect confirmation to the transfer cost function postulated and to the whole continuous approach.

We now have to consider the much more complicated problem of finding an equilibrium of the Cournot type and an overall optimum of the Stackelberg type. It should be said at the outset that we are not able to say much about this for the time being.

Let us first find out the range of variation of the total transportation cost when the partial optimality rule is followed. Substituting (46) and the value of the constant $\gamma$ into (13) yields

$$a\iint_S i\,\mathrm{d}x\,\mathrm{d}y + b\left(\iint\sqrt{i}\,\mathrm{d}x\,\mathrm{d}y\right)^2/\pi\bar{l}. \tag{47}$$

As $a$ and $b$ are constants, depending on the efficiency of vehicles, and $\pi\bar{l}$ is the given aggregate amount of road capital invested, the only factors that vary in the process of finding equilibrium and optimum are the two surface integrals. They only depend on the distribution of traffic intensity on the region.

The first one of the integrals can be identified as *total traffic on the whole region* (or total transportation work done). Obviously a small total traffic is desirable (ceteris paribus). We can also see from (47) that a small total traffic is more important when the aggregate amount of road capital, $\pi\bar{l}$, is large.

In (47) there is a tradeoff between the two integrals involved, but I am at present unable to derive the exact terms of it.

What then, can we at all say about the overall optimum for the distribution of road capital? Let us start from a situation where the distribution of road capital is uniform and see where a sequence of successive improvements leads.

We have derived the distribution of traffic for the starting case in (40). But, if the government relocates road capital in proportion to the square root of (40), then total transportation costs may be saved with this given traffic distribution.

But then transfer cost is no longer constant. It is lower in the center, and this causes the individual transporters to make the paths deviate from straight lines and become convex to the origin. As this is done in order to reduce transportation costs, the result is a further reduction of their sum, leaving unaffected the gains already obtained.

Moreover, the deflection of the paths draws even more traffic to the center and this makes further centralizations of road capital appropriate. In each stage is added a new reduction of costs and the process is continued until nothing more may be gained.

## 6. On the optimality of roads in Sweden 1973

As was said above, I am going to conclude this paper by giving some empirical evidence for the square root optimality rule. I have got statistical data for Sweden 1973 from the central road authorities concerning total length of roads in kilometers and total transportation work done in millions of vehicle kilometers for each one of the 275 'communes'. As the areas of the communes are very different, the measures of road density or road capital and of traffic intensity are obtained from the primary data by simple division by the areas in square kilometers.

As a square root relation is expected, it is appropriate to fit a power curve, or rather a regression line after linearization by taking logarithms. The result of this and the picture of it in the scatter diagram are shown [see fig. 5].

$$l = 0.84 i^{0.40}, \qquad R^2 = 0.65. \tag{48}$$

This may be compared to the theoretical curve, which, because the constant $\gamma$ can be calculated to equal 1.06, reads $l = 1.06 i^{0.50}$. The standard error for the exponent is 0.02. Hence, the degrees of freedom being 273, any confidence interval would be very narrow, $\pm 0.05$ at 99 % level.

Even though the estimation is made in logarithms the spread in the scatter is such that heteroscedasticity may be suspected. Indeed, a linear regression

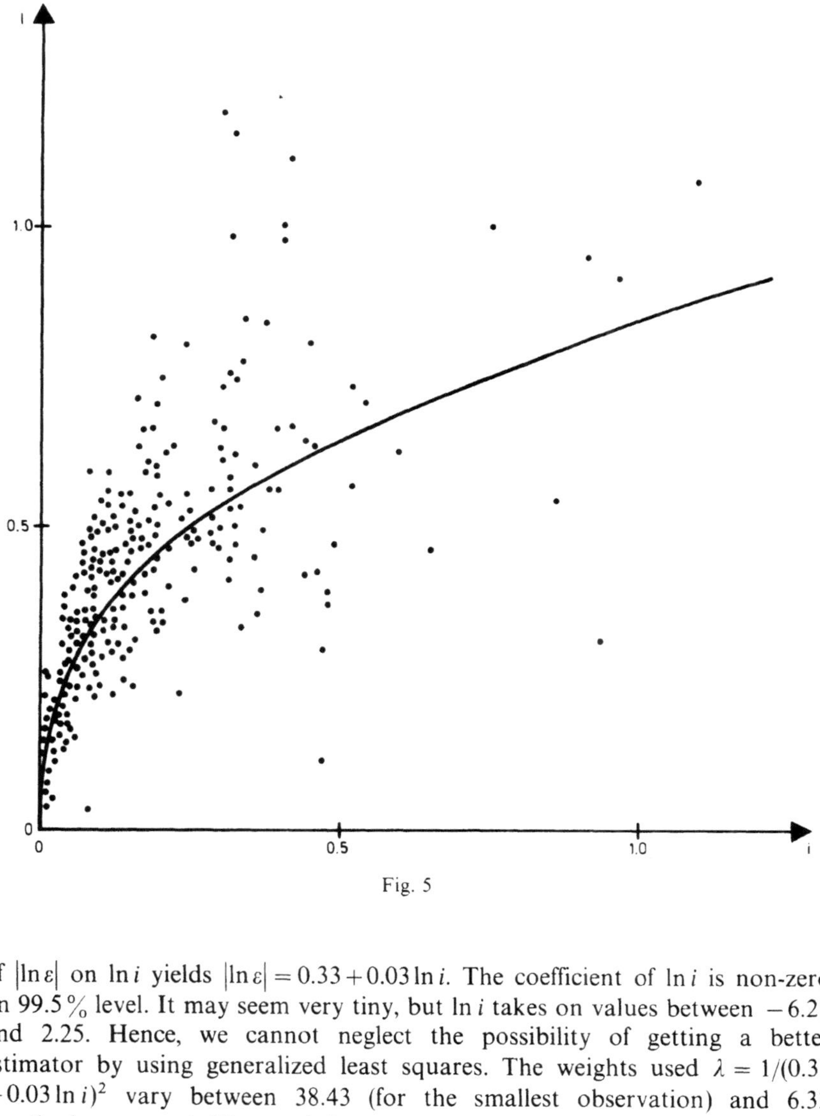


Fig. 5

of $|\ln \varepsilon|$ on $\ln i$ yields $|\ln \varepsilon| = 0.33 + 0.03 \ln i$. The coefficient of $\ln i$ is non-zero on 99.5% level. It may seem very tiny, but $\ln i$ takes on values between $-6.21$ and 2.25. Hence, we cannot neglect the possibility of getting a better estimator by using generalized least squares. The weights used $\lambda = 1/(0.33 + 0.03 \ln i)^2$ vary between 38.43 (for the smallest observation) and 6.33 (for the largest one). The result is

$$l = 0.95 i^{0.46}, \tag{49}$$

which comes even closer to the theoretical curve. The standard error for the exponent is reduced from 0.015, and hence the 99% confidence interval is $\pm 0.04$. The theoretical value is now just on the upper limit of the interval.

## References

Angel, S. and G.M. Hyman, 1970, Urban velocity fields, Environment and Planning.
Angel, S. and G.M. Hyman, 1972, Urban spatial interaction, Environment and Planning.
Angel, S. and G.M. Hyman, 1976, Urban fields – A geometry of movement for regional science.
Beckmann, M., 1952, A continuous model of transportation, Econometrica.
Beckmann, M., 1953, The partial equilibrium of a continuous space market, Weltwirtschaftliches Archiv.
Elsgole, L.E., 1961, Calculus of variations.
Fox, C., 1954, Introduction to the calculus of variations.
Johnston, J., 1972, Econometric methods.
Lam, T.N. and G.F. Newell, 1967, Flow dependent traffic assignment on a circular city, Transportation Science.
Marsden, J.E., 1973, Basic complex analysis.
Marsden, J.E. and A.J. Tromba, 1976, Vector calculus.
Palander, T.F., 1935, Beiträge zur Standortstheorie.
Stewart, J.Q., 1947, Empirical mathematical rules governing the distribution and equilibrium of population, Geographical Review.
Wardrop, J.G., 1969, Minimum cost paths in urban areas, Strassenbau- und Strassenverkehrstechnik.
Williams, H.C.W.L. and J.D. Ortuzar Salas, 1976, Some generalizations and applications of the velocity field concept, Transportation Research.
Wilson, A.G., 1967, A statistical theory of spatial distribution models, Transportation Research.
Wilson, A.G., 1970, Entropy in urban and regional modelling.

*Note added in proof:* Curls and cross products are treated as scalars. As the vectors only contain one non-zero component and all point in normal direction out from the plane, this abuse should cause no confusion.

Regional Science and Urban Economics 11 (1981) 317–333. North-Holland

# CATASTROPHIC STRUCTURAL CHANGE IN A CONTINUOUS REGIONAL MODEL

Tönu PUU

*Umeå University, S-90187 Umeå, Sweden*

This paper discusses a continuously dispersed production economy in two-dimensional space where one kind of output is produced by four primary inputs. Land is used as space and as a source of raw materials, which by the application of labour, capital equipment and energy are converted into the finished product. Land, capital and labour are available within the region, whereas energy is imported. Trade between locations is represented by continuous flows that follow routes minimizing transportation costs and are related to the local excess supplies and excess demands. The location pattern resulting from structural stability is studied. Afterwards umbilic catastrophes resulting from changes of, e.g., energy prices are discussed in detail.

## 1. Introduction

Assume we deal with the following planning problem. At every location of a bounded geographical area a simple Cobb–Douglas technology is applicable for the production of a homogeneous good. Production opportunities are equal everywhere. The single produced commodity is used for consumption and we are given a utility function according to which we can value the availability of consumers' goods at a given location. Total utility is additive so that we can integrate over locations to obtain an objective function.

The inputs used are capital, labour, land and energy. Capital and labour are assumed to be available in aggregates of given sizes and are assumed to be divided optimally between locations. Land is, of course, immobile and is available in a given quantity at all locations. If we assume that all quantities are measured per unit area the availability of land is unitary everywhere, provided that all land is developable. Energy is imported and the imports must be financed by exports of finished goods at the expense of domestic consumption. This production technology of equal opportunities may represent a case where an almost freely available raw material, such as a low-grade mineral or a common biological substance, is processed by applying energy, machinery and human labour and using land as space and a source of the raw material. Neither the substitution admitted by a Cobb–Douglas

0166–0462/81/0000–0000/$02.50 

function, nor the linear homogeneity, are too unrealistic in this simplified model.

All the inputs are also required for the production of transportation services, but here it seems more realistic to assume a Leontief technology of fixed coefficients. Imported energy must be transported within the region to the places of employment and the finished goods must be moved from local excess supply sources to local excess demand sinks, the latter including sections of the boundary where exported goods are delivered. For transportation we assume a continuous model where a scalar point function at every location specifies a set of input coefficients for moving a quantum of goods or fuel an infinitesimal distance unit (in any direction).

Along with the continuous transportation model a model of continuous flow of goods and energy is assumed. This means that the whole region is filled by sets of flow lines with smoothly changing direction and that at any location we can specify flow densities that also change in space smoothly. Flow densities change by accumulation or withdrawal from local excess supplies or demands. Naturally, local input uses, production and consumption too become smooth functions of the space coordinates. This, of course, is the continuous flow model introduced by Beckmann in the 50s.

## 2. The model

The objective function is

$$\iint_S u(q', x, y)\,\mathrm{d}x\,\mathrm{d}y, \tag{1}$$

where $x, y$ are location coordinates, $S$ denotes the region and $q'$ denotes local consumption of goods. The objective function is to be maximized subject to certain constraints that we are now going to formulate.

Production of goods, $q$, depends at every location on the use of capital services, $k$, labour services, $l$, land services, $m$, and fuel or energy consumed, $n$. These variables are interpreted as spatial densities per unit land area. The Cobb–Douglas technology prescribes that

$$q = k^{\alpha} l^{\beta} m^{\gamma} n^{\delta}, \tag{2}$$

where

$$\alpha + \beta + \gamma + \delta = 1. \tag{3}$$

Let $\phi$ and $\psi$ denote the flows of goods and energy or fuel respectively. Mathematically these are vector fields with direction and magnitude attached at all locations of the region. The directions are the directions taken by the flows at a given location and the magnitudes, or the Euclidean norms $|\phi|$ and $|\psi|$, are the flow volumes or intensities.

We can easily define unit quanta of fuel and goods such that they use up equal quantities of inputs when flow volumes are equal. Thus input requirements for transportation at any location are proportionate to the local sum $(|\phi|+|\psi|)$ of flow volumes. This is reasonable if we assume that the same transportation system is used for both flows. The fixed input coefficients for capital, labour, land and fuel are denoted $\kappa, \lambda, \mu, v$ respectively and we obtain the local uses of inputs for transportation by multiplying these coefficients by the sum of flow volumes. The input coefficients themselves vary with location as reflecting the local transportation facilities.

These preliminaries enable us to write down two constraints. If we denote the aggregates of capital and labour available by $K$ and $L$ respectively then we have

$$K=\iint_S (k+\kappa(|\phi|+|\psi|))\,\mathrm{d}x\,\mathrm{d}y, \tag{4}$$

$$L=\iint_S (l+\lambda(|\phi|+|\psi|))\,\mathrm{d}x\,\mathrm{d}y. \tag{5}$$

These constraints only tell that what is available of capital and labour in aggregate is divided between locations and at every location between production of goods and transportation services.

As for land we cannot move the aggregate around and hence have a local constraint that must hold everywhere:

$$1=m+\mu(|\phi|+|\psi|). \tag{6}$$

We next recall that according to Gauss's divergence theorem the divergence of a vector field at a point equals source density there, or, if negative, sink density. This makes it possible to relate the flows to the excess supplies and demands. As excess supply of goods is $(q-q')$, we have

$$\operatorname{div}\phi=(q-q'). \tag{7}$$

As moreover there are no local supplies of energy but everything is imported we only have excess demand of fuel:

$$\operatorname{div}\psi=-n-v(|\phi|+|\psi|). \tag{8}$$

The final constraint emerges from the fact that energy imports must be paid by exports of goods. Let $\phi_n$ and $\psi_n$ denote the outward normal components of the two flows across the boundary $\partial S$. If the normal components are inward then the sense is negative. Let us further by $p$ denote the price of the product and by $h$ denote the price of fuel. Both are defined on the boundary as determined by supply and demand in the surrounding space. We assume that this surrounding space, or world market, is vast enough to absorb any goods supply from the bounded region or furnish any fuel demand that may be considered without affecting the prices. The two prices are only defined on the boundary but there are no problems of extending the definition to the whole region provided we adhere to the boundary values.

The trade balance constraint reads

$$\int_{\partial S} (p\phi_n + h\psi_n)\,\mathrm{d}s = 0. \tag{9}$$

Assuming that the definitions of the price functions have been extended to the whole region we study the value flows, $p\phi$ and $h\psi$. These are the physical flow vector fields multiplied by the local scalar price fields. Due to Gauss' divergence theorem the path integral of the outward component of a vector field equals the surface integral of the divergence of this field on the region bounded by the closed path. Hence, from (9),

$$\iint_S (\operatorname{div}(p\phi) + \operatorname{div}(h\psi))\,\mathrm{d}x\,\mathrm{d}y = 0. \tag{10}$$

Next, by a well known identity in vector analysis, the integrand of (10) can be expanded so that the equation reads

$$\iint_S \{\operatorname{grad} p \cdot \phi + \operatorname{grad} h \cdot \psi + p \operatorname{div} \phi + h \operatorname{div} \psi\}\,\mathrm{d}x\,\mathrm{d}y = 0. \tag{11}$$

The optimization problem is now stated: To optimize aggregate utility according to (1), subject to the constraints of applicable technology, (2), availability of capital, (4), labour, (5), and land (6), the relations of goods and fuel flows to local excess supplies and demands, (7)–(8), and the trade balance relation, (11). We maximize with respect to consumption, $q'$, production, $q$, inputs used in production, $k$, $l$, $m$, and $n$, and the flows, $\phi$ and $\psi$. Before stating the optimality conditions we observe that we can substitute from (2), (7), and (8) into (11). Accordingly the Lagrangean multipliers of (2) and (7) must equal $p$ and the Lagrangean multiplier of (8) must equal $h$, provided we can put the Lagrangean multiplier equal to unity for (11). This we can do as another, non-zero, multiplier would only change all prices by a constant factor leaving all relative prices unchanged, as well as all the constraints and optimality conditions.

## 3. Optimality

After these preliminary observations we can state the remaining optimality conditions. They are

$$\partial u/\partial q' = p, \tag{12}$$

$$rk/\alpha = wl/\beta = gm/\gamma = hn/\delta = pk^{\alpha}l^{\beta}m^{\gamma}n^{\delta}, \tag{13}$$

$$(r\kappa + w\lambda + g\mu + hv)\phi/|\phi| = \text{grad}\, p, \tag{14}$$

$$(r\kappa + w\lambda + g\mu + hv)\psi/|\psi| = \text{grad}\, h. \tag{15}$$

They can be interpreted thus: Condition (12) states that marginal utility shall at every location equal opportunity cost for goods in the flow. Conditions (13) state that marginal value productivities for inputs used in production must everywhere equal local opportunity cost. For capital and labour we assumed a planning situation with costless 'relocations' of resources. As the constraints (4) and (5) thus are in integral form the corresponding Lagrangean multipliers, $r$ and $w$, rent and wages, must be constants in space. Land rent, g, is determined by the system, but as it is a Lagrangean multiplier for a constraint not in integral form, (6), it will become a function of the space coordinates. Conditions (14)–(15), finally, prescribe that the flows of goods and fuel are potential flows in the directions of the price gradients. In these directions the prices change with transportation cost as (14) and (15) imply

$$\mathrm{d}p/\mathrm{d}s = \text{grad}\, p \cdot \phi/|\phi| = (r\kappa + w\lambda + g\mu + hv), \tag{16}$$

$$\mathrm{d}h/\mathrm{d}s = \text{grad}\, h \cdot \psi/|\psi| = (r\kappa + w\lambda + g\mu + hv). \tag{17}$$

These conditions result from a planning problem, but they can be interpreted in the sense of equilibrium conditions for a competitive economy. Then (13) simply states that producers use so much of each input that profits are maximized, whereas (14)–(15) state that transporters ship goods and fuel in the directions of steepest price rise and that in these directions prices rise with transportation cost. The constancy in space of capital rent and wages means that in the long run capitalists and workers seek the place of employment of their resources where the reward is greatest. The only optimality condition that does not have any interpretation in terms of a competitive equilibrium is (12). It is in this connection interesting to note that the other optimality conditions are not affected by (12) and that a competitive equilibrium is hence Pareto-efficient. It is so, however, only in a local sense. Possibly several flow patterns may solve the marginal optimality conditions. As each of them results in a different consumption density function the value of the utility integral will be different for different solutions and only one pattern will be globally optimal. A competitive system hence ensures that a local optimum is attained, but not that the global optimum is.

We can now deduce some interesting conclusions about the local optima or equilibria. As we already noted the flow lines, i.e., the unit vector fields $\phi/|\phi|$ and $\psi/|\psi|$, are gradient fields to the potentials $p$ and $h$. Geometrically this means that the flow lines are orthogonal to the iso curves for the prices of goods and fuel.

From (13) and (2) we can derive two relations:

$$pq = rk + wl + gm + hn, \tag{18}$$

$$\alpha^{\alpha}\beta^{\beta}\gamma^{\gamma}\delta^{\delta}p = r^{\alpha}w^{\beta}g^{\gamma}h^{\delta}. \tag{19}$$

The first states the fact that with a linearly homogeneous production function revenues are exhausted in factor shares, whereas the second links the five prices of the model together. As we have seen two of the prices are to be regarded as constants in space and so (19) stipulates a functional relationship to hold between product price, $p$, land rent, $g$, and fuel price, $h$. Hence, eqs. (14)–(15) yield in view of (19) a pair of partial differential equations for product and fuel prices. For suitable boundary constraints we get a well defined boundary value problem and solving it a pair of product and fuel price functions of locations. Then (19) residually determines land rent. Along with the price potentials we get the flow lines.

In the next stage we note that, knowing the unit vector fields, the divergences in (7) and (8) depend only on flow intensities $|\phi|$ and $|\psi|$ and their partial derivatives. So, we get a new pair of differential equations in flow intensities which must be solved so that the trade balance constraints are fulfilled. The actual solution procedure for a certain case may naturally become computationally complicated, even if conceptually it is not.

Let us finally multiply (14) and (15) by $\phi$ and $\psi$ respectively to obtain

$$\operatorname{grad} p \cdot \phi = (r\kappa + w\lambda + g\mu + h\nu)|\phi|, \tag{20}$$

$$\operatorname{grad} h \cdot \psi = (r\kappa + w\lambda + g\mu + h\nu)|\psi|. \tag{21}$$

Substituting from (4), (5), (6), (7), (8), (18), (20) and (21) into (11) we arrive at the simple expression

$$\iint_S pq' \,\mathrm{d}x\,\mathrm{d}y = rK + wL + \iint_S g \,\mathrm{d}x\,\mathrm{d}y, \tag{22}$$

stating that the aggregate value of consumption evaluated at local prices equals the aggregate income sum for capitalists, workers, and landlords. Hence, in aggregate, budget constraints for the consumers of the region are fulfilled. Even if they are not fulfilled locally for the global optimum there hence exists an internal regional income transfer policy, compatible with a competitive economy and consumer's autonomy, that makes the equilibrium a global optimum.

## 4. Regional structure

The basic element of regional structure in the model presented is characterized by the system of flow lines and its orthogonal trajectories, the constant price lines. Alternatively, we can say that the same information is contained in the price potentials. We now pose the following question: Which structures in the meaning specified above are we likely to find?

As long as we deal with qualitative characteristics of the flows only we can in fact give some answers to the questions by considerations of transversality and of structural stability.

As there occur constant changes in the structure of a real economic system we can reasonably argue that only those structures that are stable to perturbations, i.e., that are only smoothly deformed but keep an easily recognizable qualitative structure, are interesting to us. Structures that are not, will vanish the moment after they have arisen. In the model considered a sufficient element of constant change can be introduced by considering the present strong changes in energy price structures.

The flow lines obtained by solving the differential eqs. (14)–(15) in phase space consist of regular points and singular points. At a regular point the flow-box theorem states that we by a smooth coordinate change can represent the flow by parallel straight lines in some neighbourhood. The case occurs whenever there passes only one solution curve through each point.

In contrast, at singular points several solution curves are incident. For linear differential equations with constant coefficients the singular points are nodes (proper and improper), saddles, and spirals (including certres) as taught in any text-book on differential equations. For more complicated systems additional types of singularities can occur, like monkey saddles, and unlike the linear case with constant coefficients the singularities need not be isolated, but can accumulate along curves or even on areas.

An important result from the generic theory of differential equations, however, states that structural stability implies that the singularities are of the simple types associated with the simple linear systems, i.e., nodes, saddles, and spirals. As the flow lines are gradients to a potential, spirals are ruled out and we are left with only nodes (stable and unstable) and simple saddles.

Geometrically the three cases are: the source from which all flow lines in a neighbourhood issue, the sink to which all lines in a neighbourhood assemble, and the simple saddle where two pairs of ingoing and outgoing trajectories separate four sectors with flow lines looking like hyperbolas. These singularities are called hyperbolic.

The generic theory also has a global result: In structurally stable flows no trajectory joins saddle points.

These two conclusions: that in a structurally stable flow all points, except a finite number of isolated hyperbolic singularities, are regular, and that no trajectory joins saddle points, makes it possible to put together a picture of the basic stable flow type. If we assume that all trajectories incident to a saddle point are incident to different nodes then we can arrange the whole set of singularities as a square lattice, where each saddle is surrounded by four nodes and each node by four saddles. In the basic graph we only need to indicate the trajectories incident to saddle points. This makes it possible to arrange the square grid. It is easy to fill in the graph with a whole set of trajectories. It should be understood that all deformations to topologically equivalent shapes of this basic grid are structurally stable as well. The basic graph is shown in fig. 1.

We have actually covered all possibilities, except that a pair of trajectories from a saddle may in fact be incident to the same node. Observe that only one pair of trajectories can be joined in this way, as the second one would have to cross the first circuit when the graph is arranged in the plane. This joining of a pair of outgoing or ingoing trajectories sets up a boundary of an isolated trade area, as no trajectory will cross this circuit. The constellation is illustrated in fig. 2.

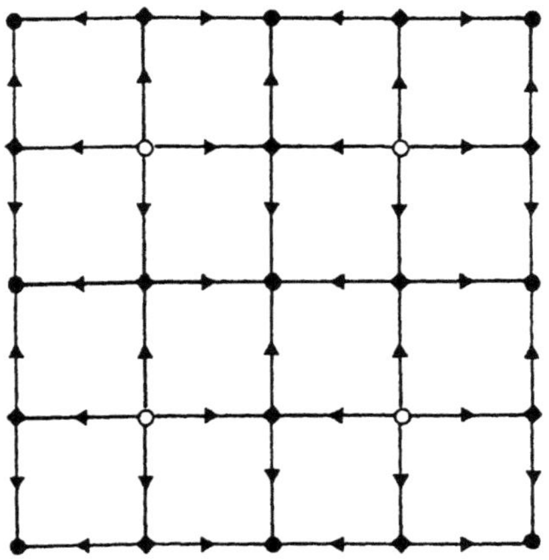

Fig. 1

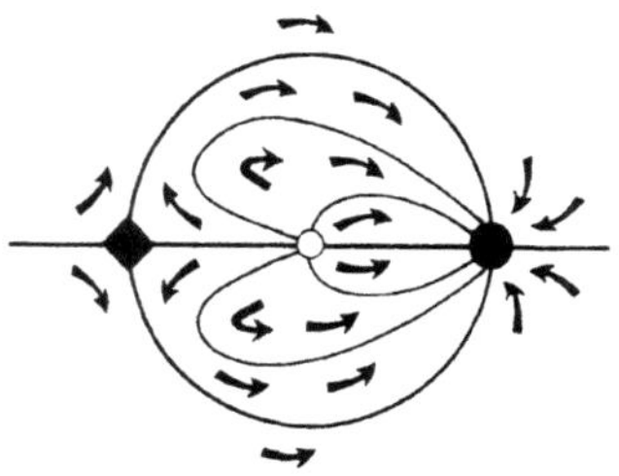

Fig. 2

Such arrangements may be inserted at any saddle-node connection in the basic graph. If we consider all possibilities of doing this, including the fact that such circuits may be nested inside each other, we cover all possibilities for structurally stable flows.

## 5. Catastrophic changes of structure

The above considerations concern which structures we are likely to find as persistent over time. The use of the concept of structural stability has been like the use of asymptotic stability of equilibria in economic theory: Stability guarantees that a disturbance of only limited duration will leave no trace of it provided the system has had sufficient time to readjust. If the equilibrium is unstable, it will never be reached again after it was disturbed. So, stability is a guarantee that equilibrium analysis is at all interesting.

The case is similar with structural stability. However, there is a particular interest in studying structurally unstable flows because when a system evolves in time it may pass a moment of unstable structure. The unstable structure itself is not interesting, as it only lasts a moment, but the fact that after this moment the system is completely different from what it was is of greatest importance. And catastrophe theory provides an instrument to analyze such sudden changes of structure.

The catastrophes involved concern flow structures and must hence have two state variables, corresponding to the two-dimensional structure of geographical space. Hence, the simplest types of catastrophes in Thom's classification are the hyperbolic and elliptic umbilics, both involving three parameters. We hence know that if there are at most three parameters in the system then all structural changes that can occur are topologically equivalent to the canonical types

$$x^3 - 3xy^2 + a(x^2 + y^2) + bx + cy, \tag{23}$$

and

$$x^3+y^3+axy+bx+cy. \tag{24}$$

To get some information about what can actually occur we can study the first one of these formulas, the elliptic umblic, at its most degenerate point, i.e., where $a=b=c=0$. The flow obtained as a gradient to the potential $\lambda = x^3 - xy^2$ is of course a monkey saddle flow. It is illustrated in fig. 3.

Let us now disturb the pattern by varying the parameter $b$ through zero value from negative to positive. As we see in figs. 4 and 5 the pattern changes completely. The trajectories take different routes and the saddle points are suddenly thrown from the positions east and west to positions north and south, after a moment of coincidence in the monkey saddle.

As in both figs. 4 and 5 there are trajectories joining the saddle points we can expect that the case is still not stable. We can try this out by introducing a change of the parameter $c$ as well by letting it take on a non-zero value.

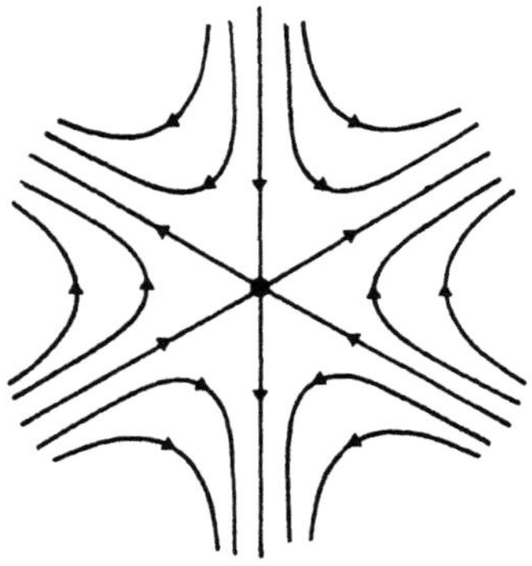

Fig. 3

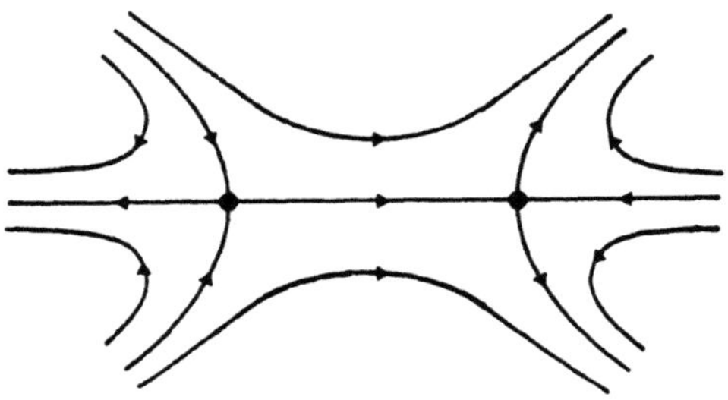

Fig. 4

What happens then is illustrated in fig. 6 where the saddle connection is broken and the isolated trade areas in north and south in fig. 4 are merged. The same happens if we disturb figs. 5, i.e., east–west trade emerges.

The illustrations cover only a small selection of the phenomena that can occur in connection with the elliptic umblic. Some more illustrations follow

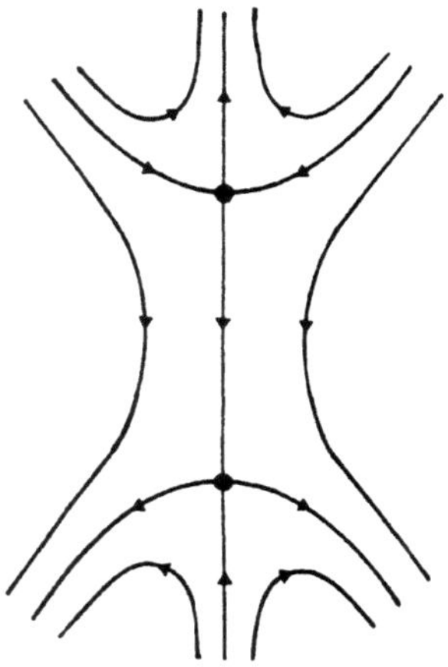

Fig. 5

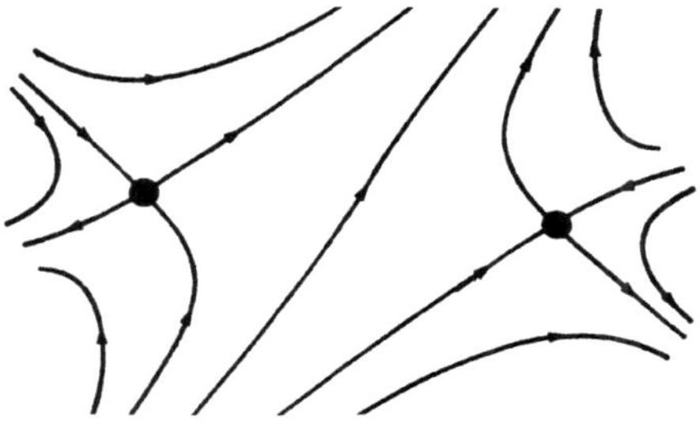

Fig. 6

in figs. 7 and 8 where we assume the parameters $b$ and $c$ to be kept constant at zero and let $a$ pass through zero from negative values to positive. The changes are even more dramatic as four singular points, three saddles and one node, fuse to the monkey saddle and then split in four again, each saddle point jumping to a position opposite to its original. We have now seen the effects of changing the linear terms and of the quadratic term, each separately. The cases can naturally be mixed.

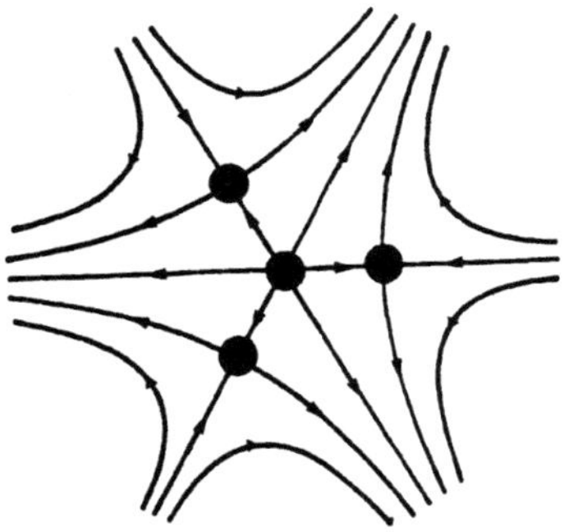

Fig. 7

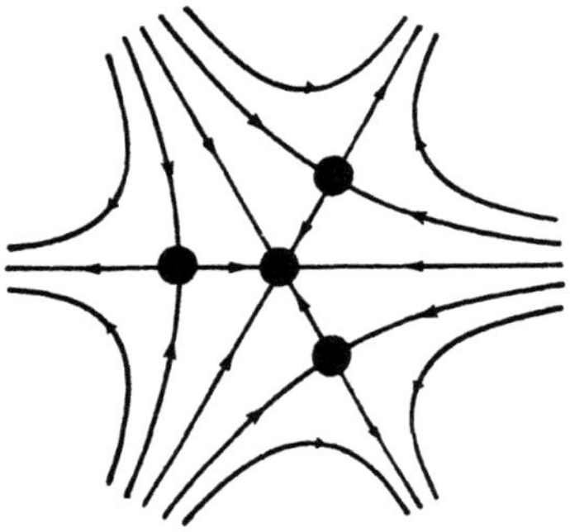

Fig. 8

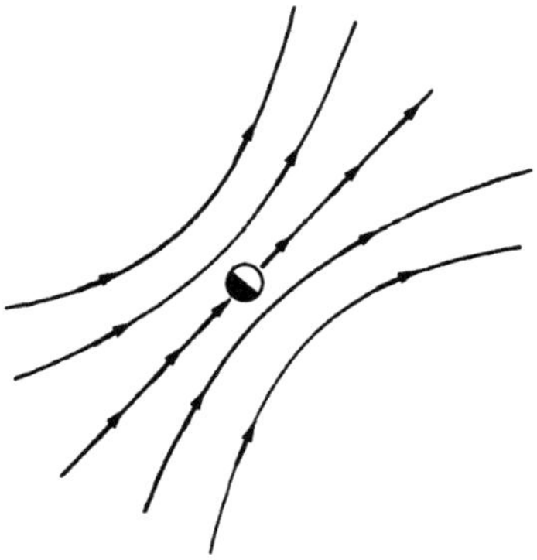

Fig. 9

Let us next study the hyperbolic umbilic. Starting with the most degenerate point again, when $\lambda = x^3 + y^3$, we see that the flow in fig. 9 at first sight resembles a flow with only regular points. There is, however, an exception: a point where the flow simply stagnates. There is a trajectory going into the node and one leaving it, whereas all other trajectories in a neighbourhood miss the point. It hence has the character of a saddle. But it is a very odd sort of saddle with only two sectors, instead of four.

If we disturb the flow by letting the parameter $a$ take on a non-zero value then the singular point splits into one node and one saddle, as shown in fig. 10. For small perturbances this pattern is stable, but if we suppose that the

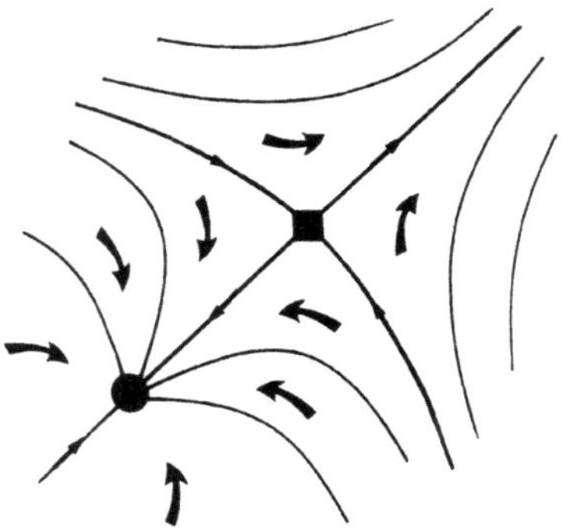

Fig. 10

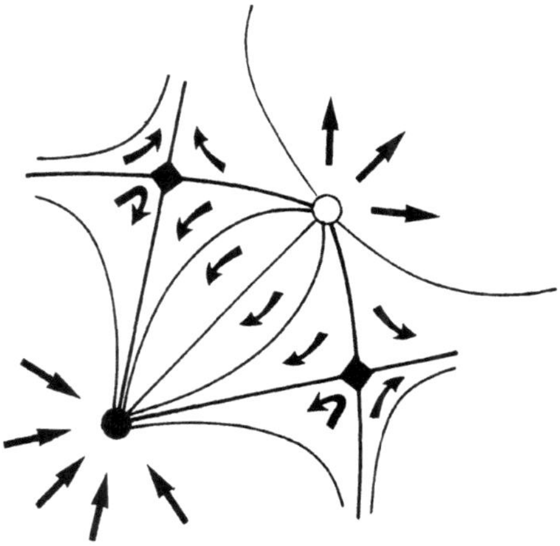

Fig. 11

parameters pass through a wider range of values still more phenomena can occur.

Suppose we have the potential $\lambda = x^3 + y^3 + 3xy - 2.25x - 2.25y$. Then the gradient flow looks like that in fig. 10. However, disturbing the flow then results in a doubling of the number of singular points as we show in fig. 11. There emerge two saddles, one source and one sink. In other ranges of parameter values the critical points can disappear altogether, so that the flow only comprises regular points where only one direction is defined everywhere.

The two cases illustrated, the elliptic and hyperbolic umbilic exhaust, up to topological equivalence, all the catastrophic phenomena that can occur with up to three changing parameters involved. The choice of three parameters is, of course, analytically convenient. With four parameters we end up with the parabolic umblic and beyond that are the limits of analysis. But the choice is not completely arbitrary. We have actually a great number of parameters in the model, but only those determining the local shipment cost influence the flow pattern. Now, the shipment cost depends on the technical fixed coefficients and on the input prices.

There are two prices in the system the values of which are determined by the world market prices on the boundary: the price of finished goods and the price of energy. The price of finished goods does not enter in the determination of transportation cost directly, but indirectly it does by influencing land rent. So, there are two changing input prices. In addition it is reasonable to assume some change of transportation technology. If we assume that technical innovations in transportation mainly increase efficiency in the use of inputs then it seems, in view of our assumption of a fixed coefficient technology, reasonable to let the input coefficients change in proportion. This adds one parameter. Observe that we need not bother about technical change in production of commodities, as such changes do not influence transportation cost. The consequence of this, like the consequence of other changes in the model, is only a change of flow intensity — not of flow direction.

This argument leaves us with exactly three strategic parameters and so the elliptic and hyperbolic umbilic exhaust all the phenomena with which we need be concerned. We therefore summarize the information in figs. 12 and 13. The elliptic umbilic is displayed in fig. 12. On the top of the figure we have drawn the familiar bifurcation set. It is, of course, displayed in the three-dimensional $a, b, c$-space. As the point representing the combination of parameter values in this space crosses the surfaces there occur changes of structure. In the small circle i.. the middle we show the flow pattern in $x, y$-space when the parameter combination corresponds to point $P$. It is the monkey saddle case and so the point $P$ corresponds to zero value of all parameters. Moving from that point to the right or left leads to a split into four critical points, whereas moving up or down in parameter space leads to a split in two critical points. According to our discussion above we suppose that the $a$-axis extends through the middle of the cuspoid cross-sections and that the $b$- and $c$-axes are in a plane orthogonal to this direction.

We observe that the flow patterns with two or four critical points are of a locally generic type. With finite changes transitions between the two- and the

Fig. 12

four-point cases can occur as the parameter combination crosses the surface. We can also note that no saddle connections are displayed. The saddle connections in fact occur on three planes through each of the three cusp lines. Every time the parameter combination passes one of these planes there occurs a transitory saddle connection.

The hyperbolic umbilic is illustrated in fig. 13. Again at the top we can see the bifurcation set. Instead of a surface that bounds an interior from an exterior as in the elliptic case we now deal with two intersecting surfaces.

There is one region above the surfaces, one below them and two between them to the right and left respectively. The difference in comparison to the preceding case is that below is now separated from above, not fused into one outside as before. Therefore the patterns are different qualitatively. In the

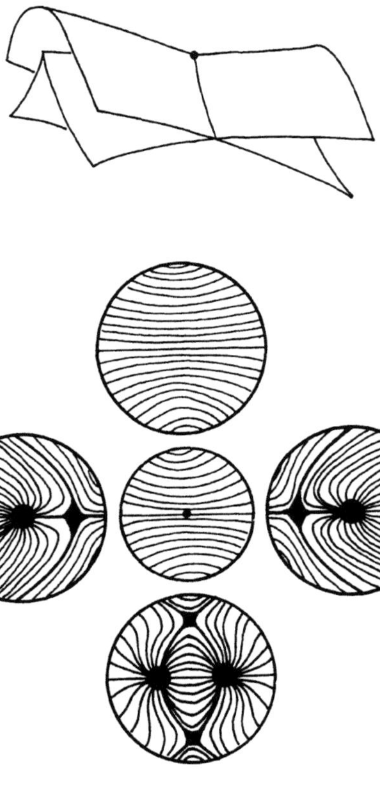

Fig. 13

central circle we show the pattern of one stagnation point in an otherwise laminar flow. This again corresponds to $P$, which is at the origin in parameter space. If we move down from $P$ in parameter space four critical points emerge, whereas if we move up the critical point disappears altogether. Moving left and right has the effect that two critical points emerge. Again, finite movements in parameter space can lead to transitions between the three cases of none, two and four critical points.

## References

The continuous model of transportation was introduced in:

Beckmann, M.J., 1952, A continuous model of transportation, Econometrica 20, 643–660.

A recent review of this is:

Beckmann, M.J. and T. Puu, 1980, Continuous flow modelling in regional science: State of the arts and new perspectives (IIASA RR, Laxenburg).

Concerning structural stability a good review is:

Peixoto, M.M., 1977, Generic properties of ordinary differential equations, in J. Hale, ed., Studies in ordinary differential equations, MAA Studies in Mathematics 14, 52–92.

A readable introduction to catastrophe theory is:

Poston, T. and I. Stewart, 1978, Catastrophe theory and its applications (Pitman, New York).

A previous use of the concept of structural stability in continuous regional flow modelling can be found in:

Puu, T., 1979, Regional modelling and structural stability, Environment and Planning A 11, 1431–1438.

Regional Science and Urban Economics 16 (1986) 81–95. North-Holland

# MULTIPLIER–ACCELERATOR MODELS REVISITED

Tönu PUU

*University of Umeå, S-901 87 Umeå, Sweden*

Received April 1985, final version received August 1985

This article discusses multiplier–accelerator models in continuous time as formulated once by Phillips. The model is placed in a continuous two-dimensional spatial setting and augmented by an interregional trade multiplier. It is seen that this produces complex patterns of change like a distributed lag system. Moreover, the action of the accelerator is made non-linear as suggested by Goodwin. This changes the system to produce limit cycles. The limit cycles may bifurcate due to parametric change. In the spatial setting it is seen that the space coordinates can cause bifurcation of the temporal limit cycle pattern.

## 1. Introduction

The objective of the present paper is to extend the multiplier–accelerator model of business cycles in two directions. *First*, it is placed in a continuous two-dimensional spatial setting with interregional trade generated by a linear propensity to import. *Second*, the idea of a floor and a ceiling, as suggested by Hicks (1950) to limit the action of the linear accelerator, is incorporated into the model in terms of a non-linear investment function. The way this is done much resembles that due to Goodwin (1951), except that in our case no mixed difference-differential equation results. The analysis is devoted to the simple Samuelson (1939)–Hicks (1950) model in its elegant continuous shape cast by Phillips (1954).

The conclusion from introducing non-linearity is the same as Goodwin's. Instead of explosion or extinction of motion as alternatives we get persistent bounded limit cycles. However, it is possible to replace Goodwin's general reasoning by results from singular perturbation theory developed by 1970 in applied mathematics. Moreover, recent developments in bifurcation and catastrophe theory make it possible to analyse bifurcations of limit cycles for only slightly more complicated investment functions than those used by Goodwin.

The introduction of space is shown to destroy the perfect periodicity of the original model, and to replace its simple harmonic motion by irregular time profiles. In the latter aspect space acts like a distributed lag system. In the first it does something distributed lags cannot do, i.e., compound cycles of non-rational period relations.

The combination of non-linearity with a spatial setting gives two main results. A general theorem on the impossibility of spatially homogeneous steady state solutions is proved. Further the model is completely solved for the case of a dispersive wave proceeding radially from the origin. It is shown that the spatial coordinate (radius vector) itself acts as a parameter causing bifurcation from an area where motion vanishes to one where limit cycles persist.

## 2. The original model

The multiplier–accelerator model was formulated by Samuelson (1939), and was later elaborated by Hicks (1950). Unlike the contemporary growth models the business cycle models were formulated as difference equations in discrete time. The choice between a discrete or continuous formulation is always one of convenience. For numerical computation or empirical study the discrete form is necessary. For analytical purposes a continuous representation of time (and space) is always superior. Therefore, the starting point will be a multiplier–accelerator model formulated by Phillips as an adaptive process in continuous time. A full account of this model can be found in Allen (1956).

The essential elements of the model are saving (or consumption) and 'induced' investments. We disregard the so called autonomous expenditures, as they only introduced a non-zero equilibrium income from which the solution of the autonomous model yields the deviations. As the particular and homogeneous solutions are additive this makes no harm, at least in the linear case, but saves unnecessary symbolism.

Savings are assumed to be a given proportion, $s$, of income, $Y$. Induced investments are proportionate to the rate of change of income, $\dot{Y}$, the proportionality factor (the accelerator) being denoted $v$. Obviously, $v$ is the fixed input coefficient of capital in a Leontief type of production function where labour is affluent and capital is always the limiting factor. Equating savings to investments, $sY=v\dot{Y}$, yields the Harrod model of balanced growth. Corresponding to the adjustment delay in the Samuelson discrete model the continuous model has adaptive adjustment, so that the rate of change of income, $\dot{Y}\propto(I-sY)$, the difference between current investment and savings, and so that the rate of change of investments, $\dot{I}\propto(v\dot{Y}-I)$, the difference between 'optimal' investments in view of income change and actual investments. The model becomes particularly simple if we, as do Samuleson and Hicks with the lagged delays, assume that the proportionality constants in these adjustment processes are equal and can be made unitary by a suitable choice of time unit. So, $\dot{Y}=(I-sY)$ and $\dot{I}=(v\dot{Y}-I)$, from which $I$ and $\dot{I}$ can be eliminated by differentiating the first equation once more with respect to time and then using the original pair of equations for the elimination. Accordingly,

$$\ddot{Y}+(1+s-v)\dot{Y}+sY=0 \tag{1}$$

is obtained. Its solutions are like those of the original Samuelson–Hicks model formulated for discrete time, i.e., they are those of a simple damped or antidamped harmonic oscillator of one definite period.

## 3. Space and interregional trade

We now place the model in the setting of continuous two-dimensional space and introduce exports $X$ and imports $M$ along with the variables $Y$ and $I$. It seems logical to assume a linear export–import multiplier along with the linear multiplier for local consumption. Denoting the propensity to import by $m$, imports are proportional to local income and exports to income 'abroad'. Accordingly, $X-M$ in each location is equal to $m$ multiplied by income difference abroad and at home. Assuming only local action between spatially contiguous locations (a first approximation equivalent to the assumption that complicated lag structures are absent in time), we still have to formalize how spatial income differences should be measured.

As demonstrated by the author in Puu (1982) and in Beckmann and Puu (1985) by Gauss' integral theorem the proper measure of spatial income differences is the Laplacian of income $\nabla^2 Y=\partial^2 Y/\partial x^2+\partial^2 Y/\partial y^2$, where $x$ and $y$ are the euclidean coordinates of twospace. Thus $X-M=m\nabla^2 Y$, or in adaptive form $\dot{X}-\dot{M}\propto(m\nabla^2 Y-X+M)$. Again assuming that adjustment speed is the same as the two previous ones, we can replace the proportionality sign by an equality.

As export surplus enters the system in the same way as do induced investments, the relations become $\dot{Y}=(I+X-M-sY)$, $\dot{I}=(v\dot{Y}-I)$, and $\dot{X}-\dot{M}=(m\nabla^2 Y-X+M)$. We can again eliminate the variables $I$, $X$, and $M$ by differentiating the first equation once more and using the original system for the elimination. In this way we obtain

$$\ddot{Y}+(1+s-v)\dot{Y}+sY-m\nabla^2 Y=0. \tag{2}$$

As demonstrated in Puu (1982) the solution separates for $Y=T(t)\ S(x,y)$, so that

$$T''+(1+s-v)T'+(\lambda m+s)T=0 \quad \text{and} \tag{3}$$

$$\nabla^2 S+\lambda S=0. \tag{4}$$

Obviously (3) is of the same form as the original model (1), so that temporal change for each given $\lambda$ is that of a damped or antidamped simple harmonic oscillator. The damping coefficient $\alpha = -(1+s-v)/2$ is independent of $\lambda$. This is not true about the period $\omega = \sqrt{(\lambda m + s - \alpha^2)}$. We note that the motion is oscillatory whenever $4(\lambda m + s) > (1+s-v)^2$.

From the general theory of eigenvalues and eigenfunctions we, however, know that there exists an infinite spectrum of ascending positive eigenvalues $\lambda$ and corresponding eigenfunctions $S(x, y)$ for any well defined region of twospace with reasonable boundary conditions. Good references about this are Courant and Hilbert (1953, Vol. 1), or Duff and Naylor (1966).

Due to the superposition principle for linear systems the solution can be written in full generality as

$$Y = \sum_i \exp(\alpha t)\{A_i \cos(\omega_i t) + B_i \sin(\omega_i t)\} S_i(x, y), \tag{5}$$

where $S_i$ are the different eigenfunctions that solve the eigenvalue problem (4) and $\omega_i$ are the periods computed from the corresponding eigenvalues $\lambda_i$.

Examples of eigenfunctions can be found in Beckmann and Puu (1985) for the rectangular, circular, and spherical regions, i.e., sines, cosines, Bessel functions, and Legendre Polynomials. As all such eigenfunction systems can be chosen so that they form an orthonormal set, it is possible to evaluate the constants $A_i$ and $B_i$ from initial conditions by the integrals

$$A_i = \iint Y(0) S_i(x, y)\, \mathrm{d}x\, \mathrm{d}y, \tag{6}$$

$$B_i = \iint Y'(0) S_i(x, y)\, \mathrm{d}x\, \mathrm{d}y, \tag{7}$$

where it is understood that the integration is on all the region in twospace for which the analysis is formulated.

It should be noted that the conclusions are not limited to the exemplified simple types of regions, but hold independent of the shapes. Moreover, as the generalized Sturm–Liouville theory demonstrates, we could even make the propensity to import location-dependent so that we replace $m\nabla^2 Y$ in eq. (2) by the far more general expression $\nabla \cdot (m\nabla Y) = m\nabla^2 Y + \nabla m \cdot \nabla Y$. Even if we thus make the expenditure diffusion by trade dependent on location to account for varying transportation facilities, all the results can be retained.

From (6)–(7) we see that *any periodic change, however irregular its time profile is, can be produced by the spatial multiplier–accelerator model.*

Moreover, as there is no reason for the eigenvalues $\lambda_i$ and the corresponding periods $\omega_i$ to take on rational proportions only, we conclude that *the period of composite cyclical motion may be varying, so that there is no periodicity in a strict sense at all.*

Accordingly, the spatial extension of the simplest business cycle mechanism of all may produce temporal change of any realistic irregularity desired, and this is attained without introducing any distributed lag structure.

However, the model still has one major deficiency, as it produces change that either is bound to go to extinction and stationary quiescence, or tends to increase beyond any limit and blow the whole system up, depending on the sign of $\alpha$. The only escape is a zero $\alpha$ when the structural coefficients are in the relation $v-s=1$, which would be a very unlikely coincidence.

## 4. Non-linearity in the original model

This strange property of explosion or extinction is a characteristic of linearity. Linearity, however, in economics as in physics or any other science, can only be a first approximation. Such linearisation is only reasonable when the variables remain within certain bounds. If the model creates change of the variables beyond any limit, then the conditions for linearisation are always violated, and the model becomes self-destructive. This is the absurdity of linear economic models of economic growth or cyclical change. Linearity holds for marginal changes, but the models implicitly claim global relevance as they are used to explain long-run development.

In addition there are strong factual reasons for making the model non-linear, given by Sir John Hicks in his reasoning of a 'floor' to disinvestments when no capital is replaced and is depreciating at its natural rate, and a ceiling to investments when other inputs than capital become binding and their own rate of growth limits investments. Hicks (1950) introduced the constraints as linear inequalities, but the analytical treatment is easier if we incorporate the non-linearity into the investment function. The simplest function, having the properties of a non-linear accelerator with a floor and a ceiling is $v \tanh \dot{Y}$ as a replacement for $v\dot{Y}$. Around zero the function is almost linear in the argument, but for large negative or positive $\dot{Y}$ it goes asymptotically to $\pm 1$.

It should be noted that the numerical values of the asymptotes or the exact form of the function are not meant to have any significance at all. Nevertheless the choice is not one of arbitrary exemplification. With respect to the qualitative behaviour of the model the choice is generic, i.e., it is topologically equivalent to the behaviour of any S-shaped curve having upper and lower asymptotic bounds. In any case where calculations are involved we replace $\tanh \dot{Y}$ by its truncated Taylor series $(\dot{Y}-\frac{1}{3}\dot{Y}^3)$, which has the same qualitative properties as the function itself as regards the behavior of the model.

Let us start by incorporating the non-linearity in the original model, without any interregional trade, as it is formalized in (1). It then becomes

$$\ddot{Y}+(1+s)\dot{Y}-v\tanh\dot{Y}+sY=0. \tag{8}$$

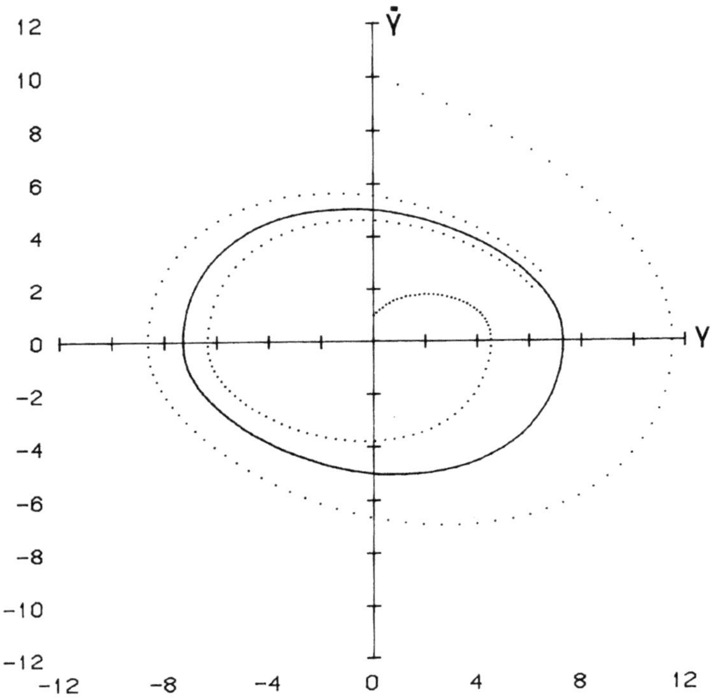


Fig. 1. Stable limit cycle.

The qualitative behaviour of this model can be inferred by sketching a phase diagram in $Y, \dot{Y}$-space. Obviously the system is damped for large $|Y|$ or $|\dot{Y}|$. In the case $v>(1+s)$, there is a neighbourhood of the origin in phase space where there is antidamping, whereas otherwise the damped zone extends to the whole plane. It is the first case that is more interesting. The combination of antidamping in the centre and damping in the periphery makes one suspect the existence of a limit cycle. Actually, numerical integration of (8), whose result is shown in fig. 1, clearly shows the limit cycle.

Another way to proceed is by using the truncated Taylor series written above. Then a change of time scale by the linear factor $\sqrt{s}$ puts the differential equation in the form

$$\ddot{Y}+Y=a\dot{Y}-b\dot{Y}^3, \tag{9}$$

where $a=\sqrt{s}(v-s-1)$ and $b=\sqrt{s}^3/3$ are positive constants. Eq. (9) is very close to Rayleigh's equation for a bowed string. See Jordan and Smith (1977) or Kevorkian and Cole (1981). It is related to the well-known van der Pol oscillator by a simple transformation, and it can be easily approximated by use of one of the singular perturbation methods. The substance of the method is that (9) is regarded as a perturbation of the linear equation $\ddot{Y}+Y=0$, which has a periodic solution of the given period $2\pi$ of arbitrary phase and amplitude. One then assumes that the non-linear equation (9) is periodic as well, so that there is a point in separating time in two variables, one fast time representing cyclic motion and one slow time representing any trend factor such as asymptotic approach to a limit cycle. Slow time is defined in relation to the coefficient of the disturbing first derivative in the right-hand side of (9) as $\tau=at$, and one attempts to find a solution of the form $Y=Y^0(\tau,t)+aY^1(\tau,t)+a^2Y^2(\tau,t)+\ldots$. Inserting this solution in (9), using the definition of slow time, and assembling terms of order 1, $a$, $a^2$ etc. gives a number of relations, the first of which are

$$\ddot{Y}^0+Y^0=0, \tag{10a}$$

$$\ddot{Y}^1+Y^1=-2Y^0_{t\tau}+aY^0_t-b(Y^0_t)^3, \tag{10b}$$

where the subscripts denote differentiation. The solution to (10a) has already been stated:

$$Y^0=A(\tau)\cos t+B(\tau)\sin t, \tag{11}$$

where the assumption that phase and amplitude depend on slow time has been incorporated in the dependence of $A$ and $B$.

To find out the exact form of the dependence of coefficients we proceed to the next equation, (10b), where the derivatives of (11) are inserted in the right-hand side. Accordingly,

$$\ddot{Y}^1+Y^1=\left(2A'+\frac{3}{4}\frac{b}{a}A(A+B)-A\right)\sin t+\left(2B'+\frac{3}{4}\frac{b}{a}B(A+B)-B\right)\cos t$$

$$-\frac{1}{4}\frac{b}{a}A(A^2-3B^2)\sin 3t-\frac{1}{4}\frac{b}{a}B(B^2-3A^2)\cos 3t,$$

where the primes denote differentiation and where we have used the usual formulas for the cubes of sines and cosines. Next we note that in the integration for $Y^1$ the $\sin t$ and $\cos t$ terms would give rise to terms of the type $t\cos t$, $t\sin t$ and hence make the series expansion non-uniform. So, we have to set the coefficients of these terms equal to zero. This results in two differential equations for $A$ and $B$, which seem to be coupled but split if we transform into polar coordinates $A=\rho\cos\phi$ and $B=\rho\sin\phi$. Then,

$$\rho'+\frac{3b}{8a}\rho^3-\tfrac{1}{2}\rho=0 \quad \text{and} \quad \phi'=0.$$

The second equation yields a constant phase angle, whereas the first one may be easily integrated, as it is of the Bernouilli type. So finally

$$Y^0 = c(1-(1-c^2/c_0^2)\exp(-at))^{-1/2}\cos(t-\phi), \tag{12}$$

where $c=\sqrt{(4a/3b)}$ is the amplitude of the limit cycle and $c_0$ is any initial value. It is seen that there is a uniform approach to the limit cycle $Y^0 = c\cos(t-\phi)$ in this first approximation. The process can be continued by deriving more terms in the power series. The calculations, however, become more and more involved, and the first approximation shows us sufficiently much of the qualitative character of the solution. It need hardly be said that there is good agreement with the result of numerical solution.

## 5. Bifurcations

We can see by inserting the definitions of $a$ and $b$ that $c=2\sqrt{((v-s-1)/s)}$. Accordingly, the amplitude of the limit cycle increases with $v$ and decreases with $s$. The dependence is continuous in character until the critical relation $v=s+1$ is fulfilled. For higher $s$ or lower $v$ the limit cycle no longer exists. The system is globally damped, as was seen above. This phenomenon is an example of a bifurcation.

More interesting examples may be obtained with a more complicated investment function, such as for instance $\tanh^3 \dot{Y}$. This may be approximated by $\dot{Y}^3 - \dot{Y}^5$. Such an investment function results in the following phenomena. Around the origin there is damping until an unstable limit cycle is reached. Outside this there is a zone with antidamping, while there is damping again outside an outer stable limit cycle. This is shown in fig. 2.

For the approximation $\dot{Y}^3 - \dot{Y}^5$ we deal with the equation $\ddot{Y} + sY = v(\dot{Y}^3 - \dot{Y}^5) - (1+s)\dot{Y}$, which after a linear change of time scale with the factor $\sqrt{s}$ takes the form

$$\ddot{Y} + Y = -(\sqrt{s} + 1/\sqrt{s})\dot{Y} + v\sqrt{s}\dot{Y}^3 - v\sqrt{s^3}\dot{Y}^5. \tag{13}$$

Using the same singular perturbation method as in the previous case, we obtain the first approximation

$$Y^0 = A(\tau)\cos t + B(\tau)\sin t. \tag{14}$$

In order that no secular terms of the type $t$ cos or $t\sin t$ should turn up in the solution of the next approximation $Y^1$ we again get a constraint on $A$ and $B$ in terms of a pair of differential equations. By introducing polar coordinates as before we arrive at the system

$$\rho' + \tfrac{5}{16}v\sqrt{s^3}\rho^5 - \tfrac{3}{8}v\sqrt{s}\rho^3 + \tfrac{1}{2}(\sqrt{s} + 1/\sqrt{s})\rho = 0 \quad \text{and} \quad \phi' = 0,$$

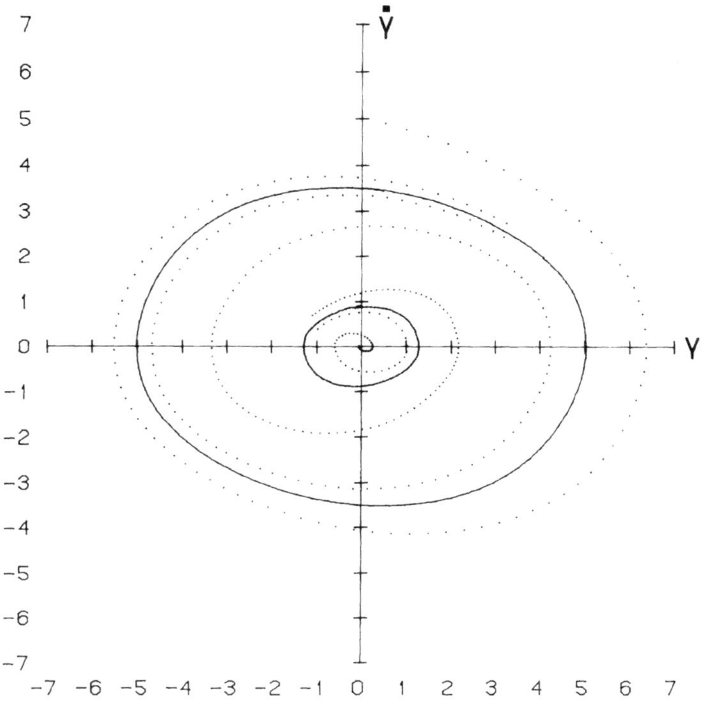


Fig. 2. Stable and unstable limit cycles.

equivalent to the pair of equations above. The second one again yields a constant phase angle, but the first is not as readily integrated as before. Therefore, let us introduce the change of variable $z = s\rho^2$, so that

$$\sqrt{s}z' = -(1+s)z + 3/4vz^2 - 5/8vz^3. \tag{15}$$

By interchanging dependent and independent variables this can be written

$$-(\sqrt{s}+1/\sqrt{s})\mathrm{d}\tau = \mathrm{d}z \Bigg/ \left( z - \frac{3}{4}\frac{v}{1+s}z^2 + \frac{5}{8}\frac{v}{1+s}z^3 \right)$$

$$= \left( \frac{1}{z} + \frac{\gamma}{\alpha - z} + \frac{\delta}{\beta - z} \right) \mathrm{d}z. \tag{16}$$

This last splitting in partial fractions works provided we choose

$$\alpha, \beta = 3/5(1 \pm \surd(1 - 40/9(1+s)/v)) \quad \text{and}$$

$$\gamma, \delta = 1/2(1 \pm 1/\surd(1 - 40/9(1+s)/v)).$$

With this choice the differential equation can be integrated to

$$k \exp(-(\surd s + 1/\surd s)\tau) = \lambda = z(\alpha - z)^{\gamma}(\beta - z)^{\delta}.$$

As an example let us choose $v = 5(1+s)$. Then $\alpha = 0.8$, $\beta = 0.4$, $\gamma = 2$, and $\delta = -1$. Accordingly

$$\lambda = \frac{z(0.8 - z)^2}{(0.4 - z)},$$

with $\lambda = k \exp(-4\tau)$ if we choose $(1+s) = 4\surd s$, i.e., $s = 0.07$. Inverting the preceding equation means solving a third degree equation

$$z^3 - 8/5 z^2 + ((4/5)^2 + \lambda)z - 2/5\lambda = 0.$$

Defining $Q = -(4/15)^2 + \lambda/3$ and $R = -(4/15)^3 - \lambda/15$ we obtain the discriminant

$$D = Q^3 + R^2 = \tfrac{3}{2}(\tfrac{4}{15})^4 \lambda - \tfrac{13}{48}(\tfrac{4}{15})^2 \lambda^2 + \tfrac{1}{27}\lambda^3.$$

Factoring $\lambda$ out leaves a positive definite quadratic form. Accordingly, the discriminant is positive or negative depending on the sign of $\lambda$. With the discriminant positive there is only one real root given by

$$z = \tfrac{8}{15} + \sqrt[3]{(R + \surd D)} + \sqrt[3]{(R - \surd D)}.$$

With a negative $\lambda$ there are three real roots, one of which is necessarily negative and hence of no interest. The positive roots then are

$$z = \tfrac{8}{15} + \surd -Q(\cos \tfrac{1}{3} \cos^{-1}(-R/\surd -Q^3) \pm \surd 3 \sin \tfrac{1}{3} \cos^{-1}(-R/\surd -Q^3)).$$

To find out the asymptotic behaviour we note that the limiting value of $\lambda$ is zero as $\tau$ increases without any bound. The limiting values are $Q = -(4/15)^2$, $R = -(4/15)^3$ and $D = 0$. Accordingly the limiting values of $z$ are 0 and 0.8.

Thus the origin and a limit cycle with amplitude 0.8 are the attractors of the system. The critical value $\beta = 0.4$ of $z$, on the other hand, represents an unstable limit cycle. There is no bifurcation in the case illustrated. However, we see from our considerations that for $9v = 40(1+s)$ we have $\alpha = \beta = 0.6$, so that the limit cycles fuse. Accordingly, the stable limit cycle of finite amplitude vanishes at this combination of structural coefficients.

Accordingly, provided the parameters $s$ and $v$ undergo continuous change so that such a coincidence of limit cycles occurs, then the system that has formerly been in motion along a limit cycle of finite amplitude suddenly collapses to stationary equilibrium.

## 6. Non-linearity in the spatial model

Let us now turn to a much tougher task, namely to introduce the non-linear investment function $v \tanh \dot{Y}$ into the spatial business cycle model (2). Little is known about non-linear partial differential equations, and what is known points at the possibilities of a wide variety of solutions some of which are manifestly strange. Anyhow, the differential equation we deal with is

$$\ddot{Y} + (1+s)\dot{Y} - v \tanh \dot{Y} + sY - m\nabla^2 Y = 0. \tag{17}$$

We can immediately see two possible solutions. One is to put $\nabla^2 Y \equiv 0$, so that the system becomes identical with (8) above. Accordingly, the limit cycle solution with income at all locations changing in phase is a possibility. Another solution is to put $\ddot{Y} = \dot{Y} = 0$ and require that the purely spatial equation $sY = m\nabla Y$ is fulfilled.

Accordingly, there seems to be a tradeoff between temporal change and spatial inhomogeneity. Suppose that we deal with a bounded region where $\dot{Y} = 0$ on the boundary. Then we multiply (17) by $\dot{Y}$, integrate over the whole region and use Gauss's integral theorem. So we obtain

$$\mathrm{d}/\mathrm{d}t \iint \dot{Y}^2 + sY^2 + m(\nabla Y)^2 \,\mathrm{d}x\,\mathrm{d}y = 2\iint v\dot{Y} \tanh \dot{Y} - (1+s)\dot{Y}^2 \,\mathrm{d}x\,\mathrm{d}y.$$

The left-hand side represents the temporal rate of change of the 'energy' of the system, as composed by temporal change and/or spatial inhomogeneity 'tension'.

The right-hand side is positive for small $|\dot{Y}|$ and negative for large $|\dot{Y}|$. Accordingly, the system gains energy when $\dot{Y}$ is predominantly small. Suppose that movement is close to extinction. Then the system must be gaining energy either in terms of increasing $|\dot{Y}|$ again, or in terms of spatially increasing tensional inhomogeneity. Movement can be frozen down in increased spatial inhomogeneity, but otherwise it can never die out, provided $v > (1+s)$. This condition is required for our reasoning about the right-hand side and it is equivalent to the condition for existence of a limit cycle in the model in section 4.

If we regard the terms involving $\dot{Y}$ as a perturbation we see that what remains is a two-dimensional variant of the linear Klein–Gordon equation. See Whitman (1974) or Nayfeh (1973). Its solution is known to produce dispersive waves. So, let us try a solution of the form $Y(\theta)$ with $\theta = k\sqrt{(x^2+y^2)} - \omega t$. Provided the dispersion relation $mk^2 - \omega^2 + s = 0$ is fulfilled the linear equation is solved. For definiteness and simplicity of calculation put $m = s = 0.5$. Accordingly, the dispersion relation allows a wave number $k = 1$ along with a period $\omega = 1$. Moreover, we put $v = 2$ and denote the spatial radius vector by $r = \sqrt{(x^2+y^2)}$. This transforms (17) into

$$Y'' + Y = 4\tanh Y' - (3 + 1/r)Y', \tag{18}$$

where $Y'$ and $Y''$ denote the derivatives of the assumed solution with respect to the argument $\theta = r - t$.

This equation is similar to (8), except for the spatial dependence on $r$, and may be dealt with by similar methods as were used for (8). Fig. 3 illustrates the limit cycles for various values of $r$. For radii less than unity the system is damped and there exist no limit cycles. For larger radii limit cycles with finite and increasing amplitude emerge, the outmost one corresponding to an

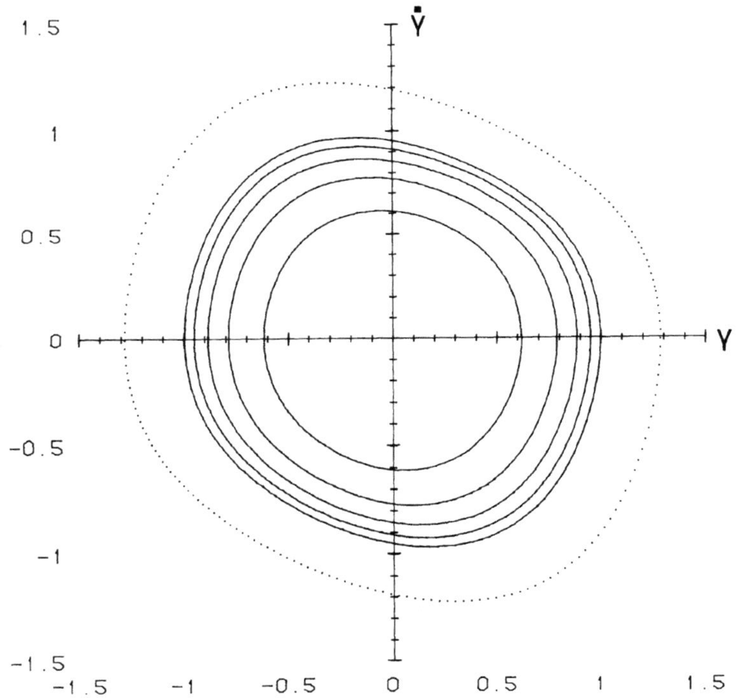


Fig. 3. Limit cycles at different distances from the origin of $x, y$ space, $r = 1.5$, 2, 2.5, 3, 3.5.

infinite radius. Although the amplitudes of the cycles increase with distance from the origin of $x, y$ space, the periods seem to be the same. This is confirmed by direct calculation according to a method used in Jordan and Smith (1977).

A first approximation to the linear left-hand side of (18) put equal to zero is a harmonic motion of period $2\pi$ and amplitude 1. So, $Y = \sin\theta$ is a solution. Next, we insert the solution in the right-hand side of (18) multiply by $Y'$, and integrate over a whole cycle to get the next approximation

$$T = 2\pi + 4\int_0^{2\pi} \tanh(\sin\theta)\cos\theta \, d\theta - (3 + 1/r)\int_0^{2\pi} \sin\theta\cos\theta \, d\theta.$$

But, the hyperbolic tangent being symmetric around zero and of the same sign as its argument, both integrals vanish. We see that not only is the period $T$ independent of $r$ up to next approximation, but the original period of the linear equation remains unchanged. This observation confirms the results of numerical solution.

Finally, we can approximate $\tanh Y'$ by $Y' - Y'^3/3$, so that (18) becomes

$$Y'' + Y = (1 - 1/r)Y' - \tfrac{4}{3}Y'^3. \tag{18a}$$

This equation may be treated with the same two-time method as was used for (9). The final solution for the first term in the series is

$$Y^0 = (1 - 1/r)((1 - (1 - 1/r)^2/c_0^2)\exp((1 - 1/r)(r - t)))^{-1/2}\cos(r - t).$$

This establishes the limit cycles of an amplitude that increases with $r$. The system obviously approaches a limit cycle provided that $r$ is at least unity, otherwise we see that the damping does not function. We also see that the approach to the limit cycle is very slow when $r$ is close to the critical unitary value.

The asymptotic solution to the first approximation is

$$Y^0 = (1 - 1/r)\cos(r - t).$$

For any given moment $t$ this gives a spatial pattern. It is illustrated by a computer diagram in fig. 4. It is interesting to note that in this case the spatial coordinate acts as a parameter that causes bifurcation in temporal behaviour. It must however be remembered that we have investigated only a few of the phenomena that the non-linear spatial model can produce.

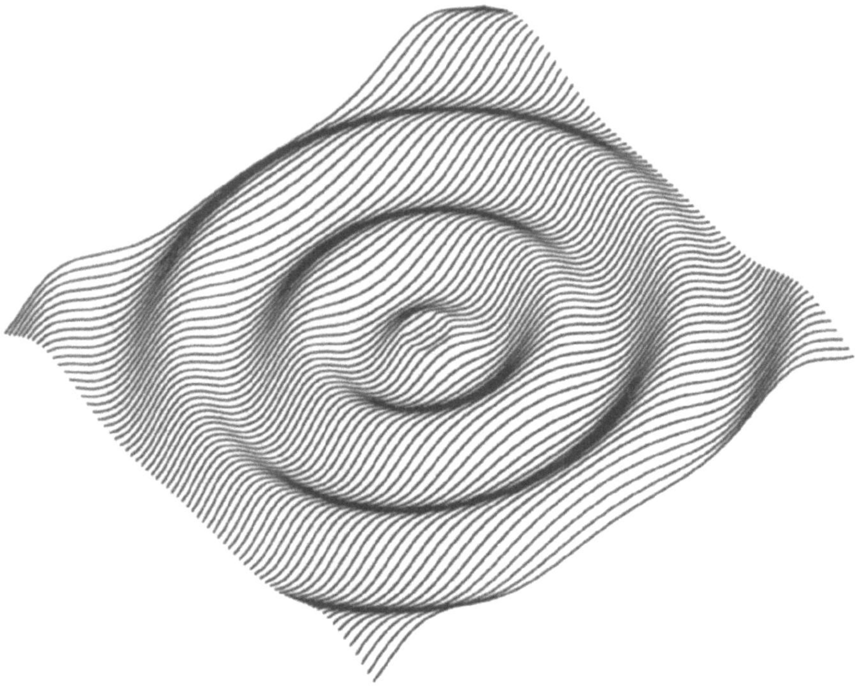

Fig. 4. Spatial pattern in the asymptotic solution.

## 7. Conclusion

We have demonstrated that two features of the original multiplier–accelerator model of the business cycle: the regularity of its solution and the tendency to explode or extinguish any dynamics in the system can be removed by putting the model in a spatial context and by making it non-linear.

## References

Allen, R.G.D., 1956, Mathematical economics (Macmillan, New York).
Beckman, M.J. and T. Puu, 1985, Spatial economics (North-Holland, Amsterdam).
Courant, R. and D. Hilbert, 1953, Methods of mathematical physics (Wiley-Interscience, New York).
Duff, G.F.D. and D. Naylor, 1966, Differential equations of applied mathematics (Wiley, New York).
Goodwin, R.M., 1951, The non-linear accelerator and the persistance of business cycles, Econometrica 19, 1–17.
Hicks, J.R. (1950), A contribution to the theory of the trade cycle (Oxford University Press, Oxford).

Jordan, D.W. and P. Smith, 1977, Non-linear ordinary differential equations (Clarendon Press, Oxford).

Kevorkian, J. and J.D. Cole, 1981, Perturbation methods in applied mathematics (Springer, New York).

Nayfeh, A.H., 1973, Perturbation methods (Wiley, New York).

Phillips, A.W., 1954, Stabilisation policy in a closed economy, Economic Journal 64, 290–323.

Puu, T., 1982, Outline of a trade cycle model in continuous space and time, Geographical Analysis 14, 1–9.

Samuelson, P.A., 1939, Interactions between the multiplier theory and the principle of acceleration, Review of Economic Statistics 21, 75–78.

Whitham, G.B., 1974, Linear and non-linear waves (Wiley-Interscience, New York).

*Chaos, Solitons & Fractals* Vol. 3, No. 1, pp. 99-129, 1993
Printed in Great Britain

0960-0779/93$6.00+.00
Pergamon Press Ltd

# Pattern Formation in Spatial Economics

T.PUU

Department of Economics
University of Umeå, S-90187 Umeå, Sweden

(*Received* 25 *September* 1992)

**Abstract** - A market economy, extended in continuous two-dimensional space, defined by the differential equations:

$$\nabla \cdot \phi = q$$

$$k \frac{\phi}{|\phi|} = \nabla \lambda$$

is studied, where $\phi$ denotes the vector field of traded commodities, $\lambda$ the scalar field of commodity prices, $q$ the scalar field of excess supply over demand, and $k$ the cost of transportation. The generic theory of differential equations is used to topologically characterize those patterns that are structurally stable, and the transitions among them are then studied by the elliptic and hyperbolic umblic catastrophes.

## 1. SPATIAL ECONOMICS

Economics is supposed to deal with three issues: *"What?"*, *"How?"*, and *"For Whom?"* shall production be arranged. If time is included in the outlook, the question *"When?"* is added to the list, and if space as well is included, *"Where?"* is added too.

There are two ways to pose the question *"Where?"*. Either, asking: *"Where should a certain activity be carried out?"*. Or, asking: *"Which activity should be carried out at a given location?"*. The first question is dealt with by *location theory*, the second by *land use theory*. There are attractive examples of both in classical economics, attractive because they involve geometric structures of a certain aesthetic appeal, and because they are particularly easy to grasp as they involve very few specialized concepts from the common creed of economists.

In 1826 Johann Heinrich von Thünen [1] considered the following question:

> *"Consider a very large town in the centre of a fertile plain which does not contain any navigable rivers or canals. The soil of the plain is assumed to be of uniform fertility which allows cultivation everywhere. At a great distance the plain ends in an uncultivated wilderness, by which it is absolutely cut off from the rest of the world.*
>
> *This plain is assumed to contain no other cities but the central town and in this all manufacturing*

*products must be produced; the city depends entirely on the surrounding country for its supply of agricultural products.*

*The question is now: How under these circumstances will agriculture be developed and how will the distance from the city affect agricultural methods when these are chosen in the optimal manner?"*

He found that agricultural production would be distributed among a set of concentric rings around the central town, according to the cost of transportation. Heavy or bulky goods, like wood for construction and heating, and cereals, would be produced closer to the city, goods more easily transportable, for instance those that have lost weight by processing and refining, like animal products, farther away.

Underlying the regular ring structure was a tacit assumption that transportation could follow straight lines everywhere, as if the whole plain was paved (as well as cultivated), and as if no other traffic (nor any production activity) put any obstacles to travelling.

The boundary circles between the rings were determined where the city market prices for the proceeds of one acre, net of transportation costs, for two production activities broke even. The width of each ring was determined by the size of demand for the product, and the order was uniquely determined by transportation cost. Heavy and bulky goods would, if anywhere at all, be produced close to the central city. This contribution remains the fundamental classic of land use theory.

Location theory as well dates back to the last century. Wilhelm Launhardt [2] in 1885 and Alfred Weber [3] in 1909 considered the location of a single production plant, using two pre-located input supplies, like ore and charcoal, and selling the product on a likewise pre-located market. The optimal location, in terms of minimal costs of transportation for inputs and output, was worked out. There could either be an inner solution, inside the triangle defined by the three pre-located corner points, or, if any of the three transportations costs dominates the sum of the others, at one of those, as in the case of a house or a bridge that is never transported to the market, but constructed right at the spot. For the minimisation problem there is a nice mechanical analogy. If holes are drilled in a piece of plywood at the three pre-located points, three threads, tied together in the same knot, are slipped through one hole each, and weights proportionate to the three transportation costs (normalized per unit of output) are suspended at the end of each thread, then the knot (in the absence of friction) moves to the optimal location. Minimum potential energy for the mechanical system is thus equivalent to minimum transportation cost. A tacit assumption was again that transportation could be along straight lines so that transportation costs were proportionate to the Euclidean distance.

Launhardt and Weber also considered the formation of market areas when several plants producing the same product were already located in some kind of lattice. The shape of this location lattice then was the problem attacked by August Lösch [4] in 1939. He realized that the ideal shape of the market area, given the Euclidean metric, was a circular disk, because of its compactness in terms of minimal average distance from the centrally located plant to all the continuously distributed consumers within it. As, however, circular disks cannot pave the plane without overlapping or interstices, he considered the regular tessellations instead: triangle, square, and hexagon, concluding that the hexagonal one was superior due to its compactness.

We find similarities and differences in the theories for location and for land use. They are similar in terms of assuming an Euclidean distance metric for transportation costs. They are also similar in terms of being based on optimization and equilibrium. They are different, as land use theory assumes a continuous distribution of agricultural producers facing a pre-located demand market in the central city, whereas location theory does the reverse, assuming a continuous distribution of consumers in the market area, at the centre of which the producing supplier is located.

The last decades geometric spatial economics fell into disrepute. Economists developed a strong inclination to equilibrium theory for a large but discrete set of commodities, where different locations in space and time were mixed up with different physical characteristics of the commodities in one single course of identification indices. This obviously was an effect of the advances in programming methods and computers. The present trend in quantitative science, where the geometric outlook is brought back, partly with the aid of computers, has yet had little influence on mainstream economics.

## 2. THE CONTINUOUS FLOW MODEL

In two seminal papers in the early 1950es [5] and [6] Martin J. Beckmann developed what could be called the ultimate generalization of spatial economic theory, like for instance the Euler-Langrange or the Navier-Stokes formalisms. As such the model is extremely elegant and versatile, being able to represent all previously known models in the field as special cases. Its weakness is a consequence of its strength; the very generality makes it almost impossible to draw any specific conclusions from it.

In particular, by entering the world of non-linearity, geometry evaporates, and results that in the linear world had the status of logically deduced theorems are degraded to the status of exemplifying special cases. Linearity was a consequence of spatially invariant (and isotropic) transportation rates, resulting in all communication being along straight lines.

Beckmann made the flow of transported commodities the corner-stone of the theory. In classical location and land use theory there is an implicit flow of trade, which, however, is trivial as it follows straight lines under the classical assumption of spatially invariant and isotropic transportation costs. Beckmann generalized the theory by removing the restrictive assumptions about transportation costs, so that curvilinear flows of trade became a rule. He also generalized from the monocentric consumption (von Thünen) or production (Launhardt-Weber and Lösch) character of the regions, admitting any distribution of supply and demand over space.

In geographical (Euclidean) two-space, co-ordinates denoted $x_1, x_2$, this trade flow can be represented by a vector field:

$$\phi = (\phi_1(x_1, x_2), \phi_2(x_1, x_2)) \tag{1}$$

The flow modulus $|\phi| = \sqrt{\phi_1^2 + \phi_2^2}$ equals the quantity of goods traded, whereas the unit direction field $\phi / |\phi| = (\cos\theta, \sin\theta)$ represents the actual direction $\theta$ of the flow as represented on a map of the geographical region dealt with.

Exactly as a flow of liquid is related to sources and sinks, the flow of traded commodities is related to the local excess supply of production over consumption. This so called excess supply function:

$$q(x_1, x_2) \tag{2}$$

is a scalar field over the region. Except being dependent on location, it can also be dependent on the price of the commodity (which will be introduced below).

The conservation of matter principle holds for traded commodities, as it does for other flows. Thus, the divergence of the flow (1) equals the local excess supply (2), i.e.:

$$\nabla \cdot \phi = q \tag{3}$$

Equation (3) can be interpreted as a condition for inter-regional trade equilibrium. In integral form it has a particularly nice interpretation:

$$\iint_A q \, dx_1 dx_2 = \iint_A \nabla \cdot \phi \, dx_1 dx_2 = \oint_{\partial A} \phi_n ds \tag{4}$$

where the last equality results from Gauss's divergence theorem. The projection $\phi_n$ of the flow, normal to the boundary $\partial A$, is the export from (or, depending on sign, negative of the import to) the region $A$, and the curve integral is thus net export over import of the commodity. The first left hand side is aggregate excess supply of production over consumption for the whole region. Thus, according to equation (4), *the total excess of exports over imports from the region equals the total excess of what is produced over what is consumed in the region.*

So far we have dealt with the equilibrium of trade, given a direction field $\phi / |\phi|$. If this is given, (3) results in a differential equation for flow volume $|\phi|$.

The next task is to derive the flow direction field. The basis for this derivation is transportation cost. Assume a transportation cost rate:

$$k(x_1, x_2) \tag{5}$$

which depends on location and may even be anisotropic, though we do not assume this in the sequel.

Beckmann defined total transportation costs as the integral:

$$\iint_A k\,|\phi|\,dx_1 dx_2 \tag{6}$$

and proposed the variational problem to minimize (6) with respect to $\phi$, subject to the local constraint (3). The resulting Euler equation was

$$k\frac{\phi}{|\phi|} = \nabla\lambda \tag{7}$$

where

$$\lambda(x_1, x_2) \tag{8}$$

was a Lagrange multiplier associated with the constraint (3). It has the interpretation of commodity price, mentioned above as a likely determinant of excess supply.

Equation (7) tells us two things. First, the unit flow field $\phi/|\phi|$ is co-directional with the gradient field $\nabla\lambda$ for commodity price, i.e., *commodities flow is in the direction of steepest price increase*. Second, the norm of the price gradient equals the transportation cost rate, i.e., *commodity price increases along the flow with accumulated transportation costs.*

Like (3) is the condition for equilibrium, (7) is the condition for efficiency of trade, resulting from competition among transportation companies. If we take squares of both sides of this vector equation we get:

$$\left(\frac{\partial\lambda}{\partial x_1}\right)^2 + \left(\frac{\partial\lambda}{\partial x_2}\right)^2 = k^2 \tag{9}$$

which can be made the basis of a constructive method for finding the flow direction field and the dual price pattern. This is illustrated in Plate I. The green circles are contours of constant price, whereas the orthogonal red radials are flow trajectories. The dashed disks have radii reciprocal to the transportation cost. They accordingly represent all the locations to which one unit of money spent on transportation can take you. The most distant points lie on the envelope to a whole family of such disks centred on a given contour of departure. Such an envelope accordingly becomes the new contour for a price, one unit of money higher. The flow trajectories, being composed of radii of the disks, obviously become orthogonal to the price contours.

The case illustrated is one where transportation cost is proportionate to the distance from the origin, i.e.

$k = \sqrt{x_1^2 + x_2^2}$. The finite graphical method is, of course, very crude, and works particularly ill close to the origin, where the radius of disks approaches infinity. In passing we note the fact that, for anisotropic transportation cost rates, the dashed disks would simply be deformed in various ways.

Plate II illustrates that the solution to (9), for a given transportation cost function, is by no means unique, but depends on the boundary conditions. A saddle-shaped structure, for both flow and price contours, is a possibility for the same transportation cost $k = \sqrt{x_1^2 + x_2^2}$ that resulted in the circular-radial structure. Formally, we now have the solution $\lambda = (x_1^2 - x_2^2)/2$, represented in Plate II, whereas $\lambda = (x_1^2 + x_2^2)/2$ was represented in Plate I.

The minimisation problem for (6) can also be posed in a different manner, natural for geographers, studying transportation rather than trade. See [7]. Suppose we minimize the curve integral

$$\int_a^b k(x_1(s), x_2(s))ds \tag{10}$$

for each trajectory separately. That the unconstrained Euler equation for this problem is equivalent to (7) was shown by the present author in [8]. It is in this context also natural to ask whether there exists a suitable curved surface on which the optimal flow lines are "straight" in the sense of being geodesics. See [7] and [8] for a discussion of this topic in terms of complex analysis and differential geometry. An interesting further development of the transportation aspects of the Beckmann model was given in [9].

The reader may realise how close all this is to the case of Fermat's law in optics, flow lines being equivalent to light rays, price contours to wave fronts, and transportation cost to the refraction index. There was even a simpler counterpart to Snell's law of refraction, proposed independently by Palander [10] and von Stackelberg [11] in the 1930es, for transportation over land and sea, where the cost minimizing route was shown to be a line, broken at the cost discontinuity along the coastline, the sines of the angles being proportionate to the costs of transportation.

We conclude that *the spatial economic structure is entirely represented by the two sets of orthogonal trajectories: the constant price contours and the direction lines for trade*. The volume of trade is of secondary interest, but it too can in principle be determined from equations (3) and (7), given suitable boundary conditions.

Beckmann's original model deals with the partial equilibrium of one spatially extended market, with a given distribution of excess supply, but it is not difficult to extend it to a production economy with many commodities produced, traded, and consumed. This program was in fact carried out by Beckmann and the present author in [12] and [13]. The most interesting outcome may have been a *specialization theorem, proving that, due to mere transversality, only one commodity (for trade, not only local consumption) would be produced at each location*. This sets up conditions for complete specialization and trade, even if the conditions for production are uniform, and is thus more general than any commonly used trade theory,

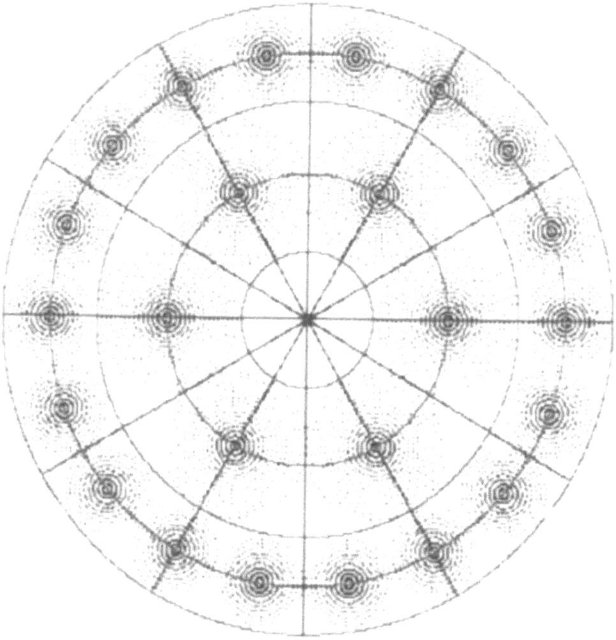

PLATE I.

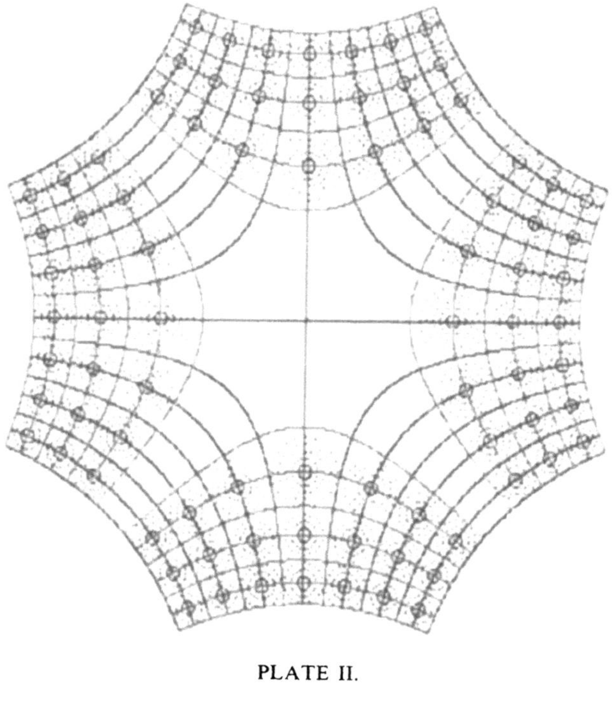

PLATE II.

PLATE III.

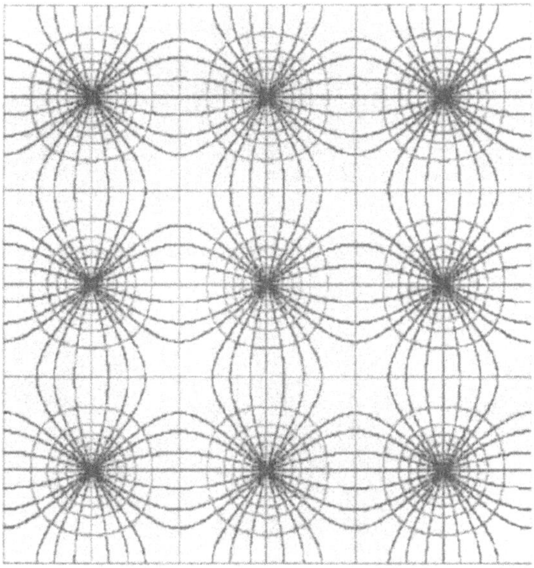

PLATE IV.

PLATE V.

PLATE VI.

PLATE VII.

PLATE VIII.

PLATE IX.

PLATE X.

PLATE XI.

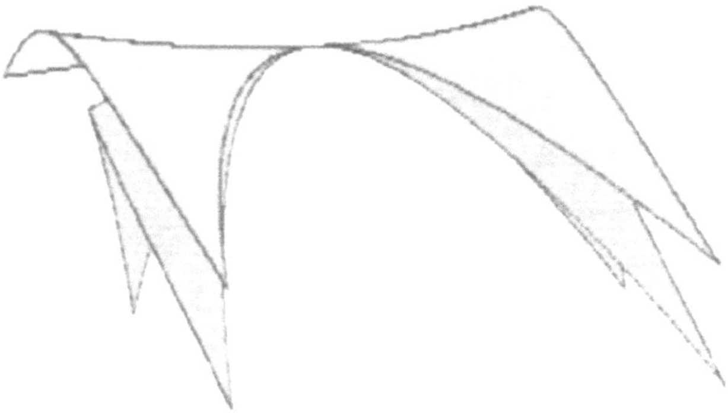

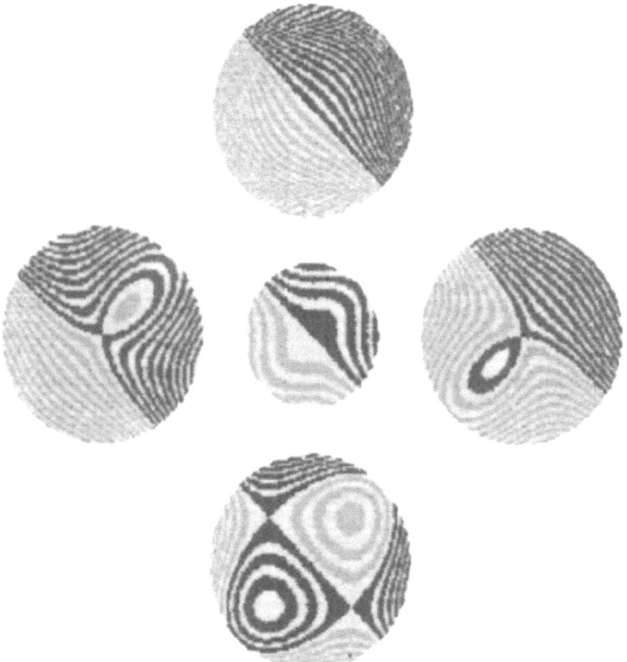

PLATE XII.

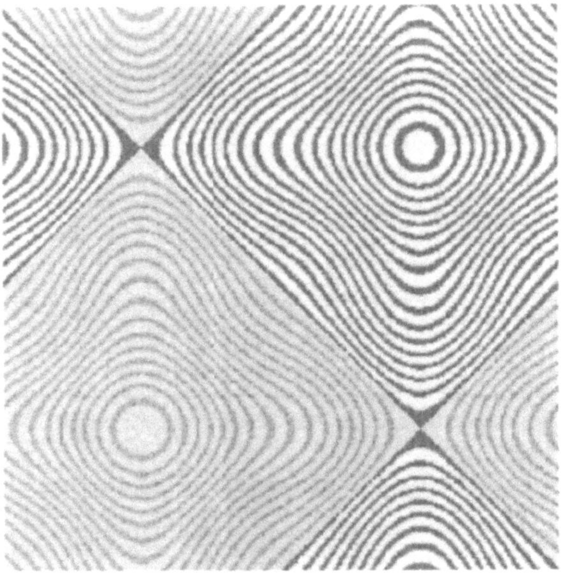

PLATE XIII.

PLATE XIV.

PLATE XV.

PLATE XVI.

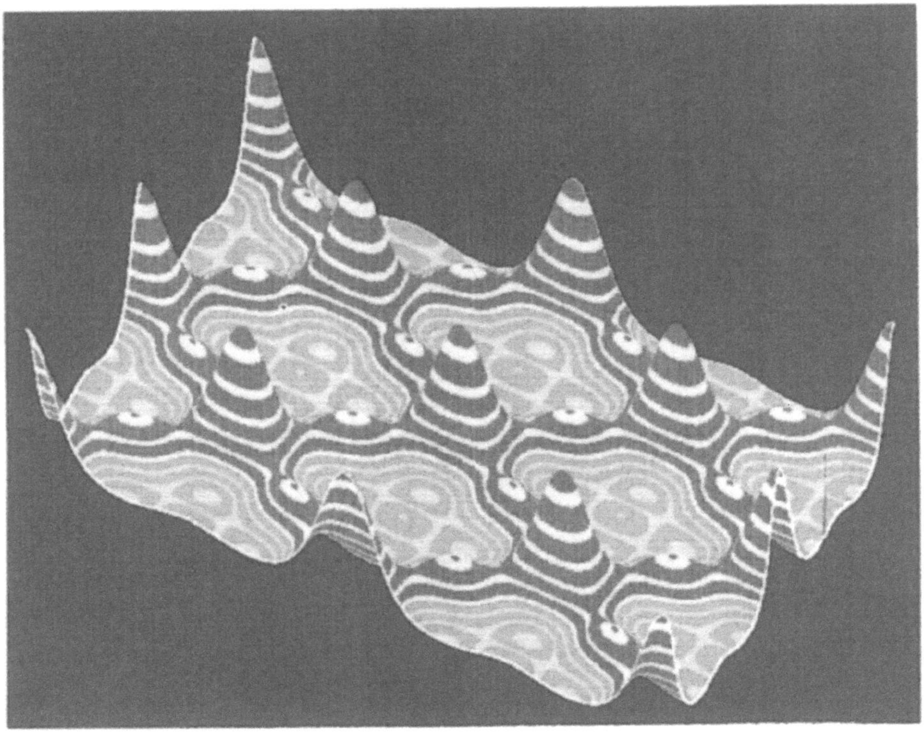

PLATE XVII.

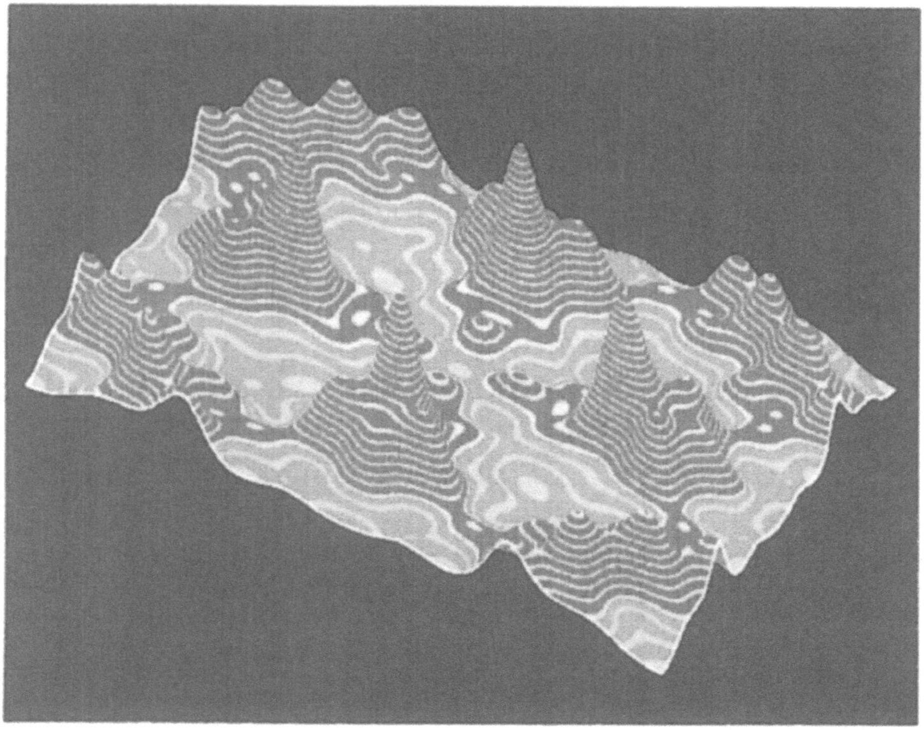

PLATE XVIII.

based on comparative advantages. The credit goes back to von Thünen, though general economics misses the point, by ignoring spatial phenomena.

The specialization theorem relates *land rent* to the profits from the most lucrative production at each location, and offers this as a *unifying factor* to study in an economic landscape where there are multiple production activities located in multiple specialization zones.

## 3. STRUCTURAL STABILITY

Let us now return to the problem mentioned in the preceding Section; the difficulty to attain any precise conclusions when the geometry of the classical spatial economics evaporates along with linearity. Beyond geometry there, however, is topology, and in particular the very strong results obtained by Peixoto in the generic theory of differential equations. See [14] and [15]. For physicists these results were disappointing, as they could not be generalized to dimensions three and higher. Geographical space, however, is two-dimensional by its very nature, and the results fit very nicely in with the Beckmann flow model. How this could be done was first shown by the present author in [16], and was later generalized in [17].

Linear systems at most have one singularity, belonging to the following types: nodes, saddles, and spirals (including centres). For nonlinear systems in general almost anything is possible. Structural stability, however, removes most of these ambiguities. There may be several singularities, but they are finite in number and have locally the same character as in the linear case. Moreover there is a useful global result concerning heteroclinic saddle connections. Peixoto's results can even be strengthened, as certain kinds of singularities (spirals and centres) are removed by optimizing behaviour, implied by the choice of optimal transportation routes.

To make things precise, assume now that we have solved for $\lambda(x_1, x_2)$ and are about to determine the orthogonal set of flow lines. Those can be derived from the set of ordinary differential equations:

$$\frac{dx_1}{ds} = \lambda_{x_1}(x_1, x_2) \tag{11}$$

$$\frac{dx_2}{ds} = \lambda_{x_2}(x_1, x_2) \tag{12}$$

where the right hand sides are the components of the price gradient $\nabla\lambda$ and $s$ is a parameter related to arc length. This set of equations is convenient for the application of results from the generic theory of differential equations.

In addition to the preceding differential equations we consider another, slightly different, set

$$\frac{dx_1}{ds} = \mu_{x_1}(x_1, x_2) \tag{13}$$

$$\frac{dx_2}{ds} = \mu_{x_2}(x_1, x_2) \tag{14}$$

"Slightly different" more precisely means that

$$|\mu_{x_i} - \lambda_{x_i}| < \epsilon \tag{15}$$

and

$$|\mu_{x_i x_j} - \lambda_{x_i x_j}| < \epsilon \tag{16}$$

hold for all $i$, $j$. In words, both the right hand sides of the systems and their derivatives differ by less than $\epsilon$. The system $\mu$ is then said to be an $\epsilon$*-perturbation* of the system $\lambda$.

For the definition of structural stability we also need the concept of *topological equivalence*. Two flow portraits are topologically equivalent, if it is possible to find a continuous one-to-one mapping between the two solution spaces, such that each trajectory can be mapped onto another trajectory and each singularity onto another singularity, flow orientations and singularity types being preserved. Intuitively, topological equivalence can be understood in terms of rubber sheet geometry. If the flow portrait is drawn on an elastic rubber sheet, then all the topological equivalents can be obtained by stretching without tearing.

Structural stability can now be defined. *A flow portrait, that is a solution to a set of differential equations, like the* $\lambda$ *set, is said to be structurally stable if a perturbed system, like the* $\mu$ *set, produces a flow portrait that is topologically equivalent to the first one.* Thus, a stable system produces flow lines that are only deformed by rubber sheet stretching as a result of small system changes.

Structural stability, as defined above, is a typical or generic property. One is unlikely to find structurally unstable patterns in reality, because they are qualitatively changed at the smallest exogenous change. In modelling reality one should avoid structural instability, because, in the idealization process involved at modelling, lots of factors are ignored that could cause such changes.

For structurally stable flows in the plane, there is an astonishingly informative characterization theorem. The reader is referred to [14] for this and other details. A structurally stable plane flow is proved to be *regular* (topologically equivalent to a set of parallel lines), except at a *finite number* of singular points. These singular points are *hyperbolic*, which in our case simply means that they are either nodes (*sinks* or *sources*) or *saddles*. In general, more types, like spirals, are admitted, but they are ruled out as the system in our case is a gradient system. This simplification results from the extremal property of least cost routes, which can never be efficient if they indefinitely whirl around the final destination. A global result is that there can be *no direct connection between saddle points*.

## 4. THE GLOBAL STRUCTURES

Knowing the types of singularities and their admitted connections, it is natural to try to organize the complete flow on the basis of a skeleton consisting of the singular points and their connecting trajectories alone. More precisely we take the trajectories incident to saddle points as organizing elements. There are only two pairs of them, incident to each saddle, so in this way we arrive at a simple graph. The nodes will be traced at the other ends of the trajectories anyhow. Had we chosen trajectories incident to the nodes, the task would have been impossibly difficult as there are infinitely many of them, and only a vanishing number of them end up at saddles.

In view of the popularity of hexagonal patterns in classical spatial economics, the natural first attempt is to find out which regular tessellations are structurally stable. Presently we deal with topology, but the different plane tessellations are, in fact, topologically different. *It came as a surprise that the basic stable pattern was square in outline, not hexagonal.* See [16].

Consider the flow skeleton shown in Figure 1, where we, as explained, only display the trajectories incident to saddle points. We take the convention to arrange them in the horizontal and vertical co-ordinate directions, a practice which in no way affects generality.

Let us start out from any saddle point, i.e. one to which both ingoing and outgoing trajectories are incident. Recalling that direct saddle connections were ruled out by stability, those trajectories must end up at nodes (a pair of sinks and a pair of sources), located S, N, E, and W of the original saddle respectively. Orienting the trajectories incident to those nodes according to their stable or unstable characters, we realize that NE, SE, SW, and NW of the original saddle point there are new singularities (if any), to which there are both ingoing and outgoing trajectories. According to the list of admitted singularities, they must be new saddle points, and we can start the process anew, thus orienting every edge, and identifying each singularity as a saddle, a sink (stable node), or a source (unstable node).

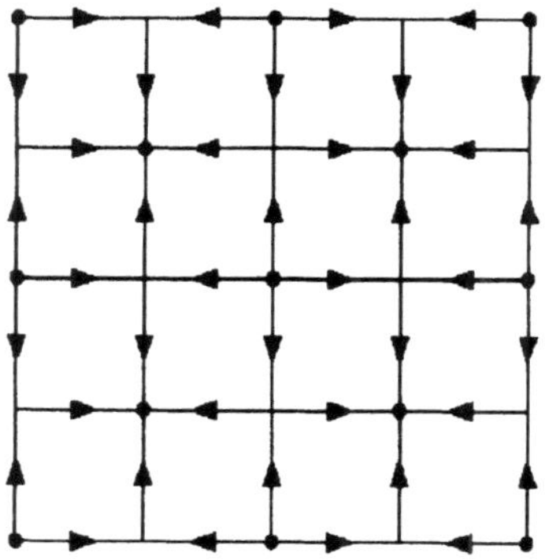

FIGURE 1. *The square flow skeleton.*

The skeleton can now be filled in with any number of trajectories, going from sources, passing close by saddles, and ending at sinks. Those can be seen in Plates III and IV, drawn in red. The plates also show the orthogonal contours for constant price, drawn in green. We note that the pattern displayed in Plate IV is a quadratic tiling. Plate III illustrates the fact that we are concerned with topological properties, by displaying a transformation of the basic square pattern. It was produced by a conformal mapping. As the two families of curves have to remain orthogonal, the conformal mappings are the appropriate transformations to use.

What plate IV could not be transformed to is a hexagonal tessellation. On the contrary, one meets considerable difficulties whenever trying to arrange a hexagonal tiling, while observing the conditions for structural stability. Manifestly unstable things, like monkey saddles, continue to turn up.

*It is also worth noting from Figure 1 that, for an infinitely extended graph, the numbers of sinks and sources are equal whereas the number of saddles equals the sum of these.*

It remains to make economic sense of these pictures. We note that the contours of constant price are the basic structural elements of the economic landscape. The boundaries of the cultivation zones in von Thünen's theory were determined where local prices, net of transportation cost, yield identical profits from different types of cultivation. Likewise, the market boundaries in Lösch's theory were determined where the local prices from several suppliers are equal. It is easy to realize that the price structure actually determines the economic landscape.

We also have to give an interpretation of the singularities. This is quite easy. The sources can be regarded as land rent maxima, like the "central town" in von Thünen's spirit, the sinks as land rent minima, like spots of maximum "wilderness". We just note that the original "isolated state" becomes an "integrated state", with several central cities and a wilderness that may recede to isolated spots, instead of just extending indefinitely far in all directions.

The saddle points then are spots, without economic significance, but with particularly good transportation facilities, as is likely in places far both from congestion at land rent maxima and poor roads at land rent minima. Around saddle points the economic landscape is sectoral rather than ring-shaped.

The square pattern of Figure 1 was obtained by assuming that there were in fact singularities at each and every possible intersection of the trajectories. Let us now consider a somewhat larger portion of the square skeleton and delete singularities in a systematic manner as shown in Figure 2.

Three pairs of adjacent sinks and saddles have been allowed to annihilate each other. We can easily check that all conditions for structural stability are still fulfilled. The new pattern is still regular, and can, as a matter of fact, be deformed into a hexagonal one as shown in Figure 3.

The letters have been inserted in Figures 2 and 3 to facilitate the identification of the topology of the two Figures.

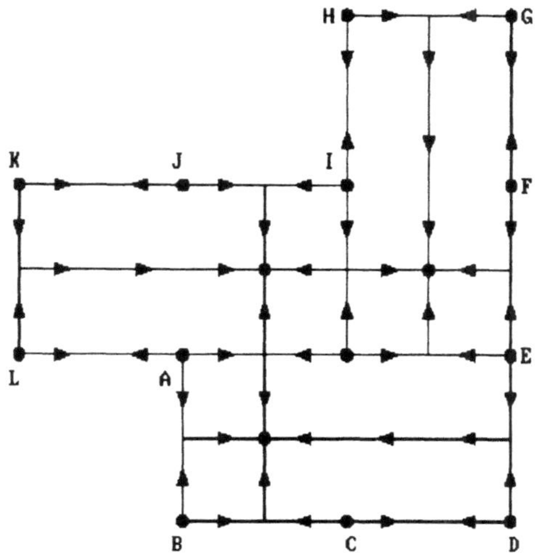


FIGURE 2. *Omission of nodes and saddles.*

By omitting every second sink and an equal number of saddles we have halved their number, while keeping the number of sources unchanged. Thus, the number of sources is now double the number of sinks, while their sum is still equal to the number of saddles. This fact, that the number of one kind of nodes is double that of the other, implies that the structure is not purely hexagonal. *It is hexagonal around sinks, but triangular around sources.*

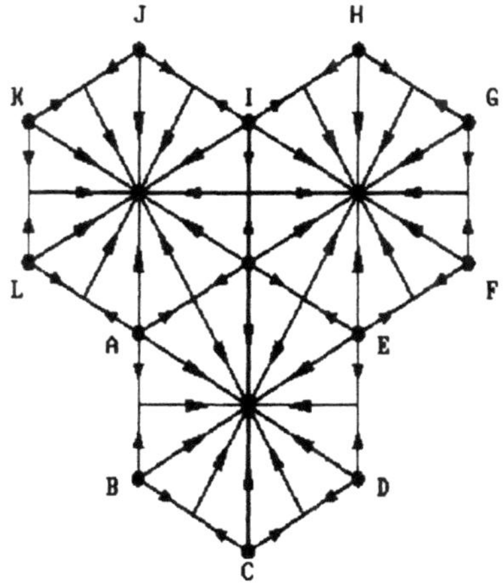


FIGURE 3. *Transformation to hexagonal pattern.*

We could obviously annihilate pairs of adjacent sources and saddles instead. As a consequence the roles of sinks and sources would be reversed, the number of sinks would become double that of the sources, and the landscape would be hexagonal around sources, triangular around sinks.

There is of course an infinity of ways of systematically omitting sets of singularities in the basic graph of Figure 1. In principle this could lead to infinitely many types of patterns, but things are simpler than that. As a matter of fact, we have already found out all there is to find out. To prove this we, however, have to proceed in the more systematic manner proposed in [17].

As a first step, note that *any polygonal structure can be triangulated*. Next, it is obvious that *a consistent orientation of the edges only admits one basic triangulation element, having just one source, one sink, and one saddle as vertices*.

To obtain regular tessellation elements - equilateral triangles, squares, and regular hexagons - the basic triangles have to be arranged cyclically, 6, 8, and 12 respectively. Observe that the basic triangle itself is not a tessellation element as it lacks symmetry. Even for the triangular tessellation, we have to arrange a cycle of six to arrive at a symmetric element. In Figure 4 we show the various tessellation elements.

Using the square tessellation element produces the grid shown in Figure 1, whereas using the hexagonal element produces the pattern shown in Figure 3. Using the triangular element produces the triangular/hexagonal tessellation, discussed only verbally, where the roles of sinks and sources were reversed. This shows that we have in fact discovered all the regular tessellations having the property of structural stability. All other omissions of singularities just produce changes in the mesh size of the pattern.

We can now sum up the discussion on structurally stable grids for flows: *Either, the grid is square with equal numbers of sources and sinks. Or, the grid is hexagonal/triangular with the number of sources half or double that of sinks. The landscape is hexagonal around the kind of nodes of which there are more, and triangular around those of which there are fewer. In either case there are as many saddles as there are nodes, sinks and sources together.*

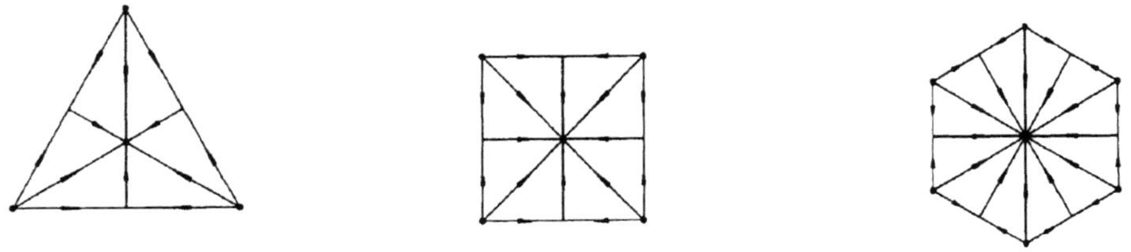

FIGURE 4. *Tessellation elements.*

The characterization of stable flow patterns has been topological, not geometrical, so we should consider all the topologically equivalent transformations along with the three stable patterns characterized. Transformations between those will be studied below by the help of catastrophe theory.

It hardly needs to be mentioned that we may obtain infinitely many non-uniform patterns by omitting singularities from Figure 1 in a non-systematic manner. These latter possibilities, though realistic, must be forsaken, as they defy any meaningful scientific classification.

## 5. CATASTROPHE

The transition from a square to a hexagonal-triangular pattern exactly corresponds to the elliptic umblic catastrophe. The reader can find mathematical detail in [18], in the discussion of the flow, generated by a six-roll mechanical mill, immersed in viscous liquid.

Suppose we have a price potential:

$$\lambda = \frac{x_1^3}{3} - x_1 x_2^2 \tag{17}$$

The pattern of flow lines corresponds to a so called monkey saddle with the hyperbola-like trajectories compressed in six sectors, instead of four as in an ordinary saddle. As the monkey saddle is not in the list of singularities, admitted under structural stability, we note that this is a structurally unstable case. We can easily see that a price potential like (17) is a solution to (9), provided the transportation cost function is $k = x_1^2 + x_2^2$.

We can expect this to be extremely unstable case. The universal form of the structurally stable flow is:

$$\mu = \frac{x_1^3}{3} - x_1 x_2^2 + \frac{a}{2}(x_1^2 + x_2^2) + b x_1 + c x_2 \tag{18}$$

We first note that, for $a$, $b$, $c$ small, (18) is an $\epsilon$-perturbation of (17), exactly in the sense meant in the Section 3. In terms of catastrophe theory, (17) is the canonical form of the elliptic umblic catastrophe, and (18) is its universal unfolding. The use of this catastrophe to study bifurcations in spatial economics was first proposed by the present author in [19].

It may be worthwhile to mention that we are able to study the bifurcations of the system in terms of catastrophe theory thanks to the fact that the differential equations (11)-(12) are derived from a potential function. This, again, depends on the fact that we are dealing with optimization of the flow of trade, by minimizing transportation costs. This is the second service from optimization. The first was to remove certain singularities (spirals and centres), thus making the procedure of constructing the global graphs of Figures 1-3 possible.

Let us now see how changing the parameters in (18), from their zero values in (17), affects the flow portrait. We have mentioned that, for all parameters $a$, $b$, $c$ zero, as in (17), the flow is a monkey saddle. For $a$ alone different from zero, the monkey saddle splits into three ordinary saddles surrounding a node. For $b$, $c$ different from zero, the monkey saddle splits into two disjoint ordinary saddles. If only one of the latter is zero the monkey saddle is split, but there remains a saddle connection. As we have seen, this is globally still an unstable situation, though, in terms of the local catastrophe theory, the system has been stabilized. For this reason we always study simultaneous changes of $b$, $c$ from their zero values.

This information is summarized in Plate V. On top of the picture, the bifurcation surface in the three-dimensional control space ($a$, $b$, $c$-space) is displayed, whereas the spatial patterns in the two-dimensional phase space ($x_1$, $x_2$-space) are shown in the five medallions below. In the middle is the degenerate flow, corresponding to the origin in control space (the waist of the bifurcation surface), whereas the different stable patterns are displayed around it, arranged in directions corresponding to the orientations implied by control space. The three saddle/one node cases are located inside, the two saddle cases outside the bifurcation surface.

We should emphasize, that what we display is not the flow, but the orthogonal structure of price contours. Different colours have been chosen according to land rent, brown where it is above average, green where it is below average. This is supposed to allude to urban and rural areas respectively. According to (17)-(18) land rent would literally be negative in the green areas. For any bounded area this absurdity can be easily removed by adding a sufficiently large constant, though we prefer not to burden the discussion with such trivial complications. The colouring convention is adhered to in the following Plates.

In order to see how the discussion concerning local change fits into the global pictures of structurally stable flows, we display the basic structurally stable square pattern in Plate VI. As a contrast, we show the unstable hexagonal pattern in Plate VII. Observe that it does not belong to the stable hexagonal/triangular variety shown in Figure 3.

In Plates VIII and IX we display its stable bifurcations, corresponding to the horizontal line in Plate V, where the parameter $a$ changes from negative to positive. The present bifurcation, like the intermediate monkey saddle case, is now global. We will see below how these global patterns can be obtained. Note that each monkey saddle splits in a node surrounded by three saddles. Depending on the sign of $a$ either the rural or the urban area will be extended. As $a$ passes from negative to positive values, three saddle points fuse with a (rural or urban) node, for a moment producing a monkey saddle, and again split in three saddles surrounding a node. Each of these central nodes changes character from urban to rural, or vice versa, thus making the number of one type double that of the other, exactly as we saw above. In the process, urban land expands on the expense of rural land, or again vice versa. The patterns shown in Plates VIII and IX are exactly the topological equivalents of the two hexagonal/triangular tessellations.

In Plates X and XI we see the global bifurcation corresponding to the vertical line of Plate V, where every monkey saddle splits into two ordinary saddles. The numbers of various nodes, sources and sinks, are now equal, and they do not change in the bifurcation, nor does the division between urban and rural land. They just change orientation from horizontal to vertical bands. We also see that the Plates represent patterns topologically equivalent to the basic square tessellation of Figure 1 and Plate VI.

It is not difficult to find a potential that produces the global monkey saddle tessellation. What we need is just a function, triply periodic over space, having a lattice of zeros on a frame of equilateral triangles, such as:

$$\lambda = \sin(2x_1)\sin(x_1 + \sqrt{3}x_2)\sin(x_1 - \sqrt{3}x_2) \tag{19}$$

Its derivatives up to second order vanish at the origin, and at all the other periodically located monkey saddles. The lowest non-zero terms in its Taylor series at those points are of the third order, viz. $\partial^3\lambda/\partial x_1^3$ and $\partial^3\lambda/\partial x_1\partial x_2^2$ so that the series indeed is locally identical with (17). The remaining terms in the unfolding, corresponding to (18), and producing the phenomena of bifurcations displayed in Plates XIII-XI, are equally easy to find.

We have dwelt on the mathematical transitions suggested by the elliptic umblic catastrophe. There is another possibility for evolution, suggested by the economic interpretation of the stable patterns, in particular their saddle points. As those attracted trajectories, but were by-passed by them, we interpreted these points as locations with good transportation facilities, but without economic significance. In the process of creation of new centres, the saddle points are obvious candidates for their location. They are thus converted into nodes, but each time this occurs they are automatically surrounded by two new saddles each. A continuing process of this kind decreases the general mesh size of the spatial structure.

Changes in mesh can also be formally modelled by the hyperbolic umblic catastrophe, where pairs of saddles and nodes are created out of the blue sky. The hyperbolic umblic catastrophe has:

$$\lambda = \frac{x_1^3}{3} + \frac{x_2^3}{3} \tag{20}$$

as its canonical form and

$$\mu = \frac{x_1^3}{3} + \frac{x_2^3}{3} + axy + bx + cy \tag{21}$$

as its universal unfolding. The singulatities are now not monkey saddles, but rather isolated stagnation points of the flow. In Plate XII we show the bifurcation surface on top and the various flows in the medallions below, exactly as this was done in Plate V. The central piece is the degenerate case, again located at the waist of the bifurcation surface. Above both membranes of the surface the flow is just laminar. Between the two membranes the isolated singularity splits into one node and one saddle, as shown in the horizontal line of Plate XII. As a further bifurcation we can obtain in all two saddles and two nodes from the isolated singularity, provided we traverse the bottom blade in the bifurcation set as well.

The global catastrophe is now represented by

$$\lambda = \sin^3(x_1) + \sin^3(x_2) \tag{22}$$

where the unfolding is again easily produced by adding suitable spatially periodic functions multiplied by the three parameters. The results are shown in Plates XIII-XVI.

We first note that the laminar flow represented in Plate XIII is again square in outline. The emerging singularities (stagnation points) are developing at the mid-pints of each side of the tiling. This is noticeable by the slight bulging of the trajectories at these points. In all there are 8 such points in the picture, one in the middle and seven along the edges. In Plate XIV each of these has split in two nodes (one source and one sink) and two saddles. The pattern, that remains square in outline, has split threefold in two directions, so that the mesh has decreased ninefold in the global catastrophe, represented in plates XIII-XIV, corresponding to the vertical line of Plate XII.

Plates XV-XVI represent the global catastrophe corresponding to the horizontal line in Plate XII. We see that each of the emerging singularities in Plate XIII has now been replaced by one node and one saddle, so we understand that we deal with cases inbetween those in Plates XIII and XIV. Though in each singularity there is only one kind of node emerging, either a source or a sink, in the plane as a whole the numbers remain unchanged.

## 6. NESTED TESSELLATIONS

Until now we have assumed one basic tessellation of the two-dimensional space, even if it was to be understood in a topological sense only. We can also, of course, as did Lösch [4], assume that there are several such tessellations superposed, resulting in a hierarchical system of economic centres of different importance. We accordingly expect the spatial extensions of the urban areas as well as the maximum values of land rent to differ among such centres.

In Plate XVII we display a system of two such levels of central places, again drawn in brown, whereas the countryside remains green. We have also added a dimension of height to represent land rent, and display the picture in three dimensions, like a mountain landscape. The case illustrated is the basic square tessellation, except that we now have nested two levels. The potential function can be written:

$$\lambda = \sum_{i=1}^{i=n} A_i \sin(ix_1)\sin(ix_2) \tag{23}$$

where $n = 2$ in the illustration. Combining higher "harmonics" we can produce additional levels in the hierarchy, and, deleting some intermediate ones, we can alter the number ratios of different types of central places. Parenthetically, we can mention that, based on theoretical as well as on empirical grounds, different laws have been suggested for these number ratios. See [22], and [23] and [24].

It should be mentioned that we have used an exponential scale for the vertical land rent dimension. This corresponds to reality where land rent maxima tend to be very sharp and land rent minima very shallow. The stratagem also removes the absurdity of negative land rents.

The way of nesting square tessellations of decreasing mesh size need not take the form represented in equation (23). For any $i$ we could also tilt the whole pattern by 45 degrees, using a linear rescaling factor of $\sqrt{2}$ In this way another sequence of square tessellations is obtained, and the two could be fit together as suggested in [24]. Formally we would have:

$$\lambda = \sum_{i=1}^{i=n} \left( A_i \sin(x)\sin(y) + B_i \sin\left(i\frac{x+y}{\sqrt{2}}\right)\sin\left(i\frac{x-y}{\sqrt{2}}\right)\right) \tag{24}$$

In Plate XVIII we illustrate a case for $n = 3$ It is interesting to note how this nesting of only few levels in the hierarchy already makes the picture look much more realistically irregular than the one displayed in Plate XVII. The nesting of hexagonal/triangular tessellations is bound to produce much more complex patterns, especially if we allow tilting by 30 degrees and the corresponding linear rescaling by a factor of $\sqrt{3}/2$.

The amplitudes $A_i$, $B_i$ in equations (23)-(24) decrease at a moderate rate, thus producing the multiple centre cases illustrated. If the amplitudes converge to zero faster, the basic shape will be retained, without any added centres. The shapes will just be deformed, like circles to squares and cones to pyramids.

Nesting sufficiently many levels obviously gives rise to the self-similarity of fractal objects, as illustrated in Figures 5-7, showing the land rent patterns according to (24) for an ascending number of nested tessellations. We note that this nesting process of eight symmetry directions introduces degenerate singularities in the centres. These should, of course, be removed, but this is easy and we prefer to display the regular figures that have a certain appeal.

FIGURE 5.
*Nested squares, n=7*

FIGURE 6.
*Nested squares, n=13*

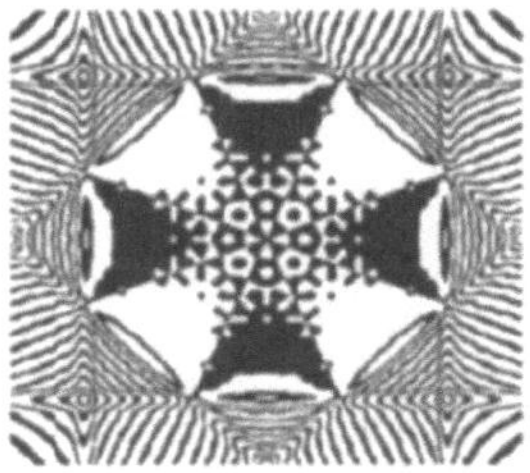

FIGURE 7.
*Nested squares, n=19*

Finally we note that, using a double sum of harmonics in stead of the single one in (23), we could, according to Fourier's theorem, produce any surface we wish.

## 7. CONCLUSION

The present discussion has focussed on structural stability as a a modelling instrument, in contrast to classical spatial economics, where optimality was always the tool to use. Hermann Weyl [20] described an experiment where lead shot is loaded into a cylinder and compressed by a piston under high pressure. The resulting packing is one of rhombic dodecahedra, familiar from beehives. Yet, Lord Kelvin, in his famous Baltimore Lectures, proved that irregular solids, tetrakaidecahedra, with slightly curved edges, represented a higher degree of compactness. Obviously, there are frictional forces operating, preventing systems in practice from reaping the last slight margins of efficiency. This is a very good reason for trying other modelling principles than optimality.

We should also stress that the outcome of considerations of structural stability is highly dependent on what these considerations are applied to. We chose to apply them to the flow pattern, inherent in the Beckmann model of the spatial economy. We could, of course, have applied it to a cell aggregate instead - like a system of market areas. Then, considering structural stability, we would conclude that, due to transversality, three, but not four, such cells are likely to meet in each corner. This, in fact, singles out the hexagonal tessellation as stable, whereas the square one is unstable. A look at any map of national boundaries, formed under the perturbations of wars and skirmishes, shows three countries meeting in each corner. Only the purely administrative borders, like those, drawn by ruler, in the United States, defy this conclusion. More about this can be found in [21].

There is a way, in terms of economic substance, to discriminate between the two outlooks. A system, where the market areas are primary, assumes a monopolistic outlook, where each producer faces a continuum of consumers. A system, where the flow field is primary, assumes sinks and sources distributed everywhere, and so equalizes the roles of consumers and producers, thus implying an atomistic competitive outlook.

## 8. REFERENCES

1. J.H. von Thünen, *Der isolierte Staat in Beziehung auf Nationalökonomie und Landwirtschaft.* Gustav Fischer, Stuttgart (1966), reprint of the 1826 edition.

2. W. Launhardt, *Mathematische Begründung der Volkswirtschaftslehre.* Leipzig (1885)

3. A. Weber, *Über den Standort der Industrien.* Tübingen (1909)

4. A Lösch, *Die räumliche Ordnung der Wirtschaft.* Kiel (1939)

5. M.J. Beckmann, A continuous model of transportation, *Econometrica* 20:643 (1952)

6. M.J. Beckmann, The partial equilibrium of a continuous space market, *Weltwirtschaftliches Archiv* 71:73 (1953)

7. S. Angel and G.M. Hyman, *Urban Fields - A Geometry of Movement for Regional Science.* Pion, London (1976)

8. T. Puu, *The Allocation of Road Capital in Two-Dimensional Space - A Continuous Approach*. North-Holland, Amsterdam (1979)

9. K.C. Mosler, *Continuous Location of Transportation Networks*. Springer-Verlag (1987)

10. T.F. Palander, *Beiträge zur Standortstheorie*. Almqvist & Wiksell, Uppsala (1935)

11. H. von Stackelberg, Das Brechungsgesetz des Verkehrs, *Jahrbücher für Nationalökonomie und Statistik* 148:680 (1938)

12. M.J. Beckmann and T. Puu, *Spatial Economics: Potential, Density, and Flow*. North-Holland, Amsterdam (1985)

13. M.J. Beckmann and T. Puu, *Spatial Structures*. Springer Verlag, Berlin (1990)

14. M.M. Peixoto, Generic properties of differential equations, in J. Hale (Ed.), *MAA Studies in Mathematics* 14:52 (1977)

15. R. Abraham and C. Shaw, *Dynamics: The Geometry of Behaviour*. Addison Wesley, New York (1992)

16. T. Puu, Regional modelling and structural stability, *Environment and Planning A* 11:1431 (1979)

17. T. Puu and W. Weidlich, The stability of hexagonal tessellations, in H. Funck and A. Kuklinski (Eds.), *Space - Structure - Economy: A Tribute to August Lösch*. von Loeper Verlag, Karlsruhe (1986)

18. T. Poston and I. Stewart, *Catastrophe Theory and its Applications*. Pitman, London (1978)

19. T. Puu, Stability and change in two-dimensional flows, in D.A. Griffith and R.D. MacKinnon (Eds.), *Dynamic Spatial Models*. Sijthoff Noordhoof, Aalphen, The Netherlands (1981)

20. H. Weyl, *Symmetry*. Princeton University Press, Princeton, New Jersey (1952)

21. T. Puu, Optimality versus stability in spatial economic pattern formation, in M. Chatterji and R.E. Kuenne, *New Frontiers in Regional Science*. Macmillan, London (1990)

22. J. Tinbergen, The spatial dispersion of production: A hypothesis, *Schweizerische Zeitschrift für Volkswirtschaft und Statistik* 46:853 (1961)

23. H.C. Bos, *Spatial Dispersion of Economic Activity*. Rotterdam University Press, Rotterdam (1965)

24. M.J. Beckmann, *Location Theory*. Random House, New York (1968)

Pergamon

Chaos, Solitons & Fractals Vol. 5, No. 1, pp. 35–44, 1995

0960–0779/95$9.50 + .00

0960–0779(94)00206–1

# The Chaotic Monopolist

T. PUU

Department of Economics, Umeå University S-90 187 Umeå, Sweden

(*Received* 15 *July* 1994)

**Abstract**—The search of a profit maximum by a monopolistic firm is studied, given a demand function with variable elasticity of demand. The system has multiple optimal solutions, so the search algorithm may result in chaotic behaviour.

## INTRODUCTION

Traditional microeconomic theory deals with two basic market types: perfect competition and monopoly. In the case of perfect competition individual firms are assumed to be so small in comparison with the entire market that they cannot noticeably influence market price on their own; they just note the current price and react accordingly with respect to their supply. Only the supply of all the numerous firms together becomes a force on the market strong enough to determine the price in a balance with the demand of all the likewise numerous and small households.

The single monopolist, facing the lot of these households, on the other hand, is assumed to deliberately choose to limit the quantity supplied so as to keep price sufficiently high to yield monopoly profit. If in addition the monopolist is able to efficiently discriminate various submarkets from each other, even different prices may be charged in all those, so as to exploit its monopoly power maximally.

The monopolist must thus know at least the entire demand curve of the market. The information needed is infinitely more complex that that needed by a competitive firm: an entire demand curve instead of just one point on it. To collect this information might be assumed to be costly, and, in view of the variability of the real world, such information collecting would have to be repeated frequently in order to yield a reliable basis for decisions.

It is more likely that a monopoly just knows a few points on the demand function, recently visited in its more or less erratic search of maximum profit. The price policy of any national transportation monopoly could testify to this, though such monopolies could always cloak up any irrational looking behaviour in an alleged pursuit of public benefit.

As to the general form of a demand function, it is assumed to be monotonically downward sloping, demand decreasing as price increases. As there are always substitutes for most goods, like driving as an alternative to using the railway, there would be a maximum price above which nobody would demand anything. Likewise, there would be a maximum saturation demand when price goes down to zero. In text book cases the demand curve is just a downward sloping straight line, but this is too simplistic. The elasticity of demand would in general vary over different sections of the demand curve, giving it a convex/concave outline. This is particularly true if the market is a composite of different submarkets with different elasticities.

The full analysis in terms of graphical reasoning was given in the pioneering work [1] by Joan Robinson in 1933.

## THE MODEL

Such a case is illustrated in Fig. 1, and can be represented by the truncated Taylor series:

$$p = A - Bx + Cx^2 - Dx^3$$

where $p$ denotes commodity price, $x$ denotes the quantity demanded, and $A$, $B$, $C$, $D$ are some positive constants.

In order that the function be invertible, i.e. that there be just one quantity demanded corresponding to each price, the curve must be down-sloping. The least steep slope is in the point of inflection, defined by:

$$\frac{d^2p}{dx^2} = 2C - 6Dx = 0$$

where the slope is:

$$\frac{dp}{dx} = -B + 2Cx + 3Dx^2$$

or, substituting for $x = C/(3D)$,

$$\frac{dp}{dx} = -B + \frac{C^2}{3D} < 0.$$

The demand curve is down-sloping, as indicated by the imposed sign requirement, provided that the condition

$$C^2 < 3BD$$

holds.

Economists usually analyse the monopolists behaviour, using the marginal revenue, $MR$, i.e. the derivative of total revenue, $d/dx(px) = p + x\,dp/dx$. For the demand curve given above the marginal revenue curve would be:

$$MR = A - 2Bx + 3Cx^2 - 4Dx^3$$

which, in fact, could lack a unique inverse, though the demand function has one. The marginal revenue curve is displayed along with the demand curve in Fig. 1. The lack of an inverse is an interesting case, because it provides an opportunity for multiple equilibria.

Now we want the marginal revenue curve to have a positive derivative at the inflection point. This point is defined by

$$\frac{d^2MR}{dx^2} = 6C - 24Dx = 0.$$

The slope is

$$\frac{dMR}{dx} = -2B + 6Cx - 12Dx^2,$$

or, substituting for $x = C/(4D)$,

$$\frac{dMR}{dx} = -2B + \frac{3C^2}{4D} > 0.$$

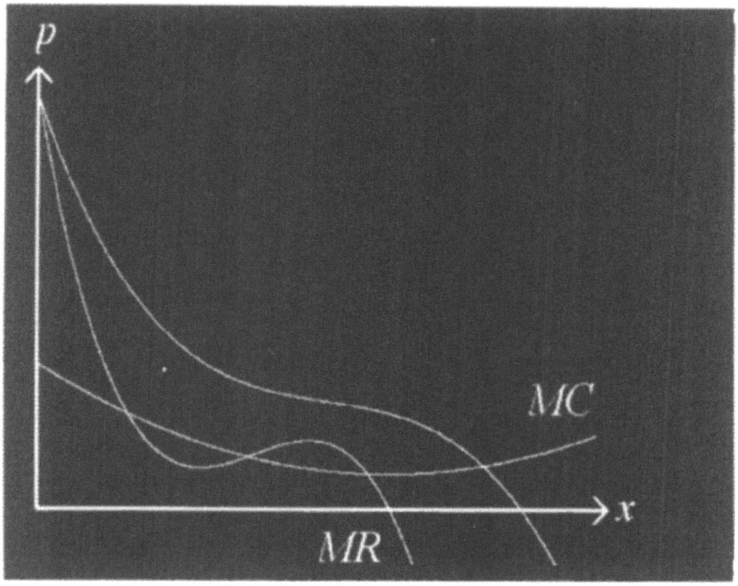


Fig. 1. Demand curve, marginal revenue and cost curves.

The condition for an upward slope at the point of inflection, i.e. for the marginal revenue curve not to have a unique inverse is:

$$C^2 > \tfrac{8}{3}BD.$$

So, there is in fact a latitude of choice for

$$C^2 \in (\tfrac{8}{3}BD, \tfrac{9}{3}BD)$$

such that the demand curve has a unique inverse but the marginal revenue curve has not.

Along with the marginal revenue curve, economists use the marginal cost curve, denoted $MC$. It is the derivative of the total cost as a function of the quantity supplied. Typically, the marginal cost curve is assumed to be concave from above, with marginal cost first decreasing with increasing supply and eventually increasing. The truncated Taylor series for the marginal cost would be

$$MC = E - 2Fx + 3Gx^2$$

where again $E$, $F$, and $G$ are positive constants and the integers are introduced for later convenience at integration.

The standard analysis would involve the condition for maximum profit, $MR = MC$, i.e.

$$(A - E) - 2(B - F)x + 3(C - G)x^2 - 4Dx^3 = 0.$$

Whenever the curves look as in Fig. 1 this equation has three distinct real roots. In theory, the monopolist would calculate these by solving the cubic, and then evaluate second order derivatives

$$-2(B - F) + 6(C - G)x - 12Dx^2$$

to check that the intermediate root is a profit minimum, whereas the higher and lower ones represent genuine maxima. Finally, the monopolist would choose between the two local maxima to identify the global profit maximum.

## ADAPTIVE SEARCH

In reality, however, the monopolist does not know more than a few points on the demand function. The marginal revenue curve, representing the derivative of an uncompletely known function, would not be known except in terms of interpolation through recently visited points. The knowledge would be of a local character and short lifetime, and the monopolist might not even know that globally there are two distinct profit maxima. As already stressed, the limits on information are due to the costliness of market research, and to the frequency of demand shifts due to changes in the markets of close substitutes.

Given this, the task would be to design a search algorithm for the maximum of the unknown profit function:

$$\Pi(x) = (A - E)x - (B - F)x^2 + (C - G)x^3 - Dx^4.$$

This would be quite easy provided the monopolist knew that the function was a quartic. The problem, however, is that nothing except a few points are known.

The simplest algorithm of all, of course, would be to estimate the difference of marginal costs and revenues from the two last visited points of the profit function, and, in the vein of Newton, to use a given step length to move in the direction of increasing profits.

Denoting the next last and last visited points by $x$ and $y$, respectively, and the step length by $\delta$, we get the next point as:

$$y + \delta\frac{\Pi(y) - \Pi(x)}{y - x}.$$

In order to avoid unnecessary numerical instability the denominator in the quotient may be factored out

$$\frac{\Pi(y) - \Pi(x)}{y - x} = (A - E) - (B - F)(x + y) + (C - G)(x^2 + 2xy + y^2) - D(x^3 + x^2y + xy^2 + y^3).$$

## NUMERICAL RESULTS

Iteration of this search process may lead to any of the two local profit maxima, to oscillating processes, or to chaos, depending on the values of the coefficients $A$ through $G$, and the step size $\delta$. The chaotic attractors may be unique, or else co-exist with different attraction basins. In the following computer simulations, as well as in drawing Fig. 1, the following values of the coefficients were used: $A = 5.6$, $B = 2.7$, $C = 0.62$, $D = 0.05$, $E = 2$, $F = 0.3$, and $G = 0.02$.

With these coefficients the profit function would be

$$\Pi(x) = 3.6x - 2.4x^2 + 0.6x^3 - 0.05x^4.$$

Equating its derivative to zero yields the equation:

$$\Pi'(x) = 3.6 - 4.8x + 1.8x^2 - 0.2x^3 = 0$$

which could also have been obtained by substituting the numerical coefficients into the $MR$ and $MC$ functions and equating. The equation has three distinct roots:

$$x = 3 \quad \text{and} \quad x = 3 \pm \sqrt{3}.$$

The iterative search process with the coefficients now introduced is defined by the mapping

$$x_{t+1} = f(x_t, y_t)$$
$$y_{t+1} = g(x_t, y_t)$$

where

$$f(x, y) = y$$

and

$$g(x, y) = y + \delta(3.6 - 2.4(x + y) + 0.6(x^2 + xy + y^2) - 0.05(x^3 + x^2y + xy^2 + y^3)).$$

Before proceeding with the simulations we note that the fixed points of this iteration, not unexpectedly, are given by the equations

$$x = y \quad \text{and} \quad 3.6 - 4.8x + 1.8x^2 - 0.2x^3 = 0$$

and that they are the maxima and the minimum of the profit function. To find out the stability of these points we calculate the Jacobian

$$\frac{\partial(f, g)}{\partial(x, y)} = \delta(2.4 + 1.8x - 0.3x^2).$$

We have used the information that $x = y$ in the fixed points. Of those we know that the profit minimum $x = 3$ is unstable, but the profit maxima

$$x = 3 \pm \sqrt{3}$$

need further discussion. Substituting any of those roots we get the Jacobian

$$\frac{\partial(f, g)}{\partial(x, y)} = \frac{3}{5}\delta.$$

Loss of stability occurs for both roots when the Jacobian is unitary, i.e. at the common value

$$\delta = 5/3.$$

This can be seen at the first branching point in the bifurcation diagram in Fig. 2 where the phase variable, $x$ (or $y$) is plotted against the parameter $\delta$.

We see the two alternative fixed points co-exist at parameter values no higher than 5/3. After that the fixed points are replaced by cycles, over a quite extensive interval, and chaotic bands, with each its own basin of attraction. After a certain point the attractors merge in a single one.

These cycles are seemingly of period three, but this is deceptive. An analysis easily shows that period three cycles are impossible in a second order process like the one we are dealing with. Repeating the simulations in a finer resolution around the middle strands of each of the 'trifurcations', we indeed find that these middle strands dissolve into two separate ones, though very close together.

Accordingly, the actual period is four, and this is also what we find in the phase diagrams, such as the one displayed in Fig. 3.

In Fig. 3 we display the approach to each of the co-existent cycles against a background of the attraction basins in different shadings. Figure 4 gives the same information in colour.

Figure 5 shows two co-existent chaotic attractors against a background of their basins. It can be noted that there is no intricacy in basin boundaries similar to the case of the Newton algorithm, though there are regions in the SW and NE where the 'wrong' basins come very close to the final attractors.

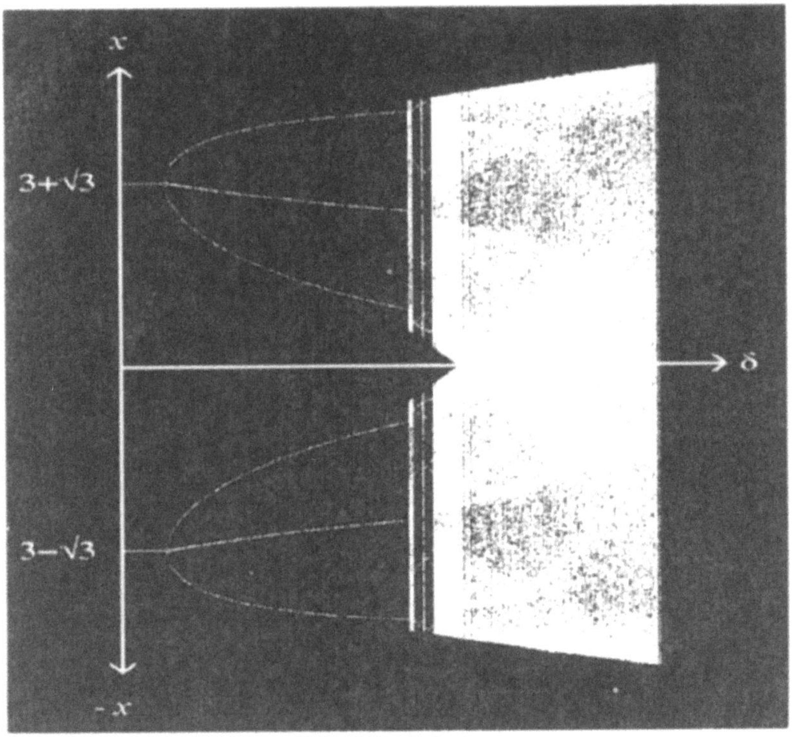


Fig. 2. Bifurcation diagram.

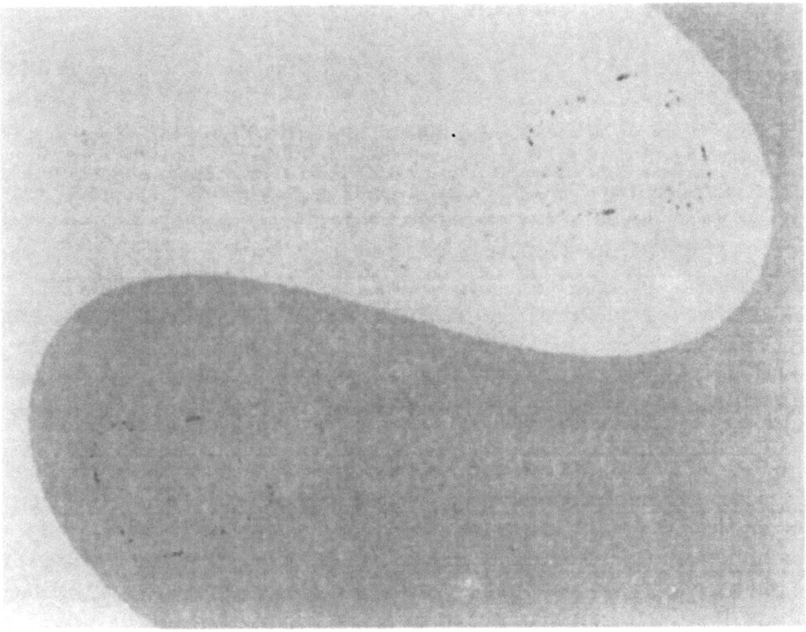

Fig. 3. Co-existent four-cycles, and their basins of attraction.

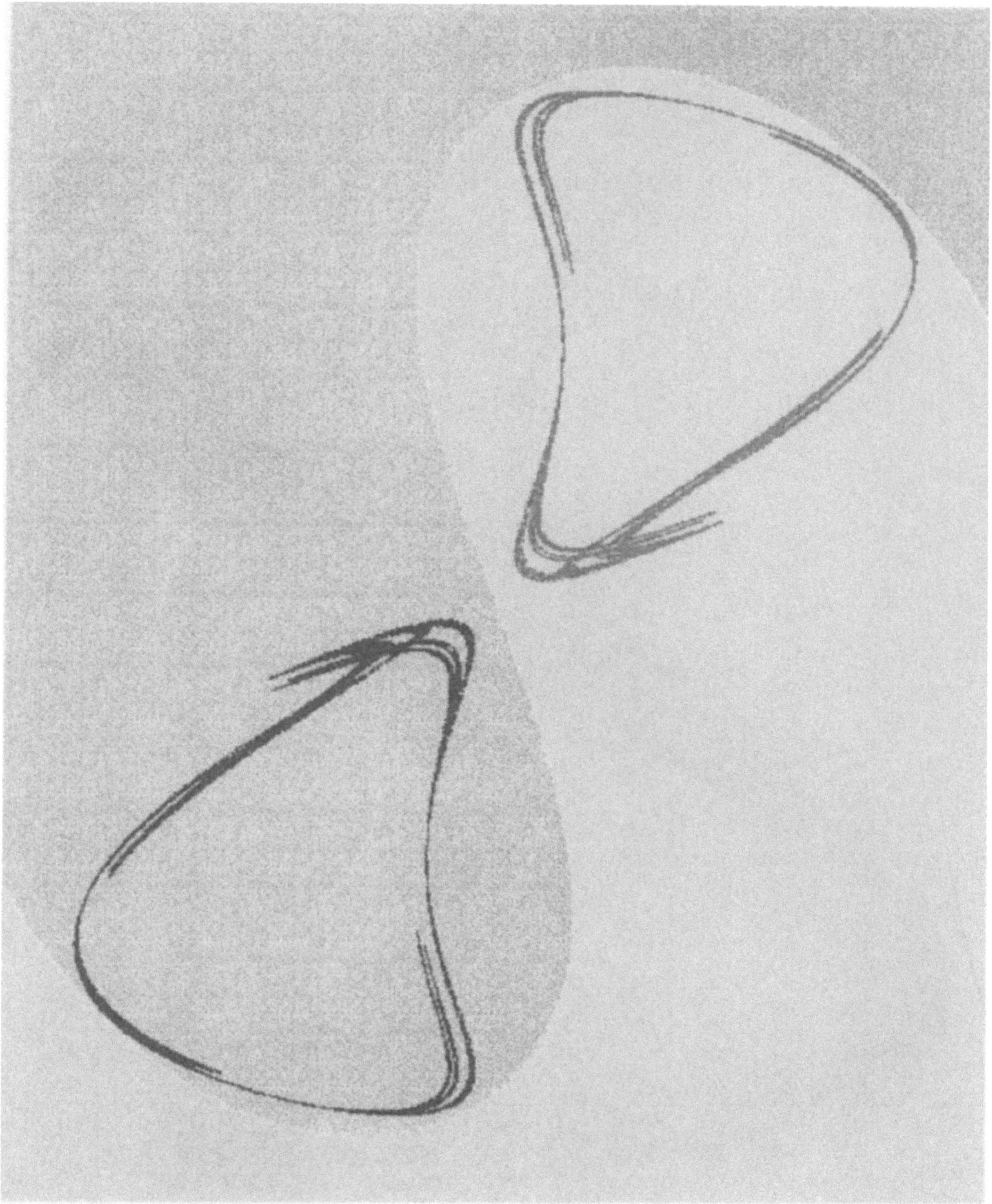

Fig. 4. Co-existent twin attractors and their basins.

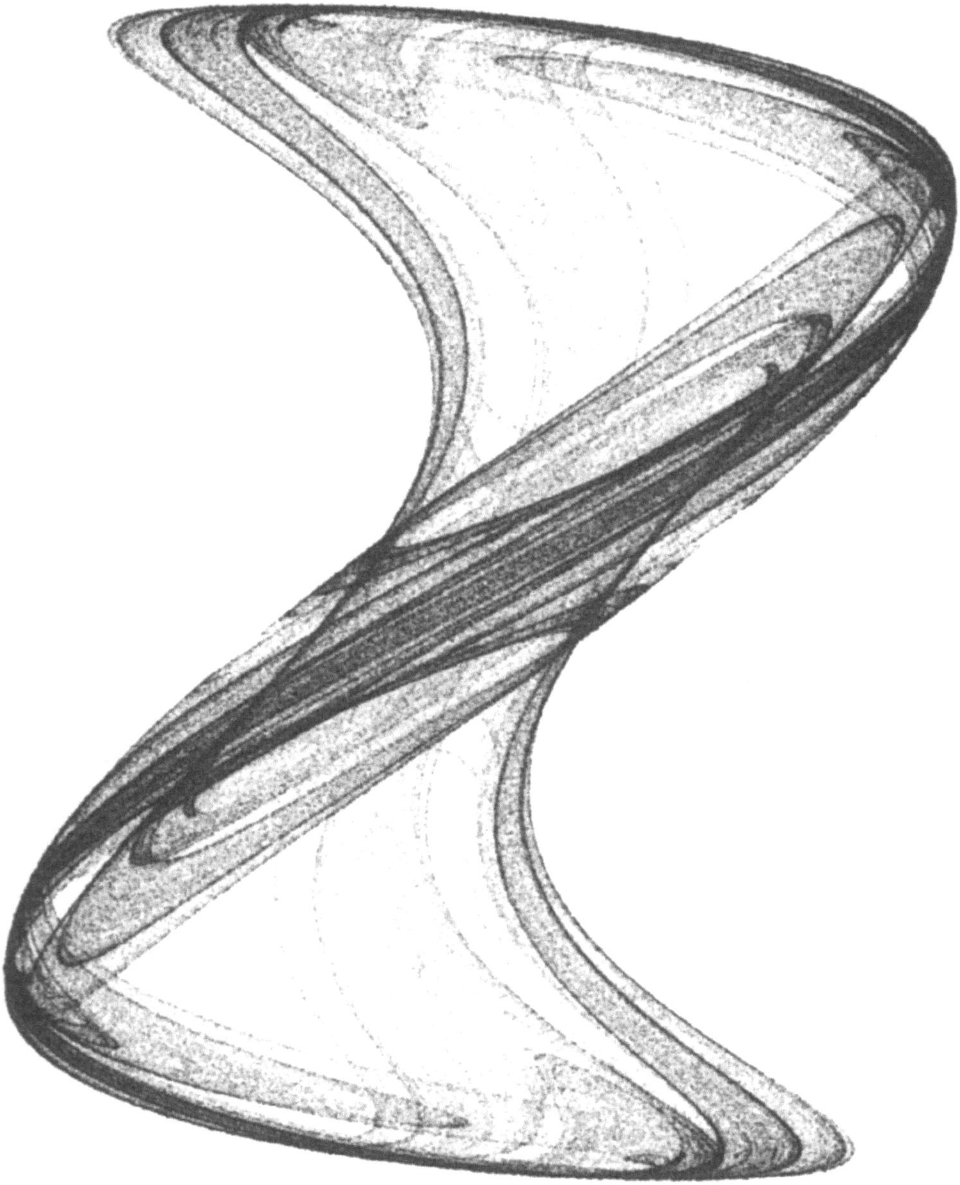

Fig. 7. Single chaotic attractor.

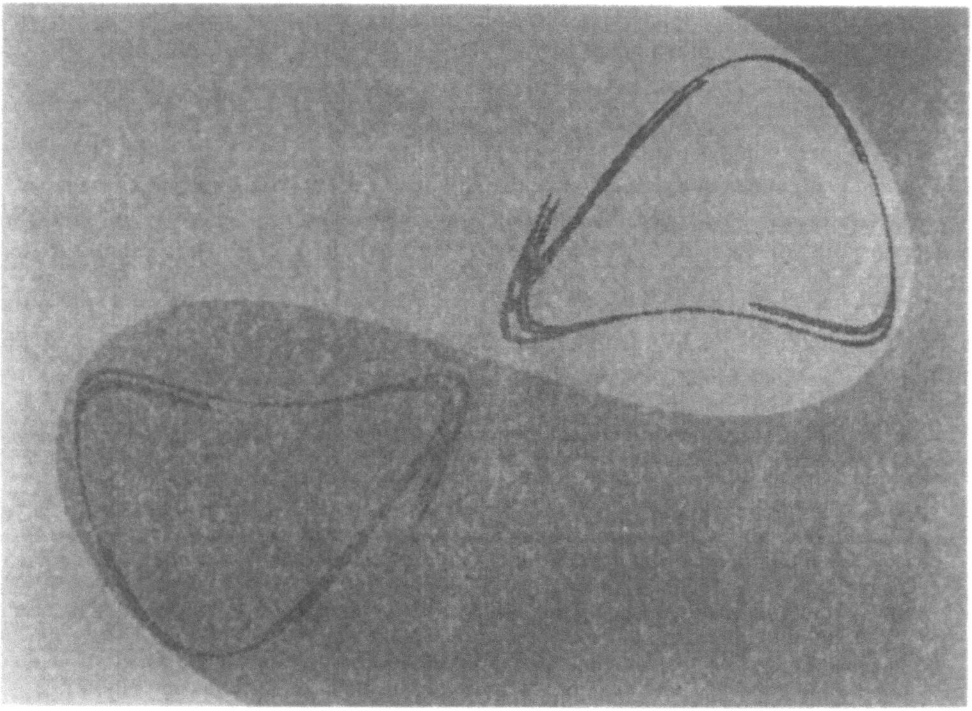

Fig. 5. Co-existent chaotic attractors, and their basins of attraction.

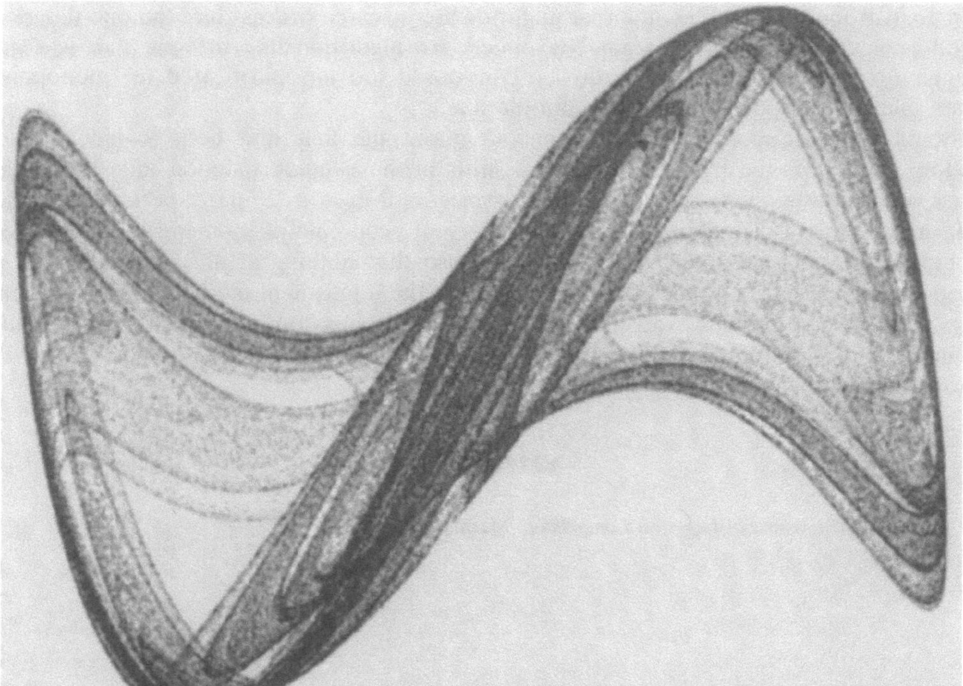

Fig. 6. Single chaotic attractor.

Figure 6 is a portrait of a single chaotic attractor extended over the entire phase diagram. It is also shown in colour in Fig. 7.

## DISCUSSION

It may be a bit difficult for economists, nourished with textbook monopoly theory, to digest that the monopolist does not know all about the market and may even behave in a way which seems erratic. But we have to admit that it can be prohibitively expensive to get all the information the monopolistic firm needs, and that the knowledge aquired may only be local. The monopolist might have no idea at all of the true global outline of the marginal revenue curve, as to how many humps there are and where they are located. Joan Robinson [1] describes the situation.

> Cases of multiple equilibrium may arise when the demand curve changes its slope, being highly elastic for a stretch, then perhaps becoming relatively inelastic, then elastic again. This may happen, for instance, in a market composed of several subgroups of consumers each with a different level of incomes. There will be several critical points at which a decline in price suddenly brings the commodity within the reach of a whole fresh group of consumers so that the demand curve becomes rapidly more elastic. The marginal revenue curve corresponding to such a demand curve may fall and rise and fall again, and there will be several points of monopoly equilibrium. The net monopoly revenue at each point would be different, but it is unlikely that any monopolist would have sufficient knowledge of the situation to enable him to choose the greatest one from among them. If the monopolist had reached one equilibrium point there would be no influence luring him towards another at which his gains might be greater.

If the monopolist has not found such an equilbrium, or if he is a little more adventurous than Joan Robinson assumes, then he might devise a search process like the one described, based on locally estimated marginal revenues. An algorithm like the one that was good enough for Isaac Newton can hardly be considered too unsophisticated for monopolistic firms, such as transportation utilities and the like.

Should the monopolist become suspicious about the fact that he is behaving like a random generator, the blame could be on shifts in the demand function, due to changing prices of substitutes or to general business cycles. Not even a regularly periodic behaviour need make him suspicious, because the imagery of economic phenomena is crowded with all kinds of regular periodic cycles. Observe also that nothing at all was said about the speed of the process, i.e. the real-time length of the adjustment step. It might accommodate to any degree of conservatism in the monopolist's behaviour we may wish to assume.

Finally, the monopoly profit might on average be quite good, despite this periodic or chaotic behaviour.

## REFERENCES

1. J. Robinson, *Economics of Imperfect Competition*. Macmillan, London (1933).

# PART III

# Philosophy of Science

# A GRAPHICAL SOLUTION OF SECOND-ORDER HOMOGENEOUS DIFFERENCE EQUATIONS

*By* TÖNU PUU

MANY textbooks on economic theory contain a chapter on the Samuelson–Hicks business cycle model.[1] The solution of second-order difference equations, however, requires more mathematics than the remainder of elementary economic theory. Thus, only numerical examples, where the time-paths of national income are computed by iteration, but not the explicit solutions of national income as functions of time, lie within the scope of ordinary textbook mathematics.

However, it is easy to construct a graph on which the character of the different kinds of solutions may be understood without anything but the simplest mathematics. The objective of the present paper is to present such a graph.[2]

Let us start with the simplest of Hicks's difference equations. It can be written in the following manner:

$$y_t = (1-s+v)y_{t-1}+(-v)y_{t-2}.$$

The marginal propensity to save is denoted by $s$ and the capital-output ratio by $v$. This linear, homogeneous second-order difference equation with constant coefficients may be divided through by $y_{t-1}$. This yields:

$$\frac{y_t}{y_{t-1}} = (1-s+v)-v\frac{y_{t-2}}{y_{t-1}}. \tag{1}$$

In the following graphs the vertical $z$-axis denotes the ratios $y_1/y_0$, $y_2/y_1$, &c., and the horizontal $x$-axis their inverses $y_0/y_1$, $y_2/y_1$, &c. Each graph contains a pair of rectangular hyperbolas with the equation $z = 1/x$. The straight line in the graphs has equation $z = (1-s+v)-vx$.

Now, let us start from the point $z = y_1/y_0$ on the vertical axis and draw a horizontal line towards the hyperbola. The horizontal coordinate of the intersection point is $x = y_0/y_1$. If we now draw a vertical line from this point towards the line $z = (1-s+v)-vx$, then the new intersection point has $z = (1-s+v)-v\ y_0/y_1$ as its vertical coordinate, which must equal $y_2/y_1$ according to equation (1). We may continue in this way and read the ratios $y_3/y_2$, $y_4/y_3$, &c., successively on the vertical axis.

[1] See the first formulation in P. A. Samuelson, 'Interactions between the Multiplier Analysis and the Principle of Acceleration', *Review of Economic Statistics*, May, 1939, p. 75, and a slightly different formulation, which we are going to discuss, in J. R. Hicks, *A Contribution to the Theory of the Trade Cycle*, 1950.

[2] An alternative graphic analysis is presented in W. J. Baumol, 'Topology of Second-order Linear Difference Equations with Constant Coefficients', *Econometrica*, 1958. The present graphical analysis is inspired by chapter 9 in J. S. Duesenberry, *Business Cycles and Economic Growth*, 1958.

Extract from Oxford Economic Papers, New Series, Oxford (1963)Vol. 15, No.1:54-58

These ratios subtracted by 1 denote the relative growth-rates. This makes it easy to 'translate' the time-path of the ratio $y_t/y_{t-1}$ into the time-path of $y_t$ itself.

The consequences for $y_t$ of different values of $y_t/y_{t-1}$ and $y_{t-1}$ are summarized in the following table:

| | $-\infty < \frac{y_t}{y_{t-1}} < -1$ | $-1 < \frac{y_t}{y_{t-1}} < 0$ | $0 < \frac{y_t}{y_{t-1}} < 1$ | $1 < \frac{y_t}{y_{t-1}} < \infty$ |
|---|---|---|---|---|
| $y_{t-1} > 0$ | $y_t < 0$<br>$-y_t > y_{t-1}$ | $y_t < 0$<br>$-y_t < y_{t-1}$ | $y_t > 0$<br>$y_t < y_{t-1}$ | $y_t > 0$<br>$y_t > y_{t-1}$ |
| $y_{t-1} < 0$ | $y_t > 0$<br>$y_t > -y_{t-1}$ | $y_t > 0$<br>$y_t < -y_{t-1}$ | $y_t < 0$<br>$y_t > y_{t-1}$ | $y_t < 0$<br>$y_t < y_{t-1}$ |

Now, the line $z = (1-s+v)-vx$ may have three qualitatively different positions with regard to the positive branch of the hyperbola, each representing a different type of time-path of $y_t$. The line may intersect the hyperbola in two points, $P$ and $Q$ in Fig. 1 $a, b$, it may be a tangent to the hyperbola in one point, $R$ in Fig. 2, and finally it may lay below the hyperbola as in Fig. 3. All the time we are discussing the positive branch of the hyperbola, because the line for obvious reasons never can intersect the third quadrant where the negative branch is located.

In order to be a tangent, the line must have a point in common with the hyperbola in which the slope of the line equals the slope of the hyperbola. The slope of the line is $-v$ and the slope of the hyperbola $-(1/x^2)$. The point of the hyperbola where its slope equals the slope of the line is determined by the equations:

$$\left.\begin{aligned} -\frac{1}{x^2} &= -v \\ z &= \frac{1}{x} \end{aligned}\right\}. \tag{2}$$

They have a unique solution because we only regard the positive branch of the hyperbola:

$$\left.\begin{aligned} x &= \frac{1}{\sqrt{v}} \\ z &= \sqrt{v} \end{aligned}\right\}. \tag{3}$$

In the case of tangency this point must satisfy the equation

$$z = (1-s+v)-vx,$$

i.e.

$$\sqrt{v} = (1-s+v)-v\frac{1}{\sqrt{v}}. \tag{4}$$

This may be written:

$$(1-s+v)^2 = 4v. \tag{4a}$$

If the hyperbola is intersected in two points by the line, the point of the hyperbola with coordinates (3) must lie below the line, i.e.

$$\sqrt{v} < (1-s+v)-v.\frac{1}{\sqrt{v}} \tag{5}$$

or

$$(1-s+v)^2 > 4v. \tag{5a}$$

The remaining case is when the line everywhere lies below the hyperbola. This means that

$$\sqrt{v} > (1-s+v)-v\frac{1}{\sqrt{v}} \tag{6}$$

or

$$(1-s+v)^2 < 4v. \tag{6a}$$

The three cases are those where the characteristic equation of the Hicksian difference equation has two equal, two real and different, and two conjugate complex roots respectively.

The case of two real and different roots is represented by Fig. 1 *a*, *b*. The intersections *P* and *Q* represent equilibrium growth-rates. If $y_1/y_0$ equals the vertical coordinate of *P* or *Q*, then the growth-rate will be unchanged, provided that no exogenous disturbances occur. These vertical coordinates of *P* and *Q* are also equal to the roots of the characteristic eqaution. This is seen if we compute these vertical coordinates from the following system:

$$\left.\begin{aligned} z &= (1-s+v)-vx \\ z &= \frac{1}{x} \end{aligned}\right\} \tag{7}$$

which gives

$$z = \frac{(1-s+v)}{2} \pm \frac{\sqrt{\{(1-s+v)^2-4v\}}}{2}.$$

Let us now see what happens if the initial condition $y_1/y_0$ does not equal any of the equilibrium growth rates. Obviously *P* is a stable equilibrium and *Q* an unstable one. For this reason *Q* represents a critical point. If $y_1/y_0$ lies between *P* and *Q*, $y_t/y_{t-1}$ converges towards *P*. The same happens when $y_1/y_0$ lies above *P*. These cases are represented in Fig. 1 *a*. When $y_1/y_0$ lies below *Q*, the ratio $y_t/y_{t-1}$ must take on a negative value for one period and then approaches *P* from above. This is illustrated in Fig. 1 *b*. As we already noted, the negativity of $y_t/y_{t-1}$ means a change of sign. If $y_{t-1}$ is positive, $y_t$ will be negative and the system will approach an equilibrium decrease-rate. Thus, if $y_t$ has decreased, or increased too little, between the first two periods, then the process will turn downwards. This is the reason why the Hicksian model may have a downturn when the 'roof' is touched.

In Fig. 2 we have represented the case where the line is a tangent to the hyperbola. This case may easily be discussed as an application of our previous discussion. The points *P* and *Q* have crept together; if $y_1/y_0$ is below $R$, the same conclusion applies as when $y_1/y_0$ is below $Q$ in the previous case. An equilibrium decrease-rate is approached. If $y_1/y_0$ lies above $R$, an equilibrium growth-rate is approached as in Fig. 1 *a*.

In the remaining case, represented by Fig. 3, the line lies below the hyperbola everywhere, and the result is an oscillatory movement. Every time $y_t/y_{t-1}$ takes on a negative value the sign of $y_t$ is changed.

*Uppsala University*

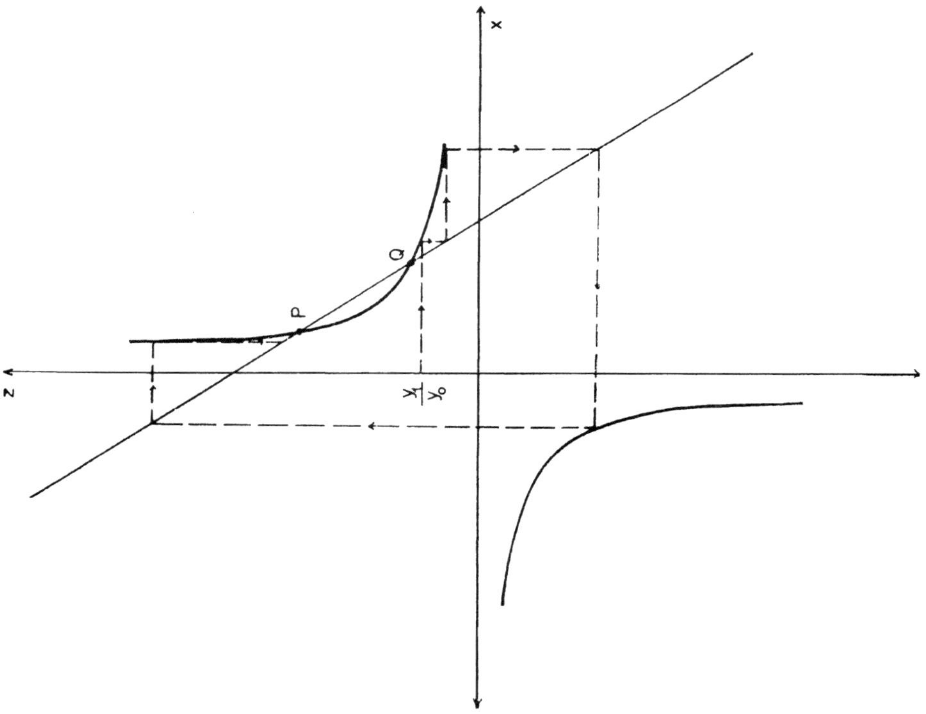


FIG. 1 *b*

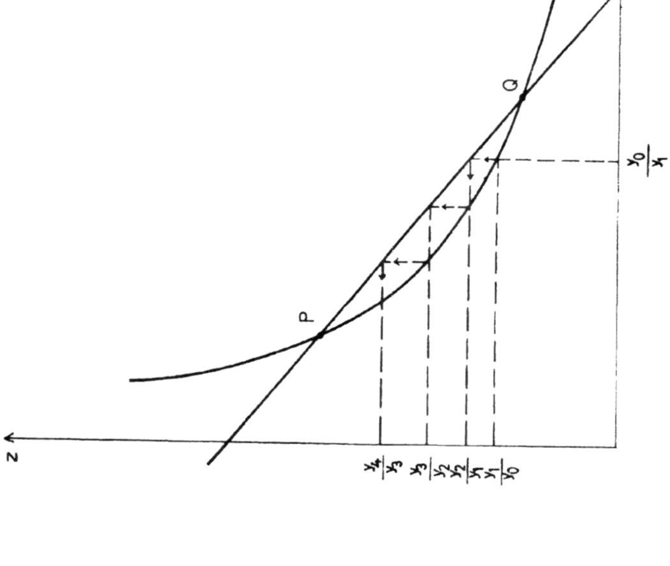


FIG. 1 *a*

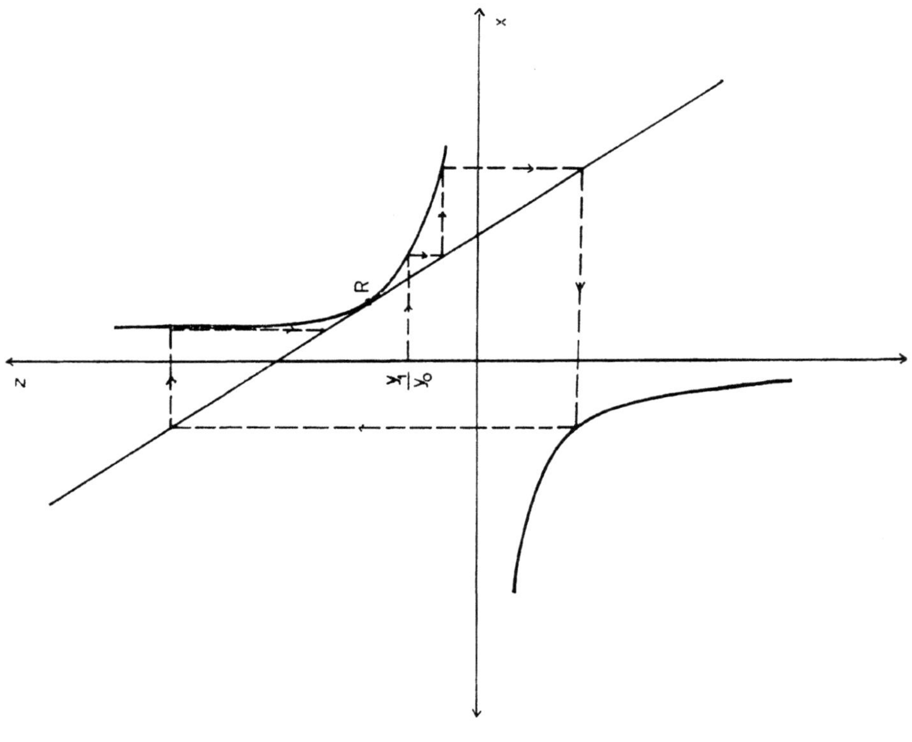


FIG. 2

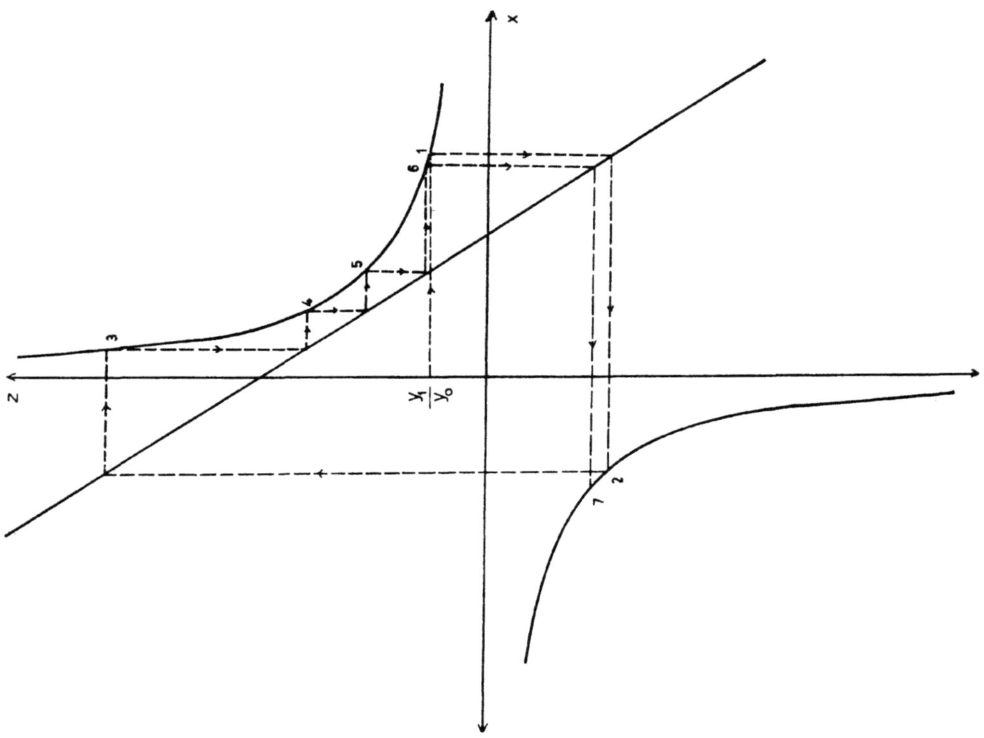


FIG. 3

# SOME REFLECTIONS ON THE RELATION BETWEEN ECONOMIC THEORY AND EMPIRICAL REALITY*

*Tõnu Puu*

Docent at the University of Uppsala, Uppsala, Sweden

## Introduction and Summary

The starting point of this methodological paper is the idea from the philosophy of science that theories in empirical sciences only become meaningful as a result of the fact that statements about empirically observable phenomena can be logically derived from them. The statements are applications in particular cases of empirical generalizations, as the hypotheses on the lowest abstraction levels are called. The empirical generalizations must contain magnitudes which have, explicitly stated or tacitly understood, operational definitions by which they can be calculated on the bases of measurements of directly observed magnitudes.

The condition for a theory to have an empirical basis is that it be possible to derive empirical generalizations from it, which are not tautologies, or logically true propositions. If they were tautologies, the impossibility of finding empirical material which could impose rejection is evident on logical grounds. It is pointed out in this article that this type of theory is rather common in economics; something which is usually associated with the tendency to introduce unspecified autonomous disturbances. Examples are provided from optimal behavior theory, the comparative static theory of price determination, the dynamic theory of "excess demand", and macroeconomic theory.

According to the philosophy of science the abstract parts of a theory need not have any other meaning than that which is obtained indirectly by their being instruments for the derivation of empirical generalizations. Because of the usual construction process of economic theory, that is isolation of the features of actual phenomena which particularly interest the constructor, and simplifying idealizations of the complicated structures of reality, the resulting theories can be construed as pictorial model "realities". This can lead to the belief that such theories have some empirical significance as a consequence of reality being the beginning material in the process of idealization. However, this is said to be an illusion, which might lead to economic theory becoming unable to give explanations of actual phenomena.

What follows represents some simple reflections which the author of this paper has made in connection with reading some of the current standard works in the philosophy of science. Within this branch of theoretical philosophy, a picture

* The author is deeply indebted to Professor Tord Palander and the members of his seminar at Uppsala University for several valuable discussions on the subject. Likewise, the author is indebted to Professor Harald Dickson, who has drawn his attention to many obscure points in the manuscript, and to Professor Håkan Törnebohm, who has suggested a more tolerant attitude to actual practice of scientific research than that, represented by the writings of logical empiricists, which inspired this paper.

of the nature of scientific explanation has been constructed which seems most easily suited to the natural sciences. This picture has been achieved through the use of a systematic concept apparatus, completely different from the rather vague notions which lie behind the speculations of the majority of researchers active in specialized areas on the methods used in their own work. Thus, it can be of some interest for economists to attempt to answer questions of the following type: To what extent is this picture relevant to the explanations which economic theory gives? Are there problems stressed by philosophers of science which are of no special significance for economic theory? Does economic theory involve specific problems of great importance that philosophers of science have neglected?

Such questions are suggested by statements by some of the philosophers of science themselves; for example R. B. Braithwaite in his statement, qualified by a somewhat unclear reservation, that the social sciences can be regarded as natural sciences as regards methodology to the extent that man can be included in nature.[1] In spite of the fact that many economists have been eminent logicians and philosophers of science—such as W. S. Jevons, J. M. Keynes, and J. S. Mill—their activity does not seem to have led to an inclusion of problems in economic explanation among the subject matter discussed in the philosophy of science. The examples from particular sciences which are discussed still come from theoretical physics and other natural sciences. As an economist, therefore, one is obliged to contemplate for oneself the structure of economic theory, its means and its relationship to reality. However, it would result in the sparing of much effort if it was possible to take over ready formulated concepts and complete lines of thought from the philosophy of science. Such a procedure as opposed to its alternative of constructing everything from the ground up, would greatly facilitate communications with philosophers of science and practitioners of other particular sciences. This is obviously, in itself, another advantage.

## A Demonstration of the Structure of Scientific Theories

The philosophy of science is usually concerned with demonstrating the formal structure of a scientific theory by discussing the role of logical deduction, the nature of abstract concepts, and the relationship of the theory to empirically observed facts expressed in rules for the establishment and rejection of hypotheses.

It seems appropriate to the following discussion to mention the essential features of Braithwaite's demonstration of the structure of scientific theories.[2] According to this, each theory in an empirical science can be considered a hierarchy of hypotheses on different levels of abstraction. The hierarchical

[1] R. B. Braithwaite, *Scientific Explanation*. Cambridge 1964, p. 1.
[2] Braithwaite, op. cit., pp. 12 ff.

construction is attained through use of the rules of logical inference, according to which the hypotheses on lower levels of abstraction may be derived from hypotheses on higher levels of abstraction. The passing from higher to lower levels of abstraction could take place through the specification of the general assumptions. The passing to lower abstraction levels also involves the elimination of such theoretical concepts as will be mentioned below. The hypotheses on the lowest level of abstraction are called empirical generalizations, and are statements about the relationships between the actual occurrences of objects or events.

Through experiments or other methods of observation, empirical material is obtained about the occurrence of events or existence of objects about which the empirical generalizations make assertions. This material can directly be confronted with the empirical generalizations and indirectly with the abstract hypotheses from which the empirical generalizations are logically derived.

Every observation in material of this sort which agrees with what the empirical generalization in question asserts, would then be an indication of the correctness of the entire theory and contribute to establishing the hierarchy of hypotheses which compose it. However, an empirical generalization—and still less the abstract hypotheses from which it is derived—could not be proved true no matter how extensive the evidence produced is.

On the one hand, the existence of a single observation within the evidence that conflicts with what the empirical generalization in question asserts would be enough to reject it and the entire hierarchy of abstract hypotheses. Consequently there exists an asymmetry in that a single observation which conflicts with the statements of the theory leads to the definite rejection of the theory as erroneous—while on the other hand the observations which agree with the assertions of the theory cannot be sufficient in number to lead to the acceptance of the theory as true. Thus the establishment of a theory is always provisional whereas its rejection is definite.

This asymmetry is due to the asymmetric nature of the logical relationship "implication".[1] As the empirical generalization, from a logical point of view, forms the premise and its prediction in a case where observations have been made, the conclusion, the establishment of the correctness of this conclusion cannot lead to an establishment of the correctness of the premise. On the other hand, the establishment of the incorrectness of the conclusion must lead to the assessment of the premise as incorrect. The establishment of the latter as incorrect is transferred via the implication relations to the hypotheses on higher

[1] About the logical concepts used in this paper see P. Suppes, *Introduction to Logic*. Princeton 1957. Related to the asymmetry mentioned are some "paradoxes of confirmation". If the objective is to establish the sentence "all ravens are black", inspection of ravens as to their color is the usual procedure. But, as the sentence is logically equivalent to the sentence "everything which is not black is not a raven", the procedure might as well be an inspection of non-black objects as to their being ravens or not. This may seem intuitively absurd. About these paradoxes, see P. Suppes, *A Bayesian Approach to the Paradoxes of Confirmation* in *Hintikka-Suppes* (Ed:s), *Aspects of Inductive Logic*. Amsterdam 1966.

levels of abstraction, all of which according to "modus tollendo tollens" must be considered incorrect.

What has been stated implies an antisymmetry between the logical structure of a theory on the one hand, where the abstract hypotheses are premises and statements about phenomena in reality are the conclusions, and the structure of the induction on the other hand, where the knowledge about phenomena in reality constitutes the "raw material" and the abstract hypotheses the results of scientific inquiry. This conflict has led to several attempts to give the inductive procedure the same logical structure as the deductive, by using the assumption that suppressed hypotheses concerning the "conformity of nature" are present at every inductive procedure. The most famous attempt in that direction has been made by D. Hume.[1] Such thoughts have, however, become more unrealistic the more remote the scientific theories have grown from the simple empirical generalizations which Hume tried to establish, and the more complicated the structures of abstract hypotheses have become.

In addition to the idea that scientific theories can in some formal way be "derived" from empirical observations, (which hardly any philosopher of science would accept now), there is a related, more subtle, idea that at least the abstract scientific terms which are found in hypotheses on higher levels of abstraction might be considered as abbreviations of complicated expressions that are solely referring to empirically observable objects and events. This notion has been presented by B. Russell in his doctrine of so-called "logical constructions".[2] F. P. Ramsey has raised objections to this. Braithwaite, whose presentation is given here, maintains that if the demand that all theoretical terms should be explicity definable in empirical entities were satisfied, theories would be reduced to mere systematizations of empirically observed facts and the development of theories would be blocked.[3] Thus the theoretical terms derive their meaning only implicitly by means of the way in which they appear in the abstract hypotheses. Like the abstract hypotheses themselves, theoretical terms ultimately obtain their meaning through the empirical generalizations which constitute the last stage of the theoretical hierarchy.

This simple presentation began with the assumptions that one single hypothesis corresponds to every level of abstraction in a theory, and that simple implication relations exist between the hypotheses on different abstraction levels. From a purely formal point of view, one can, of course, always maintain such a conception of any theory, provided that one allows the "hypotheses" of the previous account to be conjunctions of several different hypotheses. One must also include the hypotheses from higher levels of abstraction, which have

[1] About this see S. Toulmin, *The Philosophy of Science;* Swedish edition: *Vetenskapsteori.* Stockholm 1964, pp. 97 ff.

[2] B. Russell, *Mysticism and Logic and other Essays.* New York 1918, p. 146.

[3] Braithwaite, op. cit., pp. 53 ff. Wedberg writes about the "fundamental concepts" as undetermined concepts upon which the theories "pose certain general conditions". See A. Wedberg, *Filosofins historia Vol. III (Från Bolzano till Wittgenstein).* Stockholm 1966, p. 250 English edition in preparation.

not yet been used, among these conjunctions. This is always possible thanks to the reflexive property of the implications. The discussion of the structure of theories is made easier if such an arrangement is allowed, provided that one is especially clear as to what the expression "to reject a theory" actually means. When every level of abstraction contains a conjunction of several hypotheses, the rejection means rejection of all the conjunctions. This does not mean, of course, that every particular hypothesis which is included in one of the conjunctions has to be rejected.[1] It may be enough that only one hypothesis in every conjunction is either replaced or modified. Certainly, there are no mechanical rules which indicate which of the hypotheses ought to be changed, and in what way they ought to be changed, indeed just as there exists no set of mechanical rules for constructing theories out of empirical observations. The only thing, that can be said in general is that the modified theoretical system must imply the same statements as the original system in the cases where the statements agreed with the observations made; and that the modified system should in addition—unlike the original one—imply statements which agree with the observations made in those cases where disagreement was the reason for rejecting the original system.

A reservation to the preceding presentation that ought to be added is that it does not hold for theories containing probability statements. For if a hypothesis states that something holds—not generally—but only with a certain frequency among all cases, then the hypothesis should be rejected only if in a sample observed the relative frequency for which this something holds, too much deviates from the frequency which was proposed in the hypothesis. But, no matter how large one decides to make the permitted deviation, it is still possible that the frequency in the sample selected—in spite of the correctness of the hypothesis—falls outside the permitted interval and consequently a correct hypothesis is rejected. For this reason the rejection of a hypothesis, like its confirmation must be considered provisional with the possibility that it may be reconsidered upon the receipt of further information.[2]

It is true that confirmation is provisional and rejection definite for hypotheses which are universal propositions. The reverse of this, that rejection is provisional and confirmation definite must hold for the logical negations of universal propositions which are existential propositions. Probability hypotheses are intermediary cases and become statements of the types mentioned above when their assumed relative frequences take on the values zero or unity. As current economic theory, however, contains real probability hypotheses to a very limited extent, these complications can be ignored in what follows.

Two peculiar features of economic theory stand out quite clearly against the background of the previous presentation of Braithwaite's work. *Firstly* economic theory seems to have tendency towards a—real or spurious—immediate

---

[1] See Braithwaite, op. cit., p. 19, and Wedberg, op. cit., p. 21.
[2] Braithwaite, op. cit., pp. 153–163 and 255.

visuality of all of the concepts and hypotheses used. This inclination can be unwholesome to the extent that the visuality is achieved through the use of models to interprete abstract hypotheses. The interpretation by models in these cases contributes to building a spurious economic reality where subjects act and processes occur, which do not exist but which one might imagine to exist in reality. *Secondly* economic theory tends to develop in such a direction that its statements about empirically observable phenomena cover more and more of the logically possible cases. This development involves a generalization of the hypotheses of the theory in a quite special sense. In the extreme limiting cases of such a generalization process all the statements about empirically observable phenomena become logically true or tautological propositions. Such a theory with only tautological empirical generalizations can never be rejected, since for logical reasons there can not be any empirical observations which contradict the statements of the theory. In what follows below, the tendency to generalize will be treated first and after that the endeavor to visualize the content of economic theory will be discussed.

## Tendencies Towards Generalization

As a beginning it is perhaps necessary to dwell upon the question of what, in this context, ought to be understood as the generalization of a theory or a hypothesis. One can imagine several different modifications a hypothesis that all according to every-day language deserve the name generalization. A pure case is the type of generalization where a hypothesis which earlier has been used to explain a limited group of phenomena is extended, unchanged in form, to explain a broader group of phenomena. The other pure case involves a change in the form of a hypothesis which is assumed to explain an unchanged group of phenomena, so that in special cases it yields the same statements as the original hypothesis, but in other cases yeilds different statements. In reality both types of generalizations are strongly attached to the development of the empirical sciences. Thus, one does not find them in a pure state but instead combined with each other. When the research is directed to explain previously unexplained phenomena, it is natural to begin by trying the applicability of hypotheses which agree in form with those which have been established in connection with the explanation of other phenomena. As it is not always possible to retain the borrowed forms of hypotheses completely unaltered, new and more general hypotheses may be introduced which take on special forms for the different groups of special phenomena which are to be explained. Thus the phenomena within the area from which the form of the hypothesis was originally borrowed and the phenomena within the new area of explanation are arranged under the same general explanatory hypothesis. Such a procedure means considerable economy of the scientific apparatus thanks to the reduction in the number of elementary concepts and hypotheses which this procedure allows.[1]

The procedure of generalizing hypotheses in such a way that the set of derivable statements about empirically observable phenomena include more and more of the logically possible statements is, accordingly, a respectable one; subject to the condition that the generalization takes place in connection with an extention of the field of the phenomena which are to be explained. On the other hand when it is not a question of an extension of the field of explanation, such generalizations only result in an increased ambiguity of the statements; and unfortunately it is often just this type of generalization that one finds in modern economic theory.

It is necessary to understand the logical difference between the two pure types of generalizations. When the generalization is made through an extension of the field of explanation, the general hypothesis implies the original special hypothesis. When the generalization is made through an increased ambiguity of the statements, the generalized hypothesis itself is implied by the original special hypothesis. The direction of implication between special and generalized hypotheses is thus opposite in these two cases.

If, however, a special hypothesis implies a general hypothesis, it seems that one might safely adopt more general theories. More general types logically follow from special types in the cases considered. But the question which ought to be asked is; what point is there in leaving a special hypothesis, with its larger information content, for a more general type with its more ambiguous statements? The answer must nearly always be a statement of the fact that the special hypothesis in question would be rejected if confronted with the empirical observations. To the extent that this is the case, which may often be natural considering that the connection between economic magnitudes resulting from human behavior can hardly show the same exactness as say, certain physical laws of nature, it becomes clearly necessary to employ hypotheses with ambiguous statements about empirically observable phenomena. But besides this, the effort to generalize sometimes seems to be an end in itself.[2] Were that not the case, hypotheses which only imply logically true statements about empirically observable phenomena would hardly be so relatively common in economic theory. As will be shown below the information content of such theories must be considered non-existent. A theory of this type may only be used to demon-

---

[1] A good example of a generalization in both senses considered is the transformation of the acceleration law of Galilei and the planetary motion laws of Kepler into special cases of the general law of gravitation as formulated by Newton. About this see H. Törnebohm, *Fysik och filosofi.* Göteborg 1957, pp. 28–45. (This work has a detailed summary in English.) See also W. P. D. Wightman, *The Growth of Scientific Ideas.* Edinburgh 1951, pp. 72–112.
[2] Such an ambition to theories, which are general because of their lack of precision and their consequent applicability in all possible cases within a group of phenomena, is in conflict with the ambition to increased precision, which according to Nagel is a mark of distinction in scientific explanation as contrasted to pre-scientific or "common sense" explanations. See E. Nagel, *The Structure of Science.* London 1961, pp. 7–10 and 37–42.

strate that one does not know anything about systematic relationships within a group of empirically observable phenomena.—However, one hardly needs a special theory to express ones lack of knowledge on this score.

The generalizations of the type critized above can naturally be an adequate means for a thought saving disposition of a number of special hypotheses resembling each other in form, each implying nontautological statements.[1] The condition for anything like this to be meaningful is, however, that it is empirically possible to decide exactly to which special case dealt with by the theory, a certain phenomenon belongs.

Theories, such that they are consistent with all the statements about empirically observable phenomena which are logically possible can never be rejected. This follows from the fact that there cannot be empirical observations that conflict with the statements of such a theory. This is true *a priori* on purely logical grounds. It would be absurd to consider theories of this kind as empirically founded. Something of this sort would lead to very peculiar consequences. An implication, or a logical "if ... then ..." proposition is by definition true subject to the condition that at least either the conclusion is true or the postulate is false.[2] When the conclusion is logically true, that is true regardless of the truth values its sentential components, the entire implication proposition must also be logically true. In other words the implication becomes a tautology from a logical point of view, on the condition that the conclusion is a tautology. This means that empirical generalizations which are logical tautologies can be implied by, or derived from, any arbitrarily chosen assumptions, regardless of whether they are true or not. The postulates and the conclusions need not have any subject matter connection whatever with each other, in order for this to be true.

As an example one may take the following logically true proposition: "If all economists are asses, then the demand for oats must either increase or not increase when its price falls." The sentence is logically true when its conclusion is logically true, i.e. true regardless of what truth value one assigns to the assumption. As the implication is logically true one can say that the premise implies the conclusion or that the proposition "the demand for oats must either increase or not increase when its price falls" can be logically derived from the proposition "all economists are asses".

As the conclusion is logically true it is to be expected that all empirical observations about changes in the price of oats and the quantity demanded agree with this. If one generally accepts that theories whose empirical generalizations are tautologies, are to be considered empirically founded then one must also accept special hypotheses of the type "all economists are asses" as

---

[1] Such a use is probably meant by W. J. Baumol, *Economic Models and Mathematics*, in S. R. Krupp (ed.), *The Structure of Economic Science*. Englewood Cliffs 1966, p. 91. Baumol regards the general theories as "prototypes" for construction of detailed theories with more restrictive premises and less ambiguity in the conclusions.

[2] See Suppes, op. cit., pp. 6–9.

empirically founded.[1] One ought to observe that it is purely spurious that any other postulate with perhaps less offensive content and a better factual connection with the conclusion can seem to be better empirically based than the postulate above about economists.

This augumentation is thus built upon the fact that logically true propositions can be derived from any arbitrarily chosen propositions and means that every procedure where a conclusion is derived which itself must be considered true *a priori*, is regarded as meaningless. Some objections could, however, be raised against this. *For one thing* it can be said that it may still be of certain interest to know that one cannot exactly predict whether, for example, the demand of oats will increase or not when its price falls. Otherwise, one might have thought that an exact prediction was possible. *For another*, it can be asserted that "the fact" that a logically true proposition can be derived from arbitrarily chosen postulates, really only consists of an agreed definition which states when an implication proposition should be considered true. The former objection can, when expressed more exactly, easily be proved to refer to something completely different than is being discussed here. The knowledge that one cannot predict anything precisely concerning a certain group of phenomena can be of some value as empirical experience, but this need not, therefore, be true about a theory which explains why one cannot make exact predictions. The other objection leads to fundamental problems in connection with inductive inference. Both of these objections will be dealt with in turn.

In two senses an assertion that it would be of some informative value to know that it is not possible to predict anything precisely about certain groups of phenomena can be meaningful. For the one thing it is possible that one has formerly wrongly asserted that it would be possible to predict something exact about these. The error might have been due to the fact that some logical mistake had been made in the derivation of the empirical generalization from the given premises. Furthermore the incorrectness might be due to the premises being contradictory, or that they would imply empirical generalizations which conflict with factual observations. This latter point can be true regarding the particular empirical generalization in question as well as other empirical generalizations that are derivable from the theory. However, in all cases the pointing out of the error, itself, is the essential thing.

Considering the great number of cocksure beliefs in the field of economics which have no scientific basis, such a search for mistakes is highly motivated.

[1] For those readers, who for some reason are prepared to accept that the proposition "all economists are asses" is empirically founded, it may be convenient to stress that by the same argumentation, and on the basis of the same observations of changes in prices and quantities demanded of oats, it may be argued that the proposition "some economists are not asses", i.e. the logical negation of the former sentence, will be empirically founded too. It is true, that from an "instrumentalistic" point of view the maintaining of logically contradictory theories does not present any difficulties, but this tolerant view may hardly be applied in cases where *always* the negation of a theory will be empirically founded as soon as the theory itself is empirically founded. About "instrumentalism" see p. 95 below.

The attack, however, must be directly aimed at faulty theories which, in cases where the assumptions or derivations are insufficiently accounted for, must be reconstructed. In no case is it sufficient to only construct a more general theory which implies the disjunction of the thing incorrectly stated and its logical negation. The error of the incorrect construction may by no means be inferred from this new construction of the theory. On the contrary, it is true that, if a given set of hypotheses implies anything definite, it also implies the disjunction of this definite something and its logical negation. It goes without saying that the empirically established existence of cases where the definite something predicted by the incorrect theory is not true, shows that the theory is untenable. This, however, follows from empirical facts, not from some new and more general construction of the theory.

The mistake, as pointed out above, may also be of a logical nature but the faultiness can not in any case be evident from a generalized theory construction. What is said above leads to another case where one can find a relevant interpretation of the conception of the information value of theories which imply only ambivalent statements of the type that say either something definite, or its logical opposite, is true. This is the case where one can show that with a set of hypotheses given as premises at the outset, it is reasonable to believe that something definite as well as its opposite can be true for a group of empirically observable phenomena. This, however, means something entirely different from deriving a logical tautology from the premises. The closer meaning is probably that one states a new hypothesis such that it, together with the original premises, implies something definite and another hypothesis such that it together with the original premises implies the logical negation of this definite something. The statement of the two new alternative premises is, however, something completely different from the derivation of a tautology from given premises. In order for the procedure to have some meaning, it is also required that it is possible to decide empirically when one or the other of the new premises should be used.

As far as the other objection is concerned, it is certainly the case that the truth value tables of the logical sentential connectives are agreed conventions, and therefore to a certain extent are arbitrarily decided. The essential thing, however, is that the formal peculiarity that every implication is true when the conclusion is true, corresponds to a real problem with inductive inferences. The features in the defining truth value table of the implication connective, which are of any importance, are connected with the use of the implication in deductive and inductive inference.

When an implication proposition is established as being logically true, it can be used in principle in two different ways in deductive inference. If the premise can be proved true, it follows immediately that the conclusion is also true. If the conclusion can be proved false, it follows immediately that the premise is also false.

Only the latter use is relevant in inductive inference. A hypotheses for which one claims general validity within a certain area of explanations must be immediately rejected whenever a statement derived from this hypothesis is considered to conflict with empirical experience. Inductive inferences therefore become more uncertain than deductive inferences because one maintains all hypotheses as long as none of the conclusions about empirically observable phenomena actually derived, conflicts with observations actually made. The link between theory and empirical observations can therefore become very weak with inductive inference. The connection must be nonexistent if it can be decided beforehand that it is logically impossible to reject a theory on the basis of its derived empirical generalizations. In contrast to the synthetical contents of empirically founded theories, its contents are seen as merely analytic.

The researcher in an empirical science must always strive to destroy his own theories. The more effective the destructive activity is, the stronger the link between theory and empirical reality becomes for the theories that survive the process of attempted destruction. But the creation of theories indestructable at the outset is much too easy a task for serious empirical research to concern itself with.

The question of what kind of "truth" one should attach to the theories maintained in an empirical science is fundamental to this argumentation. Braithwaite points out, as mentioned above, that the abstract hypotheses and the theoretical concepts which appear in them need not, in an empirical science, have any other meaning than the one they indirectly receive through the empirical generalizations derived from them. The consequence of this becomes that the abstract hypotheses are no longer required to give a picture of reality, but instead only acquire their meaning as instruments for the derivation of empirical generalizations. This view of scientific theories is sometimes called "instrumentalism" and has been maintained with special force by the logical empiricists of R. Carnap's school.[1]

[1] See Wedberg, op. cit., pp. 250–251. The position of instrumentalists like Braithwaite seems to be somewhat paradoxical. On one hand, Braithwaite maintains that the abstract parts of theories need not have any meanings apart from those meanings derived from the use of the theories as instruments for derivation of empirical generalizations. On the other hand, Braithwaite protests against the claims on the theoretical terms to be "logical constructions" from empirical observables. A greater freedom for the formation of abstract concepts, it is argued, will prevent the theories from being merely systematizations of observed facts and will furnish a ground for further development of the theories. This view is strongly supported by the fact that such an "openness" of meaning of the theoretical terms, as is defended by Braithwaite, has been a distinctive feature of the formation of the most powerful concepts in science. However, it is not quite obvious how one should construe a theory, which derives its meaning from its use as an instrument for derivation of propositions about empirically observable facts, but nevertheless must be saved from being a mere tool for systematic description of those facts. A theory does not have any empirical truth value, but nevertheless possesses some mysterious ability to produce other useful assertions about observable facts than those for the explanation of which it was originally constructed. The question is whether such an ability is something which itself is empirically established for a number of theories constructed in the past. The next question naturally concerns the reason for this. May it be something which depends on our propensity to think with the aid of abstract schematic images and on our ability to adapt such familiar images so that they may also be used to account for new experiences? If this is so, theorizing is simply a characteristic of our way of thinking. Cf. Nagel, op. cit., p. 108.

A consistently maintained instrumentalist view involves some rather paradoxical consequences. Among other things it becomes quite reasonable to maintain several different theories in order to explain the same group of phenomena in an empirical science, provided that the theories lead to the same group of empirical generalizations. Serious problems would not arise even if the theories were logically contradictory, provided that the theories are kept apart. The fact that two theories are contradictory means that they cannot be true at one and the same time, but as the question of truth itself becomes meaningless from an instrumentalist point of view the difficulty in maintaining the two theories at the same time ceases to exist.

Economists would, in general, probably find it rather difficult to accept an instrumentalistic view of their own theories. The tendency of making things visual or pictorial, to which we will return, indicates that one likes to consider all parts of economic theory as pictures of some kind of reality.

However, the essential thing in this context is that the criticism which is presented above against theories whose empirical generalizations are logically true, will remain in a somewhat changed form even if one accepts an instrumentalistic view. It has been pointed out earlier that such theories can not possibly be considered as being empirically founded. An instrumentalist cannot claim in a related criticism that the fault with such theories was that they did not give a true picture of reality, because the instrumentalist has given up any claims upon truth of theories from the beginning. On the other hand, considering that theories are regarded as instruments for derivation of empirical generalizations, it is reasonable to assert that it is a useless occupation to construct instruments for the derivation of empirical generalization which are known to be true for logical reasons. The instrumentalist can raise similar criticism against complicated theories from which only very meagre classes of non-tautological empirical generalizations can be derived. According to the instrumentalist's criterion of simplicity, one ought to prefer the simpler instruments which it would then be possible to construct for the derivation of the few empirically testable statements. A person who prefers to think that theories give pictures of reality, would instead mean that the theories in question are weakly linked to the empirically observable reality since the statements through which a real verification can be made are so few and vague.

## Examples from Economic Theory

A number of examples from elementary economic theory can serve as illustrations of the preceding general discussion for the purpose of exemplifying cases where given hypotheses are empirically testable or cases where they may not be. As will be clear in what follows there is a strong tendency in economic research to achieve logically true statements about empirically observable phenomena by means of introducing "autonomous" changes or other types of generalizations from special hypotheses previously introduced.

It is natural to begin the series of illustrations with those theories regarding the rational behavior of private subjects—consumers and firms—under so called "quantity adjustment". For both types of economic subjects the existence of restrictions on behavior and rules for the evaluation of the alternatives considered are assumed. As far as the consumer is concerned, the restrictions consist of budget constraints determined by income and the prices of goods; and the evaluation rules of subjective preference orderings with certain specified properties. As far as the firm is concerned, the restrictions consist of production functions determined by available techniques and of given sets of factor and product prices; and the evaluation rules of the efforts to maximize profit. There are two possibilities of characterizing the given assumptions.

Firstly, they can be considered as abstract hypotheses which have nothing directly to do with empirical observations, and which only become established via the empirical generalizations which are derived from them. According to what has been asserted above, empirical generalizations must not be logical tautologies.

It does not seem impossible to find empirical generalizations in both of the stated examples which can be rejected when confronted with empirical evidence, and which therefore satisfy the requirement asserted. In consumption theory an increase in the price of one good—all other prices held constant—can lead to an increase in its consumption only if an isolated increase in income leads to reduced consumption of the good in question. In the theory of the firm an increase in the price of one output, other prices being constant, must lead to an increase in the production of that output, and an increase in the price of one input, all the other prices being constant, must lead to a decrease in the use of that input. Judging from these statements, it seems as if the empirical observations which could lead to a rejection of these statements would be few since *partial* price and income changes are extremely rare, and since these statements only concern such *partial* changes. However, it is possible to state classes of simultaneous price and income changes combined with classes of simultaneous quantity changes which must not take place if the theoretical assumptions are to escape rejection. This clearly shows that there exist empirical testing possibilities even for theories which do not refer to specified numbers, but instead to rough classes of changes that are classified as increases or decreases.

The empirical verification is carried out by means of comparisons of incomes, prices and quantities during two or three time periods, during which the theories are assumed to be valid. This means of course that consumer preferences and production functions are not specified more than by certain general characteristics, but it must be assumed that they are unchanged during the succession of periods for which the comparisons are made.

If, however, such "autonomous" changes, that economists frequently use, are introduced into the production function via "technical change" or into the preference function via a "change in tastes"—all possibilities of empirical verification of the kind stated above, disappear. This is because every statement which does not agree with empirical observations can be said to depend on the asserted fact that an autonomous change has taken place in reality. From the introduction of these changes it follows that the statements which, before, might have become the object of confrontation with empirical material, have now been replaced by logical tautologies, which only state that a quantity can either increase, remain unchanged, or decrease as a consequence of a price change combined with some "autonomous" change. In the empirical material which is collected there cannot be any observations which could lead to the rejection of the theory.

If the character of the particular autonomous changes were stated more precisely, or if their occurence at least was decided independently of the testing procedure, the result would not be quite so devastating. But it is the nature of autonomous changes to be vague, and their occurence is not usually mentioned until a hypothesis being confronted with the empirical material runs the risk of being rejected.

The same result as that produced by autonomous changes is obtained by the generalization of theories about the behavior of individual subjects so as to include planning for several periods of the esthetically very attractive type which J. R. Hicks has carried out. The consequence of such generalizations is often that the verifiable empirical generalizations are replaced by logical tautologies. The question then arises whether or not one can find other empirical grounds for the theories in question aside from those obtained by comparing factually observed changes between several periods of time.

The procedure of investigating the mental processes which preceded the economic decisions of a subject, presents just such an opportunity. If these processes had been expressed for example in the form of written profit calculations the whole thing would be easily done. In other cases it appears to be more difficult. For want of better material it may be possible for the very economists who construct decision theory to introspectively record their own experiences about ways of making decisions, and thus form the empirical material from that. In this way the introduced postulates themselves would, as a second interpretation, take on the nature of empirical generalizations, thus eliminating the need to confront statements that are derived from them with other empirical evidence.

The difficulty with this way of looking at the problem is that economists, like other people, flatter themselves on being completely rational individuals—something that modern psychology with its stress on the "subconscious" hardly supports. The question is, however, whether the rational view, which was more forgivable during the age of enlightenment than to the present day is not more harmless in the economic field than in other fields where the motivations behind people's behavior are being examined. Probably most people, in dealing with economic questions, do make an effort to behave rationally, and so rational decision theories still acquire significance by being idealized pictures which people attempt to realize, but which is only achieved to a greater or lesser extent. In spite of the fact that there are decision theories which even a computer would have difficulty realizing, most of the rationality assumptions of the common decision theories are of such a simple nature and assume so little consistency and purposefulness of action that it would not be surprising if the actual behavior came fairly close to approximating the ideal.

As for decision theories which are concerned with the behavior of an economic subject where there is uncertainty about the consequences of the act of choice, the question concerning the relationship between theory and empirical observations becomes extremely embarassing. These types of decision theories contain assumptions about the nature of uncertain expectations, and assumptions about the evaluation of particular actions whose consequences can only be anticipated with uncertain expectations of the kind assumed. As long as all the empirical generalizations which can be derived from such theories do not become logical tautologies the theory constructed is completely respectable from the point of view of the philosophy of science—even if one can say that with the introduction of uncertainty the superstructures of the decision theories in the form of abstract hypotheses become especially bulky in relation to the underlying bases of nontautological empirical generalizations. However, as decision theories that take account of uncertainty are generalizations of decision theories which do not consider uncertainty—which is clear from the fact that the former contain the latter as special cases—the danger that the empirical generalizations will be transformed into logical tautologies increases. As pointed out above, this risk is always present with all generalizations. However, their consequences become especially dangerous in those cases where the decision theories take uncertainty into consideration. While the possibility of rescuing decision theories which do not take uncertainty into consideration consisted of the assumptions themselves being regarded as empirical generalizations about which knowledge had been received in an introspective way, this possibility is hardly available to decision theories which take uncertainty into consideration. The simplest introspective reflection would give as its result that the formulation of expectations under uncertainty and the evaluations the respective acts of choice regarding whose consequences the expectations are formulated could not be separated, but instead are knit together in a complicated fashion within the mental processes which precede decisions that are actually carried out.

An exception would be choice behavior in such situations of uncertainty where expectations can be made more precise by the assignment of objective probability estimates. The replacing of objective probabilities by subjective probabilities in situations of uncertainty where there is no statistical information involves an unreasonable exploitation of analogy thinking in cases which really have only one thing in common, namely that one can not estimate in advance with certainty the consequences of acts of choice that are carried out. This is probably the best we can do at present—although it is hardly satisfactory. But, of course, these comments apply only to such theories from which only tautologically true propositions may be derived. The dichotomy between expectations and evaluations is not in itself harmful when it appears in the hypotheses on high levels of abstraction.

From theories about the behavior of individual subjects one passes most naturally to the theories of the functioning of markets. It is probably sufficient to use illustrations from the static theory of price determination under so called perfect competition. This means that prices are determined by supply and demand functions in such a way that demand and supply are exactly equal in all markets which the theory intends to treat; and therefore all economic subjects are able to simultaneously carry out their plans. At first glance it might seem as if the assertion that the supply and demand functions, determined by the behavior of individual economic subjects, fix market prices would imply that these market prices can not change at all—except possibly proportionally if it is a Walras type of general equilibrium system.

This is the case, provided that the configuration of market prices and the corresponding equilibrium quantities are empirically observable magnitudes, and provided that the asserted statement is an empirical generalization. This empirical generalization would have to be rejected as soon as a market price or a quantity changed in reality. In order to avoid this distressing result one can also introduce "autonomous" changes here. It is possible that subjects can appear or disappear. For subjects, who act on the market during all periods with which the theory concerns itself, their behavior can change due to changes in taste, technical change, and possible changes in expectations about the future. All this can displace the supply as well as the demand functions. The result of all these changes would certainly be changes in prices and turnover quantities. However, by means of the introduction of autonomous changes one is able to obtain anyone of the logically possible combinations of price and quantity changes among the statements in the new empirical generalization. Thus, it becomes a logical tautology and the possibilities of empirical falsification of the theory disappear.[1]

---

[1] One type of "autonomous" changes, leading to non-tautological propositions about changes of market prices, of demanded and supplied quantities of goods, is hinted at by K. E. Boulding, *The Verifiability of Economic Images*, In Krupp (ed.), op. cit. These changes are provided by the establishment of public price control and its complementation by rationing. A strange situation that the equilibrium theory of price formation may only be tested when the free formation process for market prices, supposed to be represented by this theory, is put out of function by government decree. Another possibility of obtaining non-tautological propositions about empirically observable phenomena from the equilibrium theory of price is provided by the cases, where the conditions on the supply side or

Alternatively the configuration of market prices and the equilibrium quantities can be regarded as purely theoretical concepts and the whole static theory of price determination as a system of purely abstract hypotheses. However, even in this case we lack possibilities of empirical testing. As will be shown in what follows, one usually introduces interpretations by models in order to visualize abstract hypotheses. These model interpretations are, however, combined with great risks of misunderstanding; a point that will be treated in the following as well.

What has been said about static equilibrium theories is, in principle, also true about their dynamic extensions of the so-called "excess demand" types. The stationary processes, corresponding to the static positions of equilibrium, form special cases among the solutions of dynamic theories. This means that the dynamic theories lack nontautological generalizations to the same extent as the static theories. That there exist several possibilities of dynamization for every static theory does not alter anything in fact, since the solutions of all the dynamized theories must contain stationary processes which correspond to the equilibrium positions of the static theories. Of course, the empirical generalizations, even in dynamized theories, do not become logical tautologies until the autonomous changes are introduced. However, there is usually not a shortage of these. This is clear from the fact that the processes, which are nearly always assumed to be convergent, need autonomous disturbances to keep them in motion. Statements about the nature of the processes of price changes are, as a rule, classifications within the groups "convergent", "oscillating", and "explosive". But these statements are supplemented at the empirical confrontation by assumptions about autonomous unexplained changes. These residually determined autonomous changes can of course be so adapted that the hypothesis one wishes to establish is made to agree with any logically possible empirical evidence.

As to economic theories which treat relationships between so called macro aggregates, the same thing applies as was said about general equilibrium theories of the Walras type. The formal difference lies in the fact that the numbers of variables in macro theories have been reduced so that the theories obtain more simplicity; while the variables themselves become complicated aggregates which can be related to immediately measurable magnitudes in alternative

---

the conditions on the demand side may be regarded as unchanged. In such cases empirical confrontation material corresponding to Patinkin's "market experiments" is obtained. See M. Blaug, *Economic Theory in Retrospect.* Homewood (Ill.) 1962, pp. 606–607, and D. Patinkin, *Money, Interest and Prices* (*2:nd ed.*). New York 1965, pp. 11–12. The necessary requirements, if such testing procedures are to be legitimate, however, are that it is empirically determinable on independent grounds when production techniques, consumer preferences and the number of economic agents are unchanged. Thus, it is not possible to choose unaltered conditions on supply side or demand side as special assumptions according to the empirical observations about price and quantity changes used to confront the propositions of quilibrium price theory. Such a testing procedure will necessarily be circular. And, it is very unlikely that independent evidence for constant supply or demand conditions may be obtained.

ways. This difference does not change anything essential regarding the question of the relationship of theories to economic reality. There are different ways of empirically establishing macro-economic theories: their adaptability is dependent upon whether one regards the theories as being true pictures of reality or as instruments for the derivation of statements about reality.

For those who would like to regard economic theory as a true picture of economic reality, micro-economic theory concerning the behavior of individual subjects and the functioning of single markets stands out as immediate knowledge upon which macro-economic theory, concerning connections between aggregates, ought to be based. The efforts to derive macro theory by logical reasoning from the assumptions of micro theory, under appropriate definitions of the aggregated magnitudes, are results of this way of looking at the problem. The many attempts to "integrate" value and distribution theory into macro theory, and to solve the specific so-called "aggregation problems" are clear expressions of this. Unfortunately, the results have, as a rule, been discouraging, as the desired aggregations can not be made with the definitions tried. Those who persist in the struggle for integration have also tried to build macro theories on micro theories by means of such assumptions as that all the so called "distribution effects" can be disregarded, or that the economic subjects can be divided into a few homogenous groups.

Quite a lot becomes different for those who regard economic theory as an instrument for the derivation of statements about empirically observable phenomena without any claims of its own upon truth. In parts, the view of the instrumentalist contrasts strongly with the view that is common among economists. When alternative theories are judged by their empirical generalizations and by the facility with which these can be derived from abstract hypotheses, the old "quantity theory" for instance becomes superior to theories of the Patinkin type. The statements would be the same, that is, the price level must be proportional to the amount of money, but the quantity theory must be considered superior thanks to its simpler structure. If, however, one attaches a truth value to every hypothesis in economic theory, it must be considered beneficial to integrate as many of these as possible, for example into more complicated quantity theory.

Many problems become simpler for the consistent instrumentalist. As pointed out above it is no great problem for him to have to work with several different theories for the same problem area even if the logical relationships between the theories are unclear. To the instrumentalist any method is sufficient with which the statements of macro-economic theory itself may be tested, without paying the slightest regard to the logical relationship between macro- and micro-economic theory. The confrontation can be a complicated thing in itself, depending on the difficulty of constructing appropriate calculation methods for the total aggregates. It must be emphasized, however, that macro-economic theory can not be considered as being empirically confrontable as long as such calculation methods have not been stated or at least tacitly understood.[1] This is also true, though to a lesser degree, about micro-economic theory due to the fact that its idealized concepts of market prices bear no relation to real transaction prices as long as calculation rules have not been made precise. We will return later to the specific nature of the idealized concepts of economic theory.

It is of course assumed that an empirically verifiable macro theory implies nontautological statements. If the only statements about the relations between macro aggregates that can be derived from the theory are tautological, then no calculation rules will be sufficient enough to achieve the possibility of empirical verification.

A macro-economic theory which only contains simultaneous relationships between aggregates whose values are fixed within the frame of the theory, quite naturally leads to predictions that the values of the aggregates must not change. When the values of the aggregates are associated with empirically measurable magnitudes via complicated calculation rules, the predictions of constancy can be associated with considerable changes in reality, especially if one has permitted a liberal margin of error in the calculations. If, however, the task of macro theory were only to supply the knowledge that all macro aggregates should have constant values, one could easily do without a special theory for that purpose. Furthermore statements such as these become, as a rule, all too specific for it to be possible to find calculation rules, thanks to which the theories manage to escape rejection, in spite of the possibility, that has already been pointed out, of certain economic changes in reality. Thus autonomous changes are introduced here too.

These can be introduced in two quite different ways. They can be introduced in a clearly specified way into the relations of the theory so that their existence is empirically determinable, or even so that their values can be calculated by special calculation rules from measurable magnitudes. Government action parameters which are found in theories complemented by the addition of the

[1] Such computation rules are generally meant by the requirement of "operational definitions". The expression originates from P. W. Bridgman, *The Logic of Modern Physics.* New York 1927. See also the complaints presented by P. A. Samuelson, *Foundations of Economic Analysis.* Cambridge (Mass.) 1947, about the scarcity of "operationally meaningful theorems" in economic science. Operationality problems in economics are also treated in F. Machlup, *Essays in Economic Semantics.* Englewood Cliffs 1963. In this connection it ought to be noticed that the modern philosophy of science does not require that every single term in scientific theories must be independently defined by way of "operations". Partly, this depends on the claims on "openness" of meaning of theoretical terms, already referred to, but another reason is a change in Logic of the requirements that definitions in general have to meet. The old claims on explicit definitions *per genus proximum et differentiam specificam* have been discarded and so called "contextual definitions" have been made legitimate. See K. G. Hempel, *Fundamentals of Concept Formation in Empirical Science.* Chicago 1952, pp. 4 and 39–50. As an example Bohr's atomic model may be taken. There the terms "electron" and "possible orbit for an electron" are not defined explicitly. Rather there are "correspondence rules" which connect the composite expression "electron jump from one possible orbit to another" with radiation of light of certain wave-lengths and with visible spectral lines. See Nagel, op. cit., p. 98.

public sector into Keynesian theories are examples of such autonomous changes. Autonomous disturbances in such cases do not have a negative influence upon empirical verifiability. Autonomous changes can also be introduced as unspecified and arbitrary changes in the forms of the relationships, in which case the possibility of empirical verification completely disappears.

It has been established above that there are risks of empirical unverifiability due to the fact that statements about empirical phenomena are logically true in theories about the behavior of individual subjects, in static equilibrium price theory, in dynamic excess demand theory, and in the theories about the connections between macro aggregates. It has also been shown that these theories can avoid such consequences, provided that a certain amount of restraint with generalizations and the introduction of autonomous changes is kept in mind.

The examples have referred to mathematically formulated variants of economic theory, which also have been such that their formal calculi have been composed of simultaneous equation systems without specified analytical function forms and naturally without numerically specified constants.

This does not mean that the risks pointed to above would not be relevant to verbally formulated theories. On the contrary, the long catalogues of factors considered to determine certain economic conditions to which institutionally disposed economists (who flatter themselves with being especially "empirical") usually apply themselves become often as meaningless as simultaneous equation systems.

Nor does specification of analytical function forms and numerical constants always help as a means for achieving empirical verifiability in mathematically formulated theories. If one only carries out the calculation of numerical values, which have not been specified in advance in a theory, from empirical material that is exactly large enough to determine the unspecified values, one can hardly be said to be making a confrontation of the statements of the theory with empirical observation material. For it to be said that a real confrontation is taking place, the empirical material must involve a stricter controle of the theory than merely that which is a deprivation of the degrees of freedom introduced at the outset by neglecting to numerically specify the values of the constants.

One often finds a tendency to divide up time series material into suitably long periods, each of which comprises just a sufficient number of observations to allow the deprivation of the degrees of freedom introduced. When the use of such a procedure for different periods yields different numerical values of the same constants that were not specified from the beginning one claims that autonomous changes have affected the values of the constants between the periods, rather than rejecting the hypothesis in question as being incompatible with the observations. Computations of this sort do not lead to any empirical confrontation since the empirical observation material is used in such a way that the theories can not be rejected.

This sort of empirical determination of numerical constants is found mostly in connection with Cobb–Douglas types of production functions; and changes in the values of the constants, which it is necessary to assume so that the functional forms that have been stipulated in advance will not need to be modified, are given the name "technical progress". One can easily imagine what a corresponding procedure would mean in physics. The classical second degree equation of kinetics for bodies in free fall could then be replaced by any other arbitrarily chosen functional form whose constants undergo autonomous changes.

As long as such a theory is used for the organization of observation material which has already been collected it is harmless if not especially enlightening, but when it is used for purposes of predictions, one must be extremely sceptical considering the fact that every assumption about special numerical values of the constants is arbitrary and without corresponding support from empirical experience.

## Tendencies Towards Pictorial Intelligibility in Economic Theory

It is appropriate here to comment in more detail on the characteristics of economic theory which above were called its attraction to a real or spurious pictoriality in the concepts and assumptions that are employed. At first it is quite obvious that economists would like to avoid concepts and hypotheses which are abstract in such a way that it is quite impossible to *imagine* types of economic reality where the concepts correspond to empirically identifiable phenomena, and the hypotheses are statements whose truth value is empirically estimatable. Instead the abstractions lie in the procedure of idealizing and abstracting, which the phenomena of the existing reality seem to undergo when they are changed into concepts and statements in economic theory.

Economists' dislike of concepts that are too obviously abstract is clear from their attitude to the concept of utility. As long as the ordinal conception of utility and the theory of revealed preferences had not yet been invented, economists seemed to accept, though with some reluctance, the concept of cardinal utility. To a certain extent this discontentment might have been due to the earlier value content of the concept and its connection for example with normative taxation theory. Since the tendency to value-oriented interpretation of some scientific terms has been demonstrated by G. Myrdal, and thus to a certain extent has been rendered harmless, another objection has been raised against the concept of cardinal utility.[1]

This is based upon the fact that one can not in an empirical way establish the existence of utility as a measurable psychological sensation in individual consumers.

---

[1] See G. Myrdal, *Vetenskap och politik i nationalekonomien.* Stockholm 1930.

Such an attitude deviates strongly from the common attitude in the philosophy of science that the profitability of the concepts employed in theories should only be judged by their ability to contribute to the explanation of empirically observable phenomena. One therefore ought to compare the role of utility in consumption theory with that of light rays in geometrical optics. Through such a comparison it can be established that utility as well as light rays, without being empirically observable entities, can be used to explain something about the consumers' actual behavior and about actual optical phenomena respectively. The frenzy with which economists have rid themselves of the concept of cardinal utility indicates that this sort of attitude is foreign to most of them.

This does not mean that economists actually do not use theoretical concepts and abstract hypotheses. The abstractions lie, however, in idealizing and abstracting as already mentioned. The assumption of homogeneity within large groups of goods, and the assumption of uniformity of actual transaction prices in the markets over considerable periods of time are examples of this. One finds other examples in the concepts of perfect competition and monopoly.

The concept of perfect competition for example is idealized and abstracted from the forms of competition observed in reality in the same way that the concept of the triangle in geometry is an idealization of observed material triangles.[1] As it is *logically* true for an idealized triangle that the sum of its angles equals 180 degrees; it is also *logically* true for a firm engaged in perfect competition that it ought to adjust its production in order to maximize profits so that marginal cost equals product price. The difficulty is knowing when the respective statements are reasonably applicable to material triangles and actual firms. The enormous difference between geometry and economics consists of the fact that geometry has found its place within the purely logical deductive world of mathematics, while economics ought to be an empirical science.[2]

The procedure of passing over from reality into theory via idealization and abstraction can create beliefs that economic theory in some way is logically constructed out of observations concerning economic reality. The connection

[1] About the idealization process in Geometry see R. Nevanlinna, *Rum, tid och relativitet.* Uppsala 1966, pp. 25–30.

[2] However, some empirical natural sciences, for example Theoretical Physics, too use abstraction and idealization. The laws obtained in Physics by reasoning about ideal cases (distinguished by absence of friction, complete rigidity of bodies etc.) are only approximately valid as explanations of real phenomena. But, according to Nagel, op. cit., pp. 508–509, it will be much easier to supply the supplementary assumptions required to make the theories applicable in Physics than it is in Economics. This is, it is argued, due to the fundamental difference in the explanation tasks between the sciences mentioned. The difference is examplified by the explanations of the motions of, on one hand, a simple, material pendulum and, on the other hand, a leaf blown by the wind over unregular ground. The latter explanation is much more difficult, due to the multitude of detailed facts about the leaf, the ground and the wind which is necessary to know and to be able to handle in order that the explanation task be properly solved. According to Nagel, op. cit., pp. 461–464, this more complicated kind of explanation is required more often in the social than in the natural sciences. In economics these complicating "supplementary assumptions" refer to the historically determined and in various forms occuring "institutional frameworks."

of the theory to empirical observations then does not become that which is described by the philosophy of science referred to in this paper. According to the philosophy of science, theories are established by confronting their statements about empirically observable phenomena with factual evidence concerning these. Economists seem to prefer to think that they start from observations about phenomena in reality, and by choosing the "essential" features and in addition through a process of idealization and abstraction logically construct an economic theory. Such a procedure can be appropriate at the construction of theories, but the procedure itself can never serve as sufficient means of empirical verification at the same time.[1] If in addition no control of empirical generalizations against observed facts is made, it is impossible to know whether the features of economic reality which were omitted from the beginning are essential or not. Sometimes economists seem to think that empirical verification can be achieved by some vague merit of experience about the actual facts of economic life, possessed by some economists who perform the transsubstantiation of economic reality into economic theory.

One might perhaps recognize a similar attitude in a famous statement by Böhm-Bawerk of which Schumpeter's account is reproduced here.[2] In it he says "that is, there is no longer a special task of collecting facts—the relevant basic facts of economic life are, as experience shows, simple and familiar to us from practical experience and they repeat themselves everywhere, if in many different forms. In any case, collecting facts recedes before the task of the intellectual digestion of these facts and of developing their implications. This cannot be done save by mental isolation of the elements of experience of interest to us, and by the abstraction of many irrelevant matters. This resulting theory, it is true, is abstract, separated by the hiatus of many hypotheses from immediate reality, as any theory is; but it is as realistic and empirical as a theory of physics."

One familiar way of economists criticizing eachothers' works also is an indication of a view of the intimated kind. It is often said about a theory that

[1] It should be noticed that the propensity to think by the help of simple schemes or "Gestalten" is a characteristic of our way of obtaining every-day knowledge. Thus, the abstract concepts are not secondary constructions from observations of individual, material objects in all complicated detail, but rather primary schemes by which our perceptions of those material objects are organized. About this see Nevanlinna, op. cit., p. 26. Theorizing by abstract concepts may therefore be regarded as a natural way of thinking in scientific research, and empirical testing as a special controlling activity. The controlling activity is of greatest importance, but it is an illusion to think it possible to explain anything without theorizing merely by "keeping to facts". In the contrary, those who believe that they never theorize often make the wildest abstractions when they try to explain something. And this is especially dangerous, because the unconsciousness makes them believe that they have discovered ultimate truth.

[2] See J. Schumpeter, *Ten Great Economists*. New York 1951, p. 157. A similar optimistic attitude to the problem of empirical truth content in economic theory is found in L. Robbins, *An Essay on the Nature and Significance of Economic Science*. London 1945. Robbins believes that nearly all postulates of economic theory are empirically founded, because they refer to every-day experience about economic matters. In contrast, T. W. Hutchison, *The Significance and Basic Postulates of Economic Theory*. London 1938, requires explicit empirical testing of all more important postulates of economic theory.

because the assumptions which are introduced are unrealistic, the conclusions are of dubious value. This statement seems to mean partly that the realism of the assumptions can be decided immediately, and partly that the value of the conclusions depends upon the realism of the assumptions. What is said here would be relevant if it was a question of purely logico-deductive inference. There one would not be able to draw the conclusions by a correctly performed inference when the premises are not fulfilled.

As to the construction of theories in an empirical science, what is said becomes enigmatic. If one can speak directly about the realism of the assumptions, the hypotheses of which they consist must be empirical generalizations. But if this were the case one could hardly derive such abstract hypotheses from them whose realism can not be determined immediately but rather must be derived from the realism of the assumptions. It then becomes difficult to understand why people refrain from speaking directly about the realism of the conclusions, if one can not presume that the critic has made a mistake and that the assumptions actually ought to be considered as abstract hypotheses—not as empirical generalizations. The fact that the process of idealization emanates from reality might, however, create illusions that all the hypotheses of the theory have an immediate empirical meaning.[1]

Sometimes not even idealization seems to be sufficient but must be complemented by pure imaginary constructions of economic "reality", such as it "might" appear. One can characterize similar creations in the language of the philosophy of science as interpretations by models of abstract hypotheses.[2]

[1] According to Hutchison, op. cit., p. 10, no propositions of economic theory may be regarded as empirically founded if they can not be empirically tested directly or deduced from other postulates which can be empirically tested. In opposition to this view it has been argued above that some propositions in the theoretical structure of a science may be meaningful, merely because it is possible to deduce empirically testable propositions from groups of theoretical propositions. But the theoretical propositions are not directly testable, because they contain concepts with a certain openness of meaning. Cf. T. C. Koopmans, *Three Essays on the State of Economic Science.* New York 1957, pp. 139–140, where it is argued that it is not reasonable to except a group of propositions from the requirement of direct verifiability. In contrast to this view, the view maintained above is that a careful partition of propositions of economic theory into genuine empirical generalizations and illusory interpretations of theoretical propositions by way of models must be made.

[2] To this group belong the "half-truths" referred to by M. Friedman, *Essays in Positive Economics*. Chicago 1953. The "half-truths" may be regarded as abstract hypotheses, to which model interpretations have conferred an illusory trait of empirical reality. If propositions about the illusory "model reality" are compared with correct propositions about similar phenomena in the actual economy in function, one may draw the conclusion that the former propositions are false, but nevertheless useful because it is possible to deduce from them other propositions, which, as compared with propositions about similar phenomena in the actual economy, are not false. The author of his paper agrees on this point with B. C. Ysander, *Truth and Meaning of Economic Postulates, Money, Growth and Methodology (in Honor of Johan Åkerman)*. Lund 1961, p. 332. Ysander maintains that questions about empirical truth must not be asked about theoretical hypotheses. Such a view, however, requires that we know exactly which propositions are empirical generalizations and which propositions are theoretical hypotheses. This is impossible if the latter are made to resemble the former as much as possible by model interpretations. A discussion of the "half-truths" of Friedman is found in E. Nagel, *Assumptions in Economic Theory, American Economic Review (Papers and Proceedings)*. 1963, pp. 211–219. The most interesting idea presented is that some hypotheses in economic theory refer to "pure cases", specified in theoretical

In order to make clear what we are concerning ourselves with here, it can be appropriate to use a demonstration. D. Patinkin's construction of L. Walras' account of the process of price determination with so called "recontracting" seems to be well suited for this purpose.[1] As is generally known this process involves an auctioneer establishing a sequence of tentative market prices while sellers and buyers sign contracts for the quantities they wish to sell or buy at every shout of a price. If the shouted price is such that there is not equilibrium of supply and demand, then the contracts are cancelled and the process continues with new prices shouted. This goes on until an equilibrium price has been found.[2]

One could of course regard the process described as an empirical generalization about the nature of price determination on actual markets. It would then be easy to establish the existence of markets without auctioneers, where no probation contracts are signed and where there is not even a uniform market price. Thus, it would be easy to reject this as an empirical generalization. The fact, however, that the construed process of price determination describes how "the uniform market price" is established, seems to indicate that the presentation instead involves model interpretation of the abstract hypothesis that market prices are determined at equilibrium between supply and demand. The uniform market price is a theoretical concept. The interpretation by the model then can not be used to determine the reasonableness of the abstract hypothesis. This evaluation must be made indirectly by means of a confrontation between such actual empirical generalizations which can be derived from the hypothesis and the empirical evidence.

It now seems appropriate to record Braithwaite's definition of the concept of a model.[3] The abstract hypotheses have been assumed to contain theoretical terms which only partially and indirectly—via the confrontation of derived empirical generalizations with empirical evidence—get their meaning through the way in which they function in the theoretical hierarchy of hypotheses. In

---

terms and thus applicable to nothing in reality; such as pure competition. According to Nagel it would be impossible to identify in empirical experience a case such as pure competition because it is specified in terms of "limits" of "nonterminating" processes. Thus, it would be impossible to understand what a "re-contracting" process of price formation designates actually; rather than the process would be a false description of actual price formation.

[1] See D. Patinkin, op. cit., p. 532.

[2] It is possible that the equilibrium price theory must be construed as a teleological explanation, maintaining that equilibrium price is attained "in order that" all economic agents may carry out their plans simultaneously. As teleological explanations often emanate from antropomorphic considerations of purposiveness, it is not surprising that a human subject is inserted in the theory to carry out the price formation process. See Nagel, op. cit., pp. 28 and 523, and H. Reichenbach, *The Rise of Scientific Philosophy*. Berkeley 1951. The connection between competitive equilibrium and Paretian optimality too supports the opinion favoured in this note. For the following argument, however, it is assumed that the theory of equilibrium price is not constructed in order to provide teleological explanations.

[3] See Braithwaite, op. cit., pp. 88–92 and P. Suppes, *The Meaning and Uses of Models, The Concept and Role of the Model in Mathematics and Natural and Social Sciences* (*ed. H. Freudenthal*), Dordrecht 1961.

order to satisfy the intellectual need for pictoriality, it is possible to give certain immediately intelligible interpretations of theoretical terms; the interpretations having nothing to do with the explanatory goal of the theory itself. Empirical generalizations then take on meanings which depend upon the interpretations given to the abstract terms in the premises.

The interpretation of a theory for the purpose of making all of its hypotheses pictorial is what Braithwaite calls a model.

Thus the particle model of structure of atoms is an interpretation of the theoretical terms, atomic nucleus and electron, and of the entire theory of chemistry. Similarly, the process of "re-contracting" is a model interpretation of the static theory of price determination. The difference appears to be that while the electrons and atomic nuclei are imagined to be so small that they could possibly exist in particle form even though one can not see them, it is difficult to imagine auctioneers being so small that their non-existence could not be established. As this author understands it, the economists' situation is more advantageous inasmuch as they should not confuse the interpretations by models with actual empirical generalizations. When this happens in cases as that of "re-contracting", it means that the confusion must be made by those who have an extremely low opinion of the model builders' knowledge of reality. The entire thing becomes embarrassingly peculiar if the creator of the model interpretation himself, begins to believe that it is an empirical generalization.

An altogether different question is that of the utility of such model interpretations. Sometimes it is maintained that the interpretations by models should be valuable in that the concepts which have been visualized in the interpretations have other features besides those that are essential for the explanatory functioning of the theory. Thus, it is argued, one can pose new questions regarding the relevance of these features to the problems which the theories are designed to explain. Such questions might supply impulses toward further developments of the theories.[1] On the other hand, the interpretations by models might contribute to further disorder especially if they are confused with empirical generalizations. The need for models has probably arisen from the general struggle to attain pictorial intelligibility which in its most grandiose form has at all times lead to innumerable attempts to build so-called world pictures with or without support from specialized sciences.

The desire for pictoriality associated with the economists' tendency to literally take the interpretations by models as empirical generalizations, can be regarded as a depreciation of the tolerance of the philosophy of science toward concepts and abstract hypotheses that are too obviously theoretical. It is a fact that the philosophy of science allows lots of room for the imagination to create very abstract hypotheses under the mild constraint that only the empirical generalizations, but not the abstract hypotheses from which they are derived,

[1] About this see R. Harré, *The Logic of The Sciences*. London 1963, pp. 98 ff., where an example from the kinetic theory of gases is supplied.

must be confronted with reality. This freedom can be abused but the connection to reality remains as long as nontautological statements about empirical phenomena can be got out of the theories. The connection of economic theory to reality via the process of idealization seems to be considerably more uncertain in spite of the spurious intelligibility of the concepts and hypotheses employed. This intelligibility is obtained by the idealization from reality and is improved by model interpretations, but it can supply a false impression of realism to the theory.[1]

With such an illusion one can comfortably settle back without ever trying to state any actual empirical generalizations that might be confronted with observed evidence. In this case economic theory would become a kind of spurious reality where subjects act and processes occur which do not exist in reality but only in the imaginary idealized world of the economists.

## The Use of Mathematics

Finally, something ought to be said about the case of mathematical methods in economic theory. There has been a lack of harmony between economists on this issue. The discord, as a rule, might be explained by differences in educational and intellectual background. And the arguments which have been raised in favor of, or against, the use of mathematical methods have been more enlightening with regard to whether the combatants have had a scientific or humanistic background than with regard to the subject-matter discussed.

The arguments which have been raised against the use of mathematical methods have not, as a rule, been very enlightening, as can be expected in discussions about the suitability of employing a large group of methods in an entire science. There is considerable resentment from economists with a humanistic background against the concentration of interest around quantitative phenomena in modern economic theory. According to these people, this concentration of interest implies a negligence of what they call "qualitative" phenomena. Every kind of quantitative treatment of economic phenomena naturally means that homogeneous groups of economic phenomena are created, and the relationships between the metric properties of the respective groups are examined. The qualitative differences between groups of phenomena can be taken into consideration when the initial division into groups takes place. This can be done in as detailed a fashion as is desired, even if the need for manageability imposes a certain temperance in this direction. Thus it is difficult to see what it is that one actually neglects by dealing with quantities in economic theory. One imagines that the backbone of the criticism is that the qualitative differences between the groups are not given enough importance in that the discussion of them is carried out in connection with the initial division into groups. This attitude is usually associated with a requirement that the qualita-

[1] Nagel stresses the point that the illusory models used in presentations of theories may never replace real "correspondence rules", linking the theory with empirically controllable propositions. Nagel, op. cit., pp. 92–97.

tive differences should be weighted according to an evaluation of their particular aspects—i.e. with a normative attitude.

Another general objection to the use of mathematics in the social sciences is that the use of differential and integral calculus is inappropriate merely because the calculus was developed as a help science to certain natural sciences.

One objects to this, partly because no universal reason has yet been advanced as to why natural sciences and social sciences should not use the same kind of methods, and partly because mathematics has ceased being merely a help science to theoretical physics and has become a general logical language of a formalized type thanks to the contributions of logicians such as G. Frege and B. Russell.

General arguments in defence of the use of mathematics such as that the precision of the language lends itself to a special clearness of thought are equally unenlightening. Mathematics can, on the contrary, under service to unclear thoughts contribute to making them even more obscure.

What needs discussion is not the general issue of whether the use of a system of methods is applicable to a science, but instead whether particular mathematical methods can be suitably employed in the explanation of particular economic phenomena. Thus, it must not be surprising if positive as well as negative answers may be received. A great deal of clarity would be gained if the discussion about methods were transferred from the general level to specific problems.

A discussion of details is, however, not the purpose of this paper. Only a general reflection regarding how the discussions of methods has to depend upon the kind of truth attributed to the theories will be mentioned here. As pointed out above, economic theory works through the abstraction and idealization of phenomena which have been directly observed in reality. The theories hereby created form an idealized, logically consistent "model reality". The struggle for pictorial intelligibility which characterizes the work of economists implies that it should be possible to comprehend the kind of economic conditions within the model reality which correspond to every hypothesis in the theory.

With this attitude in mind, it is natural that one reacts in the presence of risks of "deformation" at the translation of assumptions worded in every day language into assumptions worded in the formal language of mathematics because the structure of the latter language might seem to be suggesting certain assumptions which may not be visualized and whose economic meaning in the model "reality" is difficult or impossible to judge. Assumptions about continuity, domains, and ranges of the functions introduced and assumptions about the existence of unique solutions for equation systems introduced need to be mentioned here. Valuable works such as G. Debreu's theory of value have arisen simply for the purpose of clarifying the economic significance of assumptions *within the idealized "reality" of the model.*[1]

---

[1] G. Debreu, *The Theory of Value—an Axiomati Analysis of Economic Equilibrium.* New York 1959.

Of course it is possible as has already been established to adopt the instrumentalists' approach to things; namely that the hypotheses of the theory lack any other meaning than that which they get via empirical generalizations derived from them.

If one accepts the instrumentalists' view, it is clear that the possibility of distortions, due to the unconscious introduction of additional assumptions when verbally worded hypotheses are translated into mathematics, presents no problem whatsoever. The essential concern with the set of hypotheses introduced as assumptions is their suitability for the derivation of certain empirical generalizations.

If the empirical generalizations are correctly derived and agree with the observed reality, it makes no difference whether they have been derived from the original verbally worded assumptions or from mathematical "distortions" of them. The assumptions do not need to have an empirical meaning, and thus one cannot distort what they do not have. To the extent that mathematical formulations lead to empirical generalizations which are contradicted by actual observations, where the verbal formulations of corresponding hypotheses would not be contradicted, one can naturally say that the mathematical translation is unsuitable. But as a rule, the few nontautological empirical generalizations, which economic theory contains, are independent of the "language" in which the assumptions have been stated. As mathematical or formal logical derivations usually are easier to perform than completely correct logical arguments in every day language, the instrumentalists' second criterion—that is the facility in deriving a certain set of empirical generalizations—often gives a decision in favor of mathematical formulations.

One reason why mathematically formulated economic theories may seem especially "unrealistic" is that the postulated functions relate variables, the domains of which are intervals of the continuum of real numbers. This is necessary in order that the effective tools of infinitesimal analysis may be used. The price for this to be paid seems to be that one accepts that economic variables, i.e. prices, quantities of goods, interest rates, etc., may not only vary by infinitely small fractions of the units of measure, but even take on irrational values. For the man of practical mind it seems to be pure nonsense to talk about a quantity of a good being $\sqrt{2}$, a price being $\pi$ or an interest rate being $e$. However, these are no specific problems for economics. In direct measurements of length, time or mass by the help of an operationally given metric system it equally is impossible to obtain irrational values.[1] As far as finite, or at least denumerably infinite, classes of measurements are considered, all values resulting from such measurements may of course be expressed as finite multiples of some common unit, or at least be found among the rational numbers. Nevertheless, infinitesimal analysis has been developed by Newton in order to

[1] About different kinds of metrical systems see Hempel, op. cit., p. 57–78.

be used for problems of physical dynamics. Theoretical concepts, like "instantaneous velocity" or "instantaneous acceleration", may not be measured directly. Nevertheless they are useful in theory for the deduction of propositions about time intervals and distances in physical motion, which may be tested by direct measurement. Neither is it necessary to carry out the testing by measuring irrational time intervals or distances. Analogously the marginal concepts may be useful in economic theory; and the continuous variability of the variables is a necessary requirement for the use of those marginal concepts. The mathematical formulation of economic propositions is only a technical tool; and just because, with the use of this tool, some propositions are expressed in terms of empirically undefined concepts it will not be legitimate to require empirical testability of all propositions.[1] Thus, the reluctance of common sense to accept irrational values of variables may not interfere with the formation of abstract hypotheses. The empirical experience must only be confronted with certain classes of deduced propositions.

[1] Cf. Nagel, op. cit., pp. 103 and 131–132.

RICERCHE ECONOMICHE, XLVI, 1-2 gennaio-giugno 1992, pp. 75-90

# ON PROGRESS AND PERFECTION IN THE ARTS AND SCIENCES

TÖNU PUU
*University of Umeå*

## 1. *Introduction*

All economic development has one aspect of *quantitative increase* and another of *qualitative improvement.* Qualitative change is much more difficult to model than increased productivity. The mathematical methods through which economics asserted its supremacy among the social sciences are not in favour of formulating qualitative change, as it involves increasing diversity rather than increasing numbers of well-defined objects. Some of the most promising ideas about the nature of development, Smith's division of labour, and Böhm-Bawerk's lengthening of roundabout production, were never translated into convincing mathematical models. Even when the initial interests of the researchers may have been to find out something about qualitative improvements, they often end up modelling quantitative increase instead.

There is no doubt that the output of culture has exploded in our days, indicating increased productivity. Through the flood of printed materials, radio, television, records, sound and video tapes we are literally drowned in pictures, sound, and ideas. After the experience of pollution due to industrial mass production, we could, however, ask whether an increasing quantity of cultural production is exclusively beneficial. Without getting lost in details, we note that a constant background white noise of art could, in fact, be regarded as a pollutant of our mental environment rather than as a benefit.

Received April 1992.

Improved quality, on the other hand, could, without risking controversy, be claimed as exclusively beneficial. This is connoted by the term itself. We still have to specify what we mean by quality improvements. If we specify objects of art as bundles of relevant properties like Lancaster (1971) suggested for consumer's goods in general, we could speak of improvements only in a Paretian sense of simultaneous improvement in all these property dimensions. We are then probably bound to find that most historical events of "progress" in art rather represent improvements in certain dimensions at the expense of others. Such changes are triggered off by shifts in taste and fed back by price signals to the producers that respond by appropriate design changes of their products.

Deriving imputed prices for the various properties we could overcome the Paretian relativity by calculating the values of the product in the old and the new designs. Comparing the values we find the new product always better, as can be expected from basic economic theory. Of course, we must always apply the new prices, otherwise the outcome is reversed.

This is why contemporary observers always report progress. Theorists of visual art or music, especially in self-confident ages like the Renaissance or the Enlightenment, try to persuade us that there has, in fact, been a uni-modal development to ever higher levels of perfection. The same story is told by most historians and philosophers of science.

The curious thing is that now and then some branch of cultural production is claimed to have attained perfection, and yet there follows another development to a still higher level of perfection. The historians believing in progress only seem to be interested in the last transition. If they can claim it as an improvement they are willing to accept all the previous transitions as improvements as well on the evidence of previous chronicles. Index theory warns us that there is a problem here, as a new set of prices (reflecting new tastes) is applied in each transition. We thus have to be rather cautious in accepting the ideas of progress and perfection.

## 2. *Example: Performance Practice in Music*

To put flesh on the bones of theory we will illustrate the case by the development of musical practice during the last centuries. This sheds some light on the issue of progress, because in the revival of music of the Baroque and Classical periods we find an interesting development *back* to the original solutions, from the modern ones.

### 2.1. *Progress in Music*

We have the following aspects to consider in the development of music: the instruments in practical use have been changed, some being scrapped and others coming into prominence. To the instruments belong the solutions of temperament problems (unavoidable with all keyboard instruments and in most of ensemble playing). Other ingredients are composition practice (for instance with respect to the choice of tonalities) and performance practice (all the unwritten laws with respect to articulation and sound balance that evade any attempt of precise notation).

There has been substantial change in the musical instruments over the ages. To avoid the bewildering manifold of Medieval and Renaissance instruments, let us narrow the period to 1700-1900. We can comfortably stop at 1900, as the instruments of the "modern" symphony orchestra had in fact already been frozen fifty years earlier.

By that time we find the instruments in common use completely changed. For instance the harpsichord was replaced by the pianoforte, the string family of viols by the violin family, and the lute by the guitar. The wind instruments, originally based on the sets of natural harmonics and the few notes that could be reached by comfortably placed finger holes, remained but were provided with complicated valve systems. The recorders, once important solo instruments, not being suitable for valve garments, were banished to the exclusive abuse by school children not old enough for a "real" instrument.

In some cases the process was astonishingly quick. The famous Kirckman harpsichord workshop in London finished its last instrument in 1800, but already in the cold winter 1816 numerous harpsichords in the Paris Conservatoire were consumed as firewood. Likewise, the last great viol virtuoso Karl Friedrich Abel died in 1787, and with him died the viol. It was so well buried that it could even be re-invented by Staufer in 1823 under the name "arpeggione".

It can be objected that we still find violins from the 16th, 17th and 18th centuries in use, highly appreciated, not only as antiquities but as actual tools of the musician. This, however, is an illusion. All those Stradivaris, Amatis, and Guarneris have been rebuilt. The necks (that used to be flush with the bellies) were put at an angle, the instruments were opened to reinforce the bellies by stronger bass bars, and the delicate gut strings were replaced by steel, all in order obtain a more powerful sound. A comparison with the few violins remaining in original condition indicate that we in fact deal with a completely different instrument. The question, most pertinent to the issue discussed, is: why did the old craftsmen, who otherwise built unsurpassed masterpieces, not do this themselves? It certainly was not beyond the technical feasibility of their times. The same happened with the other members of the family, viole and celli. Of course not all instruments survived this cruel operation (especially numerous delicate masterpieces by Jacobus Stainer were destroyed).

This reconstruction of old violins was by no means a unique incident in history. In 18th century France, Flemish harpsichords, in particular those from the Ruckers workshop in Antwerpen, and English viols, by masters like Richard Meares and Barak Norman, were most highly prized. The fashion of the day in France, however, wanted the bass line to be extended down to a low *AA*. Accordingly, a 7:th string was added to the old English viols. See Hans Bol (1973). The harpsichords had to be completely rebuilt with added bass keys (involving extension of both case and sound-board). This process was so often performed that it was given a special name, "ravalement". See Frank Hubbard (1967). Again we may suppose that the masters in Antwerpen and London could have done this themselves if they had wanted.

The choice of intonation for keyboard instruments tells a similar story. As known already to Pythagoras, ascending from a note in 12 pure fifths would lead to a note $(3/2)^{12} = 129.75$, higher than ascending in 7 pure octaves to $2^7 = 128$. Thus, any tuning had to be a compromise. We think of the "modern" (equal temperament) tuning of all the fifths to $2^{7/12} = 1.498$, slightly less than the pure 3/2, as the final, mathematically egalitarian solution. It has been claimed that Johann Sebastian Bach composed his *"Das wohltemperierte Klavier"* in order to demonstrate the possibility of playing in all tonalities in such an egalitarian world. See the classic: sir James Jeans (1937). This idea is somewhat absurd as the keys make no difference except absolute pitch. Bach could have composed half of the work in *C* and half in *a*, hiring any copyist to write the whole set out with correct numbers of flats and sharps. Composing 48 preludes and 48 fugues to demonstrate the possibility of transposing on these terms seems a little futile for the greatest genius of the past.

In equal temperament the major third, another important interval in chords, becomes terribly impure, $2^{4/12} = 1.260$ as compared to the theoretical 5/4. We are, however, so accustomed to this impurity that we do not even note it. In the Renaissance, people thought thirds were more important than fifths, and so divided each of the pure thirds in 4 quite impure fifths $5^{1/4} = 1.495$, compared to 3/2. Unlike the case of equal temperament this (mean tone temperament) does not work throughout the keyboard. It was limited to 8 thirds in the most important tonalities, the rest was left as it could be. All this may seem rather technical, but it demonstrates the relativity of the concept of good intonation. The Renaissance people became as tolerant to impure fifths as we are to thirds.

Later, in the days of Johann Sebastian Bach, much more sophisticated intonation systems were in use. His pupil Kirnberger describes a system based on the fact that tuning 4 mean tone fifths and 7 pure fifths leaves just one fifth than only imperceptibly deviates from that of equal temperament. The mathematics of this tuning option is contained in the formula:

$$(5^{1/4})^4 \, (3/2)^7 \, (2^{7/12})^1 = 127.9999.$$

This way of tuning not only yields one pure third and seven pure fifths, but all the frequently used thirds in the central keys are much purer than in our present day temperament. The system may be a codification of Bach's own practice. We know that Bach was very meticulous about always tuning the instruments he played himself. The system gives the tonalities their different characters so as to make it a real challenge to compose a work like "*Das wohltemperierte Klavier*".

By now we should not be surprised to find in the sources that our "modern" tuning was in fact known already in the 15th century, but not in use as it was considered an inferior solution to the Pythagorean problem!

These examples suggest that changes like increasing the compass of keyboard instruments, reinforcing violins, or changing tuning systems are not so much improvements due to major inventions as they are changes reflecting new directions of tastes.

In the case of woodwind the Böhm valve system was claimed, and certainly is, a technical invention (though not beyond the capabilities of the old artisans as they used a few valves on bass instruments for soundholes that could not be reached by the unaided fingers). The modern valve system makes all notes and passages almost equally easy to play. This is not always an advantage. For instance, a flute solo in *c*, being terribly awkward on a historical instrument, was used in pieces, connoting great strain, whereas the easy *b* key was used for virtuoso display (like Bach's famous flute solo in BWV 1067). The difference was automatically achieved on the historical instrument, but would be extremely hard to attain artificially on the modern one where all tonalities are equal. Thus, not even an obvious technical improvement need be an improvement for artistic purposes.

We also find the instruments, except when they no longer corresponded to the paradigm of the day and so were scrapped (like recorders, viols, harpsichords and lutes), unaltered over centuries. The violin that (except the reconstruction mentioned) has been unaltered for 400 years, is a good example.

This was no result of any lack of inventiveness. See Ed. Heron-Allen (1885). All kinds of materials were tried as replacements for wood, like porcelain, brass, glass, and tanned leather. Various designs were tried, either according to simple mathematical rules or in the pursuit of some principle like increasing surface area wherever this was physically possible. As a testimony in almost any museum of musical instruments we find inflated monsters, that can be called violins in a topological sense only, like those fitted with some fancy wind instrument bell-piece instead of the neck. Nothing has, however, qualified as a real improvement. Modern industry has not even produced a glue comparable to the traditional animal glue.

Egyptian furniture from the Middle Kingdom is still intact in all joints. Yet any violin repairman can open a joint with a knife whenever something needs to be attended in an instrument. There is no synthetic glue meeting these requirements. No artificial material is equivalent to a snake-wood or pernambuco bow stick provided with stallion hair, alpine spruce for bellies, or gut for strings.

The instrument seems to be impossible to improve upon, provided we do not want something else from it than what it was once constructed for. The replacement of strings by steel to make the instrument louder is one example, and if we want to use the violin as a tennis racket, the round shape, patented in England by Collins, or the trapezoidal, suggested by Dr Savart to the French Academy, may be more appropriate than the traditional one. The extreme confirmation of the optimality of the original materials is probably provided by the hog bristles used as springs in harpsichord jacks - retaining their perfect elasticity after thousands and thousands of plucks.

## 2.2. *The Revival of Historical Music*

The story of the revival of the "historical" instruments and performance practice is most instructive as it so clearly points to the original solutions as optimal. When a more substantial number of people around 1900 got curious about how the music of the 17th and 18th centuries once sounded, there were several problems to be solved. One obviously was to reconstruct the old instruments, found in museums in unplayable condition. The great pianist Wanda Landowska is reported of having put drawing pins in the hammers of her grand piano, and finally (in 1911) she managed to persuade the Pleyel company to produce a concert harpsichord for her.

The demand for harpsichords among the enthusiasts was large enough to make it profitable for the piano industry to divert part of their production to this new brand. The point of departure, of course, was the experience of the industry: tensioning strings on a metal (or possibly a very strong wooden) frame, connected by a bridge to a sound-board, just replacing the hammers by plucking jacks. Nobody thought of the fact that in traditional harpsichords the strings were mounted on a light resonant wooden case. The experience was somewhat disappointing: a weak, muffled, metallic sound. In order to increase the power of the instrument several sets of strings were added (some of them thick as pencils), but then the frame had to be further reinforced, and the result was an even weaker sound. All those strings could, of course, not be sounded by plucking with quill plectra - particularly hard tanned leather was used, and it was physically demanding to press the keys. Had this development continued, the harpsichordist would have become an equal to the ancient Roman *pulsator organum* who played the organ in the theatre by blows of his fists. The harpsichord sound was really awkward especially with broken leather plectra. The famous conductor Furtwängler is reported to have described the sound of the harpsichord as narrating skeletons copulating on a tin roof. What it was like playing harpsichord those days is told in an amusing article by Ralph Kirkpatrick (1983).

The same story could be told about viols ("gambas"), that were modelled after celli, and lutes, that were modelled after guitars. The mock names "pianochords", "cellambas", and "luthars" were coined for these hybrids by Thurnston Dart (1954). The arrogance of our age, nursed by the idea of continuous progress, rather than ignorance, was to blame for the fact that for a long time no attention was paid to the original solutions. Sixty years after the general revival of interest in "historical" performance, industry still flooded the market by wretched instrument hybrids that had nothing to do with the originals they pretended to equal or surpass. When the pioneer Arnold Dolmetsch in 1890 gave a concert with viols, Bernard Shaw prophetically remarked: *"If we went back to old viols... I suppose we should have to make them again; and I wonder what would be the result of that... if our fiddle-makers were to attempt to revive them, they would probably aim at the sort of 'power' of tone produced by those violins which ingenious street-players make of empty Australian mutton tins and odd stool legs".*

It is surprising that the enthusiasts still persisted, despite the disappointing results. For the general public these experiments created a picture of music on "historical" or "authentic" instruments as something awkward, and bound to sound bad, an interesting academic enterprise maybe, but hardly anything artistically rewarding. The case was aggravated by the fact that few first rate musicians dared to risk their careers in this business. Mainly those whose soloist aspirations failed with respect to conventional instruments tended to specialize in a field where nobody had yet set the standards of quality. Despite this negative selection sufficiently many great musicians (like Wanda Landowska, August Wenzinger, Thurston Dart, and Nikolaus Harnoncourt to mention a few) persisted.

Then the following idea occurred to people like Frank Hubbard (1967): maybe the old craftsmen knew what they did? Perhaps it is better to start anew from scratch and copy the old instruments we find in museums? In stead of industry, small workshops grew up, where harpsichords, recorders, lutes, and viols were produced according to what could be found in museums and in literary evidence, like the famous Diderot and D'Alambert (1751-80) encyclopaedia. Even the instruments in continuous use were modified. The violins got the gut strings back and were played light bows, the celli lost the end-pins, and the double-basses were in many cases provided with frets. Flutes, oboes, and bassoons were again stripped of the valve garments.

Simultaneously the sources on performance practice from the 17th and 18th centuries were penetrated anew and the able musicians persisting in the pursuit of authentic performance could try out various long forgotten practices on instruments that now responded favourably to their efforts. Works like Carl Ph. E. Bach (1753-62), Leopold Mozart (1756), Johann Mattheson (1739), and Johann Joachim Quantz (1752), to mention only the most important treatises from mid 18th century, became so demanded that they were all spread in new facsimile reprints.

The resulting renewal not only concerned technical points (like two-finger vibrato for strings, or double-tongue techniques for woodwind), but the whole articulation of music. For the powerful sound, indispensable in large concert halls, things like crisp intonation had been sacrificed. They were now re-established, and with them the rhetorical articulation of the Baroque and Classical music. With the support of literary evidence the consequences were drawn concerning ensemble size and sound balance. Concerning all this, reading Nikolaus Harnoncourt (1982, 1984) cannot be too highly recommended.

For instance, dynamics had for a long time been handled by bulk and volume. As it is not within the capability of any conductor to make a symphony orchestra start a note at the same time, the effect of a sluggish crescendo produced by it is very different from the lightening crescendo a few musicians can produce even without a conductor. Likewise, the use of many musicians in the orchestra would have created insurmountable intonation problems had not the constant vibrato been invented. A note played by a "modern" symphony orchestra is in fact a mental construct by the listener (an averaging interpolation over time and space). Stopping the orchestra and freezing the sound at a certain moment would create an awful discord. Ensemble sizes for performing Baroque and Classical music were reduced, and vibrato again receded to become a specific embellishment of certain notes mainly in solo passages.

Vocal practice changed along with instrumental, emphasizing articulation by stressing the consonants rather than the vowels.

The music of the Baroque and Classical periods was thus after a long initial phase efficiently reconstructed within a short time span both with regard to instruments and performance practice. Of course, there is nobody to testify whether the result sounds like the historical original. But anybody can judge that the result is artistically much more satisfactory than the attempts to play Baroque and Classical music with the Romantic orchestra. And, what is interesting in this context is that *the success was due to going back to the solutions found in existent instruments and literary evidence.*

We are now at the heart of what actually once caused the transformations, away from the now rediscovered practices of the 17th and 18th centuries. It obviously was a major social change: the construction of concert halls and opera houses for very large audiences, requiring a large volume of sound. As these rooms were acoustically dry, and extreme legato playing was thus needed, things like crisp articulation were forgotten, being almost impossible anyhow. The music composed by Mendelssohn or Berlioz, no longer "speaking" but "painting", to use the words of Nikolaus Harnoncourt, was perfectly handled by the "modern" orchestra in this environment. When Mendelssohn revived Bach's works (in 1829), and Berlioz revived Gluck's (in 1859), in both cases after a century of neglect, they started the tradition of performing the old masters according to the practice of their days. The story just told indicates that the original solutions were better.

Of course this cannot imply that there never are improvements in history. No instrument, of course, springs forth like Pallas Athene from the head of Zeus, fully equipped in every respect. For each instrument there is a rudimentary beginning and a development to a final design, but this happens on a relatively fast time scale, whereas the changes we note over longer time periods rather are responses to changing tastes. Elaborating this would bring us too far, as we would have to be very careful about recognizing the recorder or viol of the Renaissance as an instrument different from its Baroque successor, each being superior in the proper context. To establish in which cases we deal with pure improvement of one instrument and in which we deal with two different ones, is quite hard in practice, especially as in more exotic cases there is yet nobody to test and judge the quality of the instruments.

## 3. *Art and Science*

The story dwelt extensively on the case of music. This after all is only one branch of culture. The visual arts are to some extent easier to deal with. Unless there has been physical deterioration, there is no ambiguity about what a painting or sculpture looks like, the objects are still there and our eyes, at least physically, are the same as those of our ancestors. There is no parallel of translating the notes into sounding music. Likewise there are no implements like the musical instruments needed to look at a painting or a piece of sculpture. The general conclusion, however, is the same.

The Early Renaissance sculptors in Tuscany developed to perfection the representation of the human body as a solid object in marble and bronze. Yet, it remained for Bernini to make sculpture something that conveyed expression and texture via light and shadow, where the sculpture no longer ideally was a solid copy of what it represented. It would be hard to claim that Bernini was superior to, say, Verrocchio. The natural conclusion is that in the theatrical age of the Baroque statues were placed in the stage of a church or a royal court, intended to be looked at from a certain respectful distance. This was quite different from a portrait sculpture of some wealthy Florentine merchant placed in the intimate surrounding of a private home.

Again, we note the change of tastes as the motive force, pushing artistic evolution in a direction where we can no longer speak of improvement or progress. This should not be so understood that everything in art is equally perfect according to the dictum *"de gustibus non est disputandum"*. Certainly there is good taste and bad taste and multitudes of sculptors that do not reach the summits of Verrocchio or Bernini, but the summits themselves we cannot compare. Regarding the history of art or music as successive transitions from one summit to another we can hardly speak of any progress.

What about science? There is a common idea that art and science are distinct activities, the former occupied with beauty the latter with truth. Art, deprived of its social function with respect to expression and meaning, condensed into pure beauty, is an absurdity. As for science, we are usually not aware of the aesthetic principles we apply, though things like the beauty contest for mathematical theorems announced in a recent issue of *"The Mathematical Intelligencer"* (1990) reminds us of their existence. Every time we speak of an "elegant" theory we refer to such principles, even if few scientists dare to be explicit on this point. Hermann Weyl was an exception when he at an old age admitted: *"My work has always tried to unite the true with the beautiful and when I had to choose one or the other I usually chose the beautiful"*. Elegance in science has to do with simplicity. The principle of Occam's razor has always been accepted as a guide for science, but there is no guarantee that it leads to absolute truth. After all we do not know if reality is simple or complex. It should be noted that beauty in a scientific theory could not be defined in terms of formal characteristics. In a mathematical theorem, for instance, the proof is an integral part of the aesthetics. Among the hottest candidates in the beauty contest mentioned was the Eulerian formula:

$$\frac{1}{1^2} + \frac{1}{2^2} + \frac{1}{3^2} + \dots = \frac{\pi^2}{6}$$

Any claim to beauty would most certainly evaporate if this series merely was used to define $\pi$, though the formal properties of the expression would still be the same.

Aesthetic principles have been extremely important in the history of science. There is no better example of this than the case of optimality in various fields.

In physics the principle of least action led to the important advent of Euler-Lagrange dynamics, at the same time as it gave rise to the absurd metaphysical principles due to Leibnitz (the world as the best of all possible worlds) and Maupertuis (Nature minimizing the action needed for changes of whatever kind). See Anthony Tromba (1985) about the amusing dispute between Maupertuis and Voltaire.

In biology Darwin ascribed the labour and wax minimizing cells of the hive bee to the "*wonderful instinct*" of the bees, cultivated by the process of natural selection favouring the most economical of the bees, concluding: "*Beyond this stage of perfection in architecture natural selection could not lead; for the comb of the hive-bee is absolutely perfect in economizing labour and wax*". See D'Arcy Wentworth Thompson (1942), and Hermann Weyl (1952).

In economics we have the parallel case of the hexagonal market areas as possessing the optimum properties of compactness (hence minimum transportation cost). See August Lösch (1939). It is obvious that Adam Smith's "*invisible hand*" is ubiquitous, organizing men in pursuit of individual self interest to achieve common good, equivalent to the "*wonderful instinct*" of the thrifty bees of Darwin, to the economizing Nature of Maupertuis and to God as the architect of the best of all possible worlds of Leibnitz.

It would be wrong to assign too much importance to all these optimizing subjects, thus classifying the theories as metaphysical. Rather, we should see optimality in science as an application of aesthetic principles. It is important to note that science has made considerable progress on this road, despite incorporating seemingly unnecessary aesthetic constraints.

Likewise, Bach's frugality in highly emotional music was in no way hampered by his incorporation of intellectual constraints, like the case of the "*Matthäuspassion*" where for instance in very numerous places the number of semiquavers in the bass line refers to the exact place in the Bible text.

In the very definition of a creative activity lies that there are degrees of freedom (in the contrast to a mechanical procedure carried out according to a certain pre-determined succession of rules). In scientific theorizing the degrees of freedom are used for idealized theoretical constructs and aesthetic principles, in the arts intellectual constraints and riddles fill the gap. This certainly is an indication that science should be included among the arts. The day science is equivalent to mechanically collecting facts and organizing them, it also ceases to be exciting.

Accordingly, the relativity of progress should also be applied to science, and we should recognize it as a common misunderstanding that development always is towards ever higher degrees of perfection, in art with respect to beauty, in science with respect to truth and understanding.

In the philosophy of science we often learn that scientific theory is modified, and thus refined, every time a contradiction with observed fact is noted. See for instance Richard Braithwaite (1964), or Sir Karl Popper (1959). A favourite example is the replacement of classical dynamics by Einstein's relativity theory due to the Micheelsen-Morely measurement on the constancy of the speed of light.

The reference to the event of relativity at most gives part of the truth. The transition from Aristotelian dynamics gives a different picture. Not only was it perfectly possible to explain the movements in celestial dynamics by the complicated epi-cycles, but the general dynamics for moving bodies must be said to have been more sophisticated before than immediately after the Copernican revolution. The system of concentric spheres (stone, water, air, and fire), creating a tendency for each object to return to its own sphere, could explain all known movements: the fall of the stone through air and water, the rise of air through water, or the rise of fire through air. Compared to this the original Galielan explanation, now mercifully forgotten, of why a stone continued to move after the initial impact, given in terms of air displaced by the stone, closing behind it and giving small further pushes, does not seem to be an improvement.

To explain changes of paradigm like the Copernican revolution Thomas Kuhn (1962) introduced the concept of "*normal science*" and extra-scientific factors causing paradigmatic changes. Kuhn argued that a dominant paradigm, whichever it is, tends to become so modified and refined in the course of time that it can hardly at all be refuted. Accordingly, a change like the one due to the Micheelsen-Morely experiment can seldom overthrow a dominant paradigm, and should thus be regarded as an exception rather than as a rule in the history of science.

For us as economists it is worthwhile to note that the ideas ascribed to Kuhn were anticipated in Joseph Schumpeter (1954). Schumpeter identified certain "*classical situations*" (equivalent to Kuhn's normal science) when science was regarded as having achieved perfection, presenting an aspect of repose and finality "*like a Greek temple that spreads its perfect lines against a cloudless sky*".

## 4. *Development*

We have argued that development is not necessarily progress, either in arts or in science, and that perfection is an evasive goal for development. What then is development, for things obviously change over time? A good analogy is the biological development tree for the species. Manmade products of any kind (musical instruments or other tools), like living organisms, can for any practical or scientific purpose be exhaustively represented by a finite set of measurements concerning form and function, like consumer's goods were regarded in Lancaster (1971). Just take such a property space of sufficiently many dimensions and place a Darwinian development tree in this setting, where the dimensions and their metric properties, unlike the case of the original biological tree, have significance.

Like biological development starts with organisms at a low level of differentiation, technological development starts with multi-purpose tools (for instance not differentiating between the operations of cutting, sawing and scraping). These tools develop over time, but in addition there are particularly interesting moments when the development tree branches and the tools become differentiated for certain purposes (the knife becomes distinct from the saw and the scraper). There is thus a slow evolution as well as sudden branchings, and particularly the latter deserve closer attention.

The evolution of both kinds may be regarded as being directed by parameters pertaining to the total economy or ecology (represented by for instance price signals). As the price signals undergo a slow and smooth development the products respond by an adjustment of design and physical properties. This adjustment process may be assumed to be pretty quick. In the case where the adjustment responds smoothly we hardly notice it. When a new "niche" is opened up, or when several components can be combined in effective symbiosis we notice a sudden branching.

As the response to changed environmental signals is quick we understand that product development to perfection in each environment is a fast process, and that substantial changes (like the rebuilding of violins, or the Böhm valve system for woodwind), rather than being improvements along a one-dimensional scale, are responses to new price signals that favour loudness and extreme legato playing. We obviously deal with a branching point as the change mentioned was associated with a major institutional transformation, the construction of huge acoustically "dry" concert halls for large audiences.

For the analysis of the branching points it is worthwhile to note that inventions, like mutations in biology, tend to come repetitively at a steady rate. The airplane was, as is well known, invented many times, but became a reality only when the airfoil wing could be combined with a, with respect to its weight, sufficiently powerful engine. Almost always we deal with critical threshold values concerning power to weight and bulkiness, material strength, and the like in components to be combined for the real take-off of an invention.

Likewise, the computer of any capacity was a possibility ever since Pascal. If space required for the machine, the cost of materials needed, and the time of computation were not constrained, the super-computer could have been built long ago. The case of the computer represents an issue of economic feasibility, the case of the aircraft one of technical feasibility, but in essence they are alike.

There is an obvious parallel between artistic or scientific development and the development of physical products. Scientific tools and artistic practices too are developed for specific purposes, and they need not be scrapped once a new tool has seen daylight. They may remain rather perfect for the purpose for which each of them was developed. In practice we still calculate the trajectory of a missile by the old laws of ballistics, rather than using general relativity theory. Such a pluralistic, or instrumentalistic, view goes with abandoning the idea of unimodal progress to ever higher levels of perfection.

## 5. *Perfection*

It has been indicated above that, along with the idea of progress, we nurse that of actually attained perfection, though the two ideas are in potential conflict. According to Schumpeter we have an exaggerated appreciation of well organized classical systems at the expense of more turbulent processes of scientific (or artistical) renewal.

Actual research always takes the direction from the particular to the general. Galileo's acceleration law and Kepler's laws of planetary motion *preceded* Newton's laws. In all text-books, however, the system is taught deductively, starting with Newton's laws and deriving the more specific laws as special cases. The aimed scientific ideal is something like Euclid's "*Elements*". The extreme expression of this is the reductionistic view of the whole body of different sciences advocated by Auguste Comte (1830), where ideally the social sciences should be derived from psychology, psychology from biology, biology from chemistry, and chemistry from physics.

In pursuit of such an ideal, Gauss is reported of having destroyed all the intermediate (generally clear and accessible) reports of his investigations, publishing only the magnificent final products of high indigestibility, like the foundations of differential geometry, "*Disquisitiones generales circa superficies curvas*". It is amusing that the project started as a commission of land surveying. In this way all the humble traces of the actual research process were cleared away.

This is not a concern of physics and mathematics alone. In economics, we never start a micro course by the paradox of value, which would immediately invoke the interest of every student, then passing to the equilibrium of supply and demand, and finally ending up with the factors determining production and consumption. We always start at the top of the pyramid with the axiomatics of ordinal utility. By thus taking the student in the direction *reverse* to that taken by actual research we deprive the student of the satisfaction of finding the *way* to the general principles.

The general idea seems to be to display perfection and completeness of the body of science. There is, however, a general warning for such aspirations to be derived from the fate of the most ambitious integration program of our days, the Hilbert program and the Russell-Whitehead "*Principia Mathematica*" where the whole body of mathematical knowledge should ultimately be based on a few logical principles. As is well known, Gödel finally proved that if a system of logic is powerful enough to produce all true theorems, then it is also self-destructive! This story is told in a most amusing way by Douglas Hofstadter (1979).

### *REFERENCES*


D'ALEMBERT, J. and D. DIDEROT (1751-80): *Dictionnaire raisonné des sciences, des arts et des métiers*. Paris.

D'ARCY WENTWORTH THOMPSON (1942): *On Growth and Form*. Cambridge: Cambridge University Press.

BACH, C. PH. E. (1753-62): *Versuch über die wahre Art Klavier zu spielen*. Berlin.

BOL, H. (1973): *La basse de viole du temps de Marin Marais et d'Antoine Fourquerais*. Bilthoven: A. B. Craighton.

BRAITHWAITE, R.B. (1964): *Scientific Explanation. A Study of the Function of Theory. Probability and Law in Science*. Cambridge: Cambridge University Press.

COMTE, A. (1830): *Cours de philosophie positive*. Paris.

DART, T. (1954): *The Interpretation of Music*. London: Hutchinson.

HARNONCOURT, N. (1982): *Musik als Klangrede. Wege zu einem neuen Musiverständnis*. Salzburg: Residenz Verlag.

HARNONCOURT, N. (1984): *Der Musikalische Dialog. Gedanken zu Monteverdi, Bach und Mozart*. Salzburg: Residenz Verlag.

HERON ALLEN, E. (1885): *Violin-Making - as it was and is*. London.

HOFSTAEDTER, D. (1979): *Gödel, Escher, Bach: An Eternal Golden Braid*. New York: Vintage Books.

HUBBARD, F. (1967): *Three Centuries of Harpsichord Making*. Harvard: Harvard University Press.

JEANS, J. (1937): *Science and Music*. London: Cambridge University Press.

KIRKPATRICK, R. (1983): "Fifty Years of Harpsichord Playing", *Early Music*, 11, pp. 31 ff.

KUHN, T. (1962): *The Structure of Scientific Revolutions. International Encyclopaedia of Unified Science*. Chicago: University of Chicago Press.

LANCASTER, K. (1971): *Consumer Demand. A New Approach*. New York: Columbia University Press.

LÖSCH, A. (1939): *Die räumliche Ordnung der Wirtschaft. Eine Untersuchung über Standort. Wirtschaftsgebiete und internationalen Handel*. Jena.

LUCIE SMITH, E. (1981): *The Story of Craft. The Craftsman's Role in Society*. Oxford: Phaidon.

MATTHESON, J. (1739): *Der vollkommene Kapellmeister*. Hamburg.

MOZART, L. (1756): *Gründliche Violinschule*. Augsburg.

POPPER, K. R. (1959): *The Logic of Scientific Discovery*. London: Cambridge University Press.

QUANTZ, J. J. (1752): *Versuch einer Anweisung die Flute Traversiere zu spielen*. Berlin.

SCHUMPETER, J. A. (1954): *History of Economic Analysis*. London: Allen and Unwin.
TROMBA, A. (1985): *Mathematics and Optimal Form*. New York: Scientific American Books.
WEYL, H. (1952): *Symmetry*. Princeton: Princeton University Press.

*Summary* JEL Z1

## ON PROGRESS AND PERFECTION IN THE ARTS AND SCIENCES

This article discusses the nature of development in culture. It is particularly emphasized that cultural objects have many dimensions, and that development often means progress in some of those at the expense of others. Development must thus be seen as a response to changing tastes rather than as technological progress in a strict sense. Performance practice in music is taken as an example.

*Riassunto* JEL Z1

## PROGRESSO E PERFEZIONAMENTO NELLE ARTI E NELLE SCIENZE

Questo articolo tratta della natura dello sviluppo nella cultura. Si mette in particolare evidenza che gli oggetti culturali sono di diverse dimensioni e che sviluppo spesso significa progresso in alcuni di essi a discapito di altri. Lo sviluppo deve perciò essere visto come una risposta al cambiamento di gusti piuttosto che come progresso tecnologico in senso stretto. La pratica dell'esecuzione musicale è utilizzata quale esempio.

# Curriculum Vitae

Tönu Puu was born in 1936 in Tallinn, Estonia, and emigrated to Sweden in 1944.

After studies at the University of Uppsala, Sweden, he finished his dissertation in 1964 with Professor Tord Palander as supervisor. The title was "*Studies in the optimal choice of assets*" (published in Swedish), and was given the grade "Laudatur" by the faculty, a grade which was used twice before in economics in Sweden during the Century. It was also awarded the "Erik Lindahl Prize".

He was appointed associate professor (docent) in 1964, but worked mainly as acting full professor in economics in Uppsala.

In 1971 he was appointed ordinary full professor in economics at the University of Umeå by Royal patent, a position he still holds. For seventeen years he was chairman of the department.

He belongs, or has belonged to, the boards of editors of the following journals "*Annals of Regional Science*", "*Journal of Regional Science*", "*Regional Science and Urban Economics*", "*Chaos, Solitons & Fractals* ", "*International Journal of Shape Modeling*", "*Discrete Dynamics in Nature and Society*", "*Nonlinear Dynamics, Psychology & Life Sciences*". He is associated as reviewer with the "*Mathematical Reviews*", and belongs since 1975 to the administrative board of "*The Scandinavian Journal of Economics*".

His published production, over a period of thirtyfive years, comprises works on portfolio selection, investments, Keynesian macroeconomics, production theory, philosophy of science, natural resources, spatial economics, economics of culture, nonlinear dynamic processes, biography, and general textbooks.

In his first published works he used portfolio selection theory for deriving demand functions for financial assets and money. They were published in 1962, and were among the first integrating Harry Markowitz's portfolio analysis into general microeconomics with prices, price expectations and budget constraints.

In the dissertation he also extended traditional investment analysis, as developed by Erich Schneider, to imperfect markets when the borrowing and lending rates differed, and demonstrated the general theorem that, given such market imperfections, present value dominance of an alternative under all permutations of lending and borrowing rates became the correct decision criterion. He was also early in deriving general formulas for the relations between expected short term interest rates and the term structure, generalizing results by Sir John Hicks and Friedrich Lutz.

His work during the years in Uppsala was mainly devoted to production theory. The best known results were a Slutskian decomposition of price effects in the theory of the firm and certain aggregation results. Leif Johansen based part of the analysis of his "*Production Functions*" (North-Holland 1972) on those aggregation results.

The work on the philosophy of science stems from the same period, and was inspired by the logical empiricism. It can be seen as an expository application of the doctrine to economic theory, and some of it was used for years in the courses taught by Sir Karl Popper in London.

His later work deals with spatial economics and with nonlinear dynamics, documented in five mongraphs (North-Holland 1979 and 1985, Springer-Verlag 1990, 1993, and 1997), two of them co-authored with Martin J. Beckmann

In most of the works on spatial economics Beckmann's continuous space market model is an important building block, where Puu's contributions specify what can be said by topological methods, using genericity and structural stability as tools for the characterization of spatial patterns, thus generalizing the ideas from Paul Samuelson's correspondance principle.

His current work deals with nonlinear business cycle models, based on the multiplier and accelerator, where coupling through interregional trade produces frequency locking, quasiperiodicity and chaos, and other nonlinear dynamic models, such as oligopoly models, where complex dynamics arises. This research has been documented in three sold out editions of his monograph on nonlinear economic dynamics.

The most recent works are three books: one advanced textbook on mathematical spatio-economics, published by Springer-Verlag, another book on the economics of culture, and the complete revision of his Springer book on nonlinear dynamics appearing in June 1997.

Puu is married since 1972 to Gertrud Puu (née Nässén 1945), who is PhD in biochemistry and senior researcher at the Research institute of the Swedish Defence. They have two children, Margareta born 1974 and Magnus born 1981.

Puu's main side interest is music, in which field he is a maker and restorer of historical instruments and an amateur violist. He also works part of his time since 1987 as a producer and artistic director of the biannual Nordic Baroque Music Festival in Nordmaling. He is currently chairman of the professors' union at his university.

# The Collected Scientific Works of Tönu Puu

1. "Mikroteori för det enskilda subjektets optimala förmögenhetssammansättning I", Scandinavian Journal of Economics 64:157-175 (1962)
2. "Mikroteori för det enskilda subjektets optimala förmögenhetssammansättning II", Scandinavian Journal of Economics 65:13-53 (1963)
3. "A graphical solution to second order homogeneous difference equations", Oxford Economic Papers 15:53-58 (1963)
4. "Studier i det Optimala Tillgångsvalets Teori" (Almqvist och Wiksell, Uppsala 1964)
5. "Second order conditions for the monopolist's optimum at differentiated prices", Scandinavian Journal of Economics 66:208-214 (1964)
6. "The effects of monetary and fiscal policy", Studia OEconomica Upsaliensia 1:1-75 (1965)
7. "The theory of consumption for several time periods", Scandinavian Journal of Economics 67:74-79 (1965)
8. "A simple graphic method for estimating the yield on bonds" in Hahn, Brechling (Eds.), The Theory of Interest Rates (Macmillan, London 1965)
9. "Les effets de substitution et d'expansion dans la théorie de la production", Révue d'Economie Politique 74:57-91 (1966)
10. "The theories of choice between alternative investment opportunities" Weltwirtschaftliches Archiv 99:107-125 (1967)
11. "The relation between economic theory and empirical reality", Scandinavian Journal of Economics 69:85-114 (1967)
12. "Les théories economiques: structure, formalisme mathématique et contenu d'information", Révue d'Economie Politique 76:173-211 (1968)
13. "Complementarity, substitutivity and regressivity in the theory of production", in Paelinck (Ed.), Récherches Récents sur la Fonction de Production 97-131 (Presses Universitaires Notre-Dame de la Paix, Namur 1968)
14. "Causal versus teleological explanation in economics", Scandinavian Journal of Economics 71:111-126 (1969)

15. "Production under risk", Scandinavian Journal of Economics 71:84-93 (1969)
16. "The neoclassical theory of production and distribution", Scandinavian Journal of Economics 72:230-240 (1970)
17. "Matematik för Ekonomer" (Rabén och Sjögren, Stockholm 1971)
18. "On inferior (regressive) inputs", Scandinavian Journal of Economics 73:241-251 (1971)
19. "Free entry and efficient distribution of inputs", Metroeconomica 24 :70-85 (1972)
20. "Algunas reflexiones acerca de le relacion entre la teoria economica y la realidad", Revista Espanola de Economia 11:347-385 (1972)
21. "Factor demand functions in the long run equilibrium", Rivista Internazionale de Scienze Economiche e Commerciali 20:1209-1229 (1973)
22. "On the profitability of exhausting natural resources", Journal of Environmental Economics and Mangement 4:185-199 (1977)
23. "A proposed definition of traffic flow in continuous transportation models", Environment and Planning A9:559-567 (1977)
24. "On traffic equilibrium, congestion tolls, and the allocation of transportation capacity in a congested urban area", Environment and Planning A10:29-36 (1978)
25. "Towards a theory of optimal roads", Regional Science and Urban Economics 8:225-248 (1978)
26. "On the existence of optimal paths and cost surfaces in isotropic continuous transportation models", Environment and Planning A10:1121-1130 (1978)
27. "The Allocation of Road Capital in Two-Dimensional Space", (North-Holland Publishing Company, Amsterdam 1979)
28. "Regional modelling and structural stability", Environment and Planning A11:1431-1438 (1979)
29. "The Economics of Technological Progress" (Ed.), (Macmillan, London 1980)
30. "Structural stability and change in geographical space", in Griffith, McKinnon (Eds.), Dynamic Spatial Models 242-255 (Sijthoff-Noordhoff, Alphen aan den Rijn 1981)
31. "Catastrophic structural change in i continuous regional model", Regional Science and Urban Economics 11:317-333 (1981)
32. "Structural stability and change in geographical space", Environment and Planning A13:979-989 (1981)

33. "Continuous flow modelling in regional science", in Studies in Regional Science and Urban Economics 8:251-258 (North-Holland Publishing Company, Amsterdam 1982)
34. "Outline of a trade cycle model in continuous space and time", Geographical Analysis 14:1-9 (1982)
35. "Structurally stable flows and patterns of location", IIASA Research Report RR-82-42, (International Institute of Applied Systems Analysis, Laxenburg, Austria 1982)
36. "The general equilibrium of a spatially extended market economy", Geographical Analysis 14:145-154 (1982)
37. "Equilibrium in the spatial production and exchange economy" Sistemi Urbani 3:499-534 (1983)
38. "A model of spatial flows and growth of capital and labour stocks", Journal of Applied Mathematics and Computation 14:3-9 (1984)
39. "On the art of successful analogy formation", in Krelle, Hauptmann, Mosler (Eds.), Operations Research and Economic Analysis 175-179 (Springer Verlag, Berlin Heidelberg 1984)
40. "The long run equilibrium of a continuous spatial exchange economy", in Studies in Regional Science and Urban Economics 11:15-30 (North-Holland Publishing Company, Amsterdam 1984)
41. "The structure of specialization and trade in the space economy", Environment and Planning A16:1339-1347 (1984)
42. "What can be learned from continuous models of the space economy?", Papers and Proceedings of the Regional Science Association 56:21-36 (1985)
43. "A simplified model of spatiotemporal poulation dynamics", Environment and Planning A17:1263-1269 (1985)
44. "Spatial Economics: Potential, Density, and Flow" (North-Holland Publishing Company, Amsterdam 1985).
45. "Multiplier-accelerator models revisited", Regional Science and Urban Economics 16:81-95 (1986)
46. "The stability of hexagonal tessellations", in Funk, Kuklinski (Eds.), Space, Structure, Economy 133-158 (von Loeper Verlag, Karlsruhe 1986)
47. "Complex dynamics in continuous models of the business cycle", in Lecture Notes in Economics and Mathematical Systems 293:227-259 (Springer Verlag Berlin Heidelberg 1987)
48. "Relations between continuous transportation models and networks", in Yadav (Ed.), Perspectives in Urban Geography 4:156-178 (1987)
49. "A model of interdependent continuous space markets for labour, capital, and consumer's goods", in Yadav (Ed.), Perspectives in Urban Geography 4:139-153 (1987)

50. "On the equilibrium distribution of population and land value", in Yadav (Ed.), Perspectives in Urban Geography 13:215-228 (1987)
51. "Palander, Tord Folkeson", in Eatwell, Milgate, and Newman (Eds.), The New Palgrave. A Dictionary of Economics 3:788 (Macmillan, London 1987)
52. "Catastrophe theory applied to refraction of traffic", Journal of Computational and Applied Mathematics 22:315-318 (1988)
53. "Structural stability as a modelling instrument in spatial economics", Journal of Computational and Applied Mathematics 22:369-379 (1988)
54. "Resursfördelningsteori" (Studentlitteratur, Lund 1989).
55. "On spatiotemporal dynamics of capital and labour", in Studies in Regional Science and Urban Economics 20:121-131 (North-Holland, Amsterdam 1989)
56. "Nonlinear economic dynamics", Lecture Notes in Economics and Mathematical Systems 336 (Springer, Berlin 1989)
57. "On growth and dispersion of populations", Annals of Regional Science 23:171-186 (1989)
58. "On the unity of arts, crafts, and sciences", Journal of Cultural Economics 14:19-34 (1990)
59. "Optimality versus stability in spatial economic pattern formation", in Chatterji and Kuenne Eds.), New Frontiers in Regional Economics 1:25-37 (Macmillan, London 1990)
60. "Spatial structures", Advances in Spatial and Network Economics 1 (Springer, Berlin 1990).
61. "Order and Disorder in the Business Cycle", Socio-Spatial Dynamics 1:1-19 (1990)
62. "Några reflexioner över nationalekonomin idag", in K. Fridjonsdottir (ed.), Svenska samhällsvetenskaper 109-112 (Carlsson Bokförlag, Stockholm 1990)
63. Nonlinear Economic Dynamics, 2nd revised and enlarged edition (Springer, Berlin 1991)
64. "Hotelling's migration model revisited", Environment and Planning A23:1209-1216 (1991)
65. "Structural change in flow-based spatial economic models - A survey", Socio-Spatial Dynamics 2:1-17 (1991)
66. "Tord Palander and the Uppsala milieu", in V.A. Economics at Uppsala University, Uppsala (1991)
67. "On technological progress in cultural production", Journal of Cultural Economics (1991)

68. "Chaos in business cycles", Chaos, Solitons, and Fractals 1:457-473 (1991)
69. "Chaos in duopoly pricing", Chaos, Solitons, and Fractals 1:573-581 (1991)
70. "Order and disorder in business cycles", Annals of Operations Research 37:169-183 (1992)
71. "On progress and perfection in the arts", Ricerche Economiche 46:75-90 (1992)
72. "A chaotic process with slow feed back: the case of business cycles", in "Economic Evolution and Demographic Change", Lecture Notes in Economics and Mathematical Systems 395:3-34 (Springer-Verlag, Berlin 1992)
73. "On time and space in economic theory", in T.R. Lakshmaman and P. Nijkamp (eds.), "Structure and Change in the Sapce Economy" 11-24, (Springer-Verlag, Berlin 1992)
74. "Tord Palander och Uppsalamiljön", Ekonomisk Debatt 20:221-228 (1992)
75. Nonlinear Economic Dynamics, 3rd revised and enlarged edition (Springer-Verlag, Berlin 1993)
76. "Pattern formation in spatial economics", Chaos, Solitons, and Fractals 3:99-129 (1993)
77. "Om samband mellan kort och lång ränta", Ekonomisk Debatt 20: (1993)
78. "The chaotic monopolist", Chaos, Solitons and Fractals 5:35-44 (1995)
79. "The chaotic dupoplists revisited", Journal of Economic Behviour and Organization (1996)
80. "Mathematical Land Use and Location Theory; An Introduction", Springer-Verlag (1997)
81. "Conference on Bifurcation and Chaos in Economic and Social Systems", Pergamon Press (Ed.) (1996)
82. "The Economics of the Arts, the Crafts, and the Sciences - A Safari", forthcoming
83. "Complex dynamics with three oligopolists", Chaos, Solitons, and Fractals 7:2075-2081 (1996)
84. "Economic Development, Darwin, and Catastrophe Theory", forthcoming
85. Nonlinear Economic Dynamics, 4th thoroughly revised and enlarged edition (Springer-Verlag, Berlin 1997) in print

MIX
Papier aus verantwortungsvollen Quellen
Paper from responsible sources
FSC® C105338

If you have any concerns about our products,
you can contact us on
**ProductSafety@springernature.com**

In case Publisher is established outside the EU,
the EU authorized representative is:
**Springer Nature Customer Service Center GmbH**
**Europaplatz 3, 69115 Heidelberg, Germany**

Printed by Libri Plureos GmbH
in Hamburg, Germany